A guide to
Practical Techniques

ROBERT CARRIER'S KITCHEN

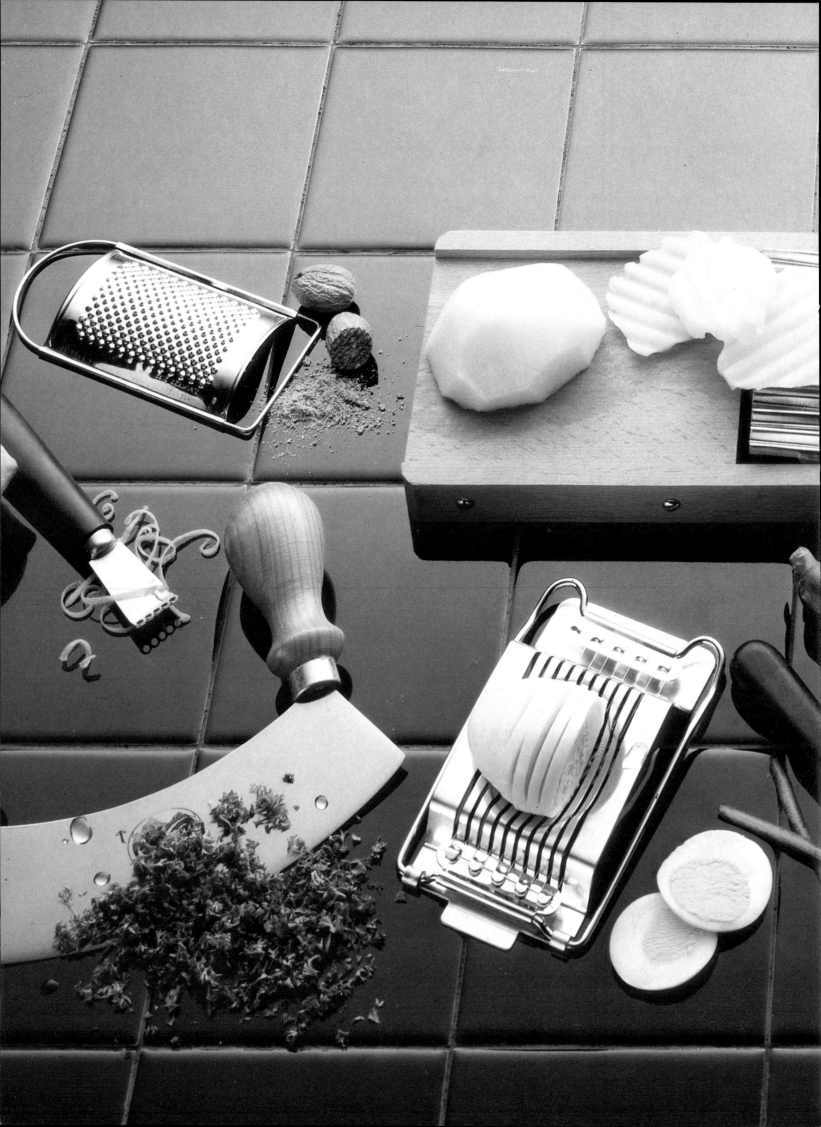

A guide to Practical Techniques

Marshall Cavendish   London Sydney & New York

Editor	Roz Fishel
Editorial Staff	Carey Denton
	Caroline Macy
	Penny Smith
	Kate Toner
Art Editor	Ross George
Series Editor	Pepita Aris
Production Executive	Robert Paulley
Production Controller	Steve Roberts

Photography
Bryce Attwell: 22, 46, 66
Tom Belshaw: 42, 53
Paul Bussell: 2, 12, 24, 29, 35, 63, 71, 82, 107
Laurie Evans: 19, 43, 52, 55, 72, 83, 102, 104
John Harris: 110
James Jackson: 36, 58, 59, 68, 74, 75, 94
Michael Kaye: 25
Chris Knaggs: 18, 49 (lower), 50, 56, 57, 60, 64, 69, 76, 77, 79 (column 3), 80, 84 (top), 91
David Levin: 9, 10, 11, 100
Peter Myers: 13, 21, 32, 39, 40, 41, 44, 48, 49 (top), 88, 90, 92, 96
Iain Reid: 30, 31
Theo Bergstrom: Cover picture, 34
Paul Webster: 14, 15, 78, 79 (columns 1, 2), 84 (below), 85, 86
Paul Williams: 8, 17, 28, 39, 51, 73, 98, 108

Weights and measures
Both metric and imperial measurements are given. As these are not exact equivalents, please work from one set of figures or the other. Use graded measuring spoons levelled across.

Time symbols
The time needed to prepare the dish is given on each recipe. The symbols are as follows:

 simple to prepare and cook

 straightforward but requires more skill or attention

 time-consuming to prepare or requires extra skill

 must be started 1 day or more ahead

On the cover: Chicken pie with green olives, page 35
Kitchen knife from Dickens & Jones (Harrods) Ltd, London W1; other equipment from David Mellor, London SW1

This edition published 1985
© Marshall Cavendish Limited 1984/1985

Printed in Italy by
L.E.G.O. S.p.a. Vicenza
Typeset by Quadraset Limited, Midsomer Norton, Bath, Avon

Published by Marshall Cavendish House
58 Old Compton Street London W1V 5PA
ISBN 0 86307 264 X (series) ISBN 0 86307 401 4 (this volume)

Contents

No matter how fresh or high-quality your ingredients are, unless you use them in the right way the results may be disappointing. *A Guide to Practical Techniques* is packed with information on the best ways to use ingredients, with detailed instructions on how to make anything from pastry to preserves.

As a good sauce will lift many a dish, I have included a section that explains how to master sauce-making. I tell you how to make the three classic French sauces — Bechamel, Velouté and the brown Sauce espagnole — from which so many other sauces are derived.

For those of you who are keen to try out some complicated dishes there are helpful hints on sophisticated skills. These include delicate French cooking with aspic, clear and helpful information on how to prepare game birds for cooking, and a guide to elegant cake decoration — skills which, once acquired, will hold you in good stead for many special occasions to come.

In cooking, the appearance of a dish is always important, but never more so than in *nouvelle cuisine*. Here the ingredients are lightly cooked so that they maintain their fresh form and natural flavour. They are presented in an artistic style borrowed from the Japanese, as in Légumes panachés, which literally translated means 'stylish vegetables'. Or, for more foods with a foreign flavour, I also show you just how easy Chinese *wok* cookery can be.

Simple sponges are wonderfully versatile cakes, so in the chapter on Cakes & Breads I give a step-by-step guide to light, airy sponges and how best to serve them. Also, there are comprehensive instructions on bread-making, which tell you the best ingredients and method to use for mouth-watering results.

All in all I think you will find *A Guide to Practical Techniques* a very useful book. The methods it includes are ones which you will use regularly, so I am sure you'll want to refer to this book time and time again.

Happy cooking and bon appétit!

Robert Carrier

Sauces

MASTERING CLASSIC WHITE SAUCE

Learn to make a perfectly smooth, creamy white sauce and you have the key to making many successful dishes: from tasty fillings for crêpes and quiches, subtle sauces for pasta and other elegant dinner party delights.

Nothing is, apparently, more straightforward or more versatile than a simple white sauce! Most white sauces are a combination of butter and flour — which, when heated together, make a *roux* — simmered with milk or stock, seasoned with salt and pepper, and sometimes a hint of nutmeg. The flavour can be varied with a little grated Cheddar for a cheese sauce; a handful of parsley and capers for caper sauce; chopped onion for onion sauce; or a packet of frozen prawns for prawn sauce.

To start the section, then, I show you how to make my special bechamel sauce. Flavoured with onion and ham or veal, the sauce is then reduced to strengthen the flavour before being enriched with reduced wine and stock. For a plain, but delicious, white sauce simply spark it with lemon juice or Tabasco, or mellow it with Madeira or cognac.

The basic bechamel sauce can also be used as the basis for many different recipes. At its most simple all you need to do is add chopped ham to your bechamel to make a creamy sauce to go over pasta, or a tasty filling for crêpes.

Making a roux

Almost every classic white sauce recipe starts off with the phrase 'make a roux'. A roux is nothing more than equal quantities of butter and flour, blended over a low heat. The cells of starch in the flour burst and the starch combines completely with the melted butter to form a paste capable of absorbing many times its own weight in liquid when it is cooked.

For the more delicate sauces I often use clarified butter. This is because unclarified butter always contains a little milk which, when brought to a high heat, is apt to burn and make a sauce gritty or slightly discoloured. To make clarified butter, heat the butter until it foams. The foam will sink to the bottom of the pan and the clear, clarified butter can be poured off, leaving the sediment behind in the pan.

If you have ever had trouble with a roux, or are new to bechamel, I can tell you that one of the secrets of easy sauce-making is to cook the roux over water in the top pan of a double boiler. Though this takes longer than the conventional method, you can be confident that it will not cook too quickly, or take on unwanted colour or burn, and that the end result will be a completely smooth white sauce.

Melt the butter in the pan and when it begins to bubble, add the sieved flour. Stir with a wooden spoon or wire whisk for 2–3 minutes until the mixture is smooth but has not changed colour. This length of time for cooking gets rid of the raw flour taste. I like to keep a bowl of this cooked roux in the refrigerator, so that it can be used at any time to make delicious sauces.

The all-important liquid

Hot liquid is stirred into the roux a little at a time. The liquid is what gives a sauce much of its particular character. It may be simply milk and cream, or a flavorsome stock — home-made beef stock, or stock made from veal, fish or poultry — but it is most important to the quality and flavour of your finished sauce.

No sauce is ready as soon as it thickens. Sauces should be cooked much longer to allow the flavour to improve by careful reduction. It is no secret that French chefs use almost twice as much liquid as the quantity needed in the recipe for any sauce. This sauce is then simmered for much longer than usual in order to reduce it and so concentrate the flavour.

I have two methods for this reducing process. Either you can cook the roux-thickened sauce, made with extra liquid, in the top pan of a double boiler for about 30 minutes, or you can put the sauce in a heat-proof measuring jug in a pan of simmering water — this way you can see exactly when it

has reduced to the correct volume. Either way, the flavours infuse and the quantity of liquid is reduced, thickening the sauce. As a result of this concentration and the blending of flavours, the sauce is more suave, more transparent and more delicious.

Adding the highlights

In professional kitchens we sometimes use a few chef's tricks to embellish a sauce. First, liquid flavourings are added. Both wine and stock are used. Each one is reduced to just a tablespoonful or two, for extra concentration of flavour, before being stirred into the finished sauce.

Taste the sauce after these additions; if it seems too bland, add just a squeeze of lemon or a dash of Tabasco. On the other hand, if you think it is too sharp, a teaspoon of Madeira or cognac will soften and enhance the flavour.

Ringing the changes on bechamel

The thickness of any sauce can be varied according to the purpose for which it is to be used by adding more or less liquid. When required for coating a piece of meat or fish, it should be thick enough to adhere to the back of a spoon. When the sauce is to be poured, it should be thin enough to flow smoothly.

Before adding egg yolks to a sauce, remove the saucepan from the heat, allow it to cool slightly, then beat in the yolks. Cook it in the top of a double boiler over a very low heat and whisk the yolks thoroughly into the sauce. Do not allow the sauce to come to the boil again or it will curdle. When lemon juice is to be added to a sauce containing milk or cream, add the lemon juice last and do not allow the sauce to boil again.

Finishing the sauce

Always strain a finished bechamel sauce before adding chopped ingredients of other flavourings. For a finer sauce with a smooth glossy appearance, line the strainer with a well wrung out, damp muslin cloth.

French chefs often incorporate extra butter into a sauce to make it thicker and more flavorsome. The butter is finely diced and whisked in with a wire whisk after the sauce has been taken from the heat, just before serving. The pan must not be returned to the heat after this addition of butter, or the sauce will separate and become fatty.

Reserving the sauce

To keep a sauce warm, cover the saucepan to prevent a skin forming, then stand it in a larger saucepan containing hot, not boiling, water. This is called a *bain marie*. With thicker sauces a spoonful of liquid — water,

Chicken breasts with tarragon cream

Making white sauce

Stir the flour into the melted butter to make a roux; cook for 2–3 minutes.

Off the heat, pour the scalded liquid onto the roux, stirring thoroughly.

stock or milk — or melted butter may be run over the top. Just before serving, whisk this protective covering into the sauce. If you are leaving a sauce to become cold, transfer it to a narrow-necked jug and stir occasionally while it is cooling. In this way there will be less surface area on which a skin can form.

Storing the sauce

Sauces containing milk, cream or eggs should be refrigerated for not more than 1–2 days before being used.

Bechamel sauce

 45 minutes

Makes 275 ml /10 fl oz sauce
40 g /1½ oz butter
30 ml /2 tbls finely chopped onion
30 ml /2 tbls finely chopped ham
  or veal
30 ml /2 tbls flour
425 ml /15 fl oz milk
¼ chicken stock cube
½ bay leaf
6 white peppercorns
a good pinch of freshly grated nutmeg
For accenting the flavour
60 ml /4 tbls dry white wine
60 ml /4 tbls chicken stock, home-made or
  from a cube
salt and white pepper
15 ml /1 tbls lemon juice (optional)
2–3 drops Tabasco (optional)
5–10 ml /1–2 tsp Madeira or cognac
(optional)
a pinch of sugar (optional)
25 g /1 oz butter (optional, see below)

1 Put the butter in a small pan over a low heat. Melt the butter, then add the finely chopped onion. Sauté very gently until the onion is soft, without letting it colour. Stir in the finely chopped ham or veal and the flour and cook for 2–3 minutes, stirring constantly with a wooden spoon. (If you do not feel too confident, it is safer — but slower — to make

the sauce in a double boiler over gently simmering water.)
2 Scald the milk (that is, bring it almost to boiling) in another pan. Stir one-quarter of the heated milk into the cooked roux, off the heat. Return it to a low heat and bring the sauce to the boil, stirring vigorously.
3 As the sauce begins to thicken, add the remainder of the milk, a little at a time, stirring briskly. Continue stirring until the sauce bubbles and is cooked.
4 Add the crumbled stock cube, bay leaf, peppercorns and nutmeg. The sauce must now infuse and reduce in quantity to 275 ml / 10 fl oz. An easy way to see when the sauce has reduced to exactly this quantity is to pour it into a heatproof measuring jug. Stand this in a pan of gently bubbling water and simmer gently, stirring from time to time, until the sauce is exactly 275 ml /10 fl oz. Alternatively, if you are using a double boiler leave the pan at the back of the stove over gently simmering water for about 30 minutes, stirring occasionally. The sauce can be used at this point if you wish; add a little salt and go straight to step 8.
5 If you wish to accent the flavour of your sauce subtley, prepare any additions while the sauce is infusing. Boil 60 ml /4 tbls wine in a small saucepan until reduced to 15 ml /1 tbls. Stir this into the sauce. Then boil 60 ml / 4 tbls chicken stock until reduced to 15 ml / 1 tbls; add this to the sauce, too.
6 Taste the sauce. If it needs pointing up, add a little salt and pepper and a squeeze of lemon juice and/or a drop of Tabasco. If, on the other hand, the flavour seems sharp and strong, soften it with 5–10 ml /1–2 tsp Madeira or cognac and a pinch of sugar.
7 Strain the sauce through a fine sieve.
8 If the bechamel is about to be served, dot the surface with butter and do not return the pan to the heat. Whisk the butter in just before serving. Leave out this step if you are using any of the variations below.

Variations on bechamel

● For cream sauce, to serve with fish, poultry, eggs and vegetables, add 30 ml / 2 tbls thick cream to the hot bechamel sauce

in the top of a double boiler and bring the mixture almost to boiling point. Flavour with a few drops of lemon juice if wished.
● For a rich mornay sauce, to serve with fish, vegetables, poached eggs and pasta, mix 1 lightly beaten egg yolk with 30 ml /2 tbls cream and stir this into the hot bechamel sauce. Cook over a gentle heat, stirring constantly, until it reaches boiling point. Remove the pan from the heat, add 25 g / 1 oz butter and 30–60 ml /2–4 tbls grated cheese (Parmesan or Gruyère cheese is best), then stir until the cheese has melted.
● Aurore sauce, a subtle pink sauce, is excellent with eggs, chicken or shellfish. Flavour the hot bechamel sauce with 15–30 ml /1–2 tbls tomato purée.
● For a mild curry sauce, delicious with fish, poultry, eggs and vegetables, add 15 ml /1 tbls curry powder and ½ tart apple, peeled, cored and diced into the bechamel sauce. Cook over a medium heat, stirring constantly, until it reaches boiling point.
● For a Nantua sauce, start by adding 30–60 ml /2–4 tbls thick cream to each 275 ml /10 fl oz hot bechamel sauce. Blend well, strain through a fine sieve and add salt and white pepper to taste. Heat without boiling, then stir in 30 ml /2 tbls diced cooked prawns, shrimps or scampi.
● Cube a 10 mm /½ in thick slice of cooked ham and add it to the bechamel sauce. Heat through gently and use as a tasty sauce for pasta, such as tagliatelle (see picture).

Bechamel-based fillings
Use the four bechamel-based recipes which follow to fill pastry cases, crêpes, folded omelettes and flans. Add 3 egg yolks to any of the mixtures and you have a quiche filling.

Financière filling

🔪🔪🔪 making the bechamel sauce, then 30 minutes

Makes 850 ml /1½ pt filling
275 ml /10 fl oz bechamel sauce (see recipe)
225 g /8 oz sweetbreads
salt and freshly ground black pepper
12 dried mushrooms
10 mm /½ in thick slice cooked ham
100 g /4 oz button mushrooms
30–45 ml /2–3 tbls butter

1 Wash the sweetbreads very carefully. Put them in a pan with cold salted water to cover. Bring this to the boil over a moderate heat and cook for 2 minutes. Drain, and cool by standing the covered pan under cold running water. Next, cut the sweetbreads into 10 mm /½ in dice.
2 Soak the dried mushrooms in a small bowl with hot water to cover.
3 Cut the ham into 10 mm /½ in dice and cut the button mushrooms into quarters, or dice them about the same size as the ham. Squeeze the soaked mushrooms dry and cut them into pieces.
4 Sauté the sweetbreads, ham and mushrooms in butter until tender. Season with salt and freshly ground black pepper to taste. Add the bechamel sauce and heat through. Use immediately.

Primavera filling

🔪🔪🔪 making the bechamel sauce, then 35 minutes

Makes 1 L /1¾ pt filling
275 ml /10 fl oz bechamel sauce (see recipe)
225 g /8 oz green beans, trimmed
salt
250 g /9 oz frozen broccoli, defrosted
2 medium-sized courgettes, peeled
75 g /3 oz butter
1 garlic clove, finely chopped
15 ml /1 tbls finely chopped fresh parsley
freshly ground black pepper
100 g /4 oz frozen peas, defrosted

1 Cook the beans in boiling salted water for 3–5 minutes. Drain, rinse in cold water and then drain again. Cook the broccoli in boiling salted water for 2–3 minutes. Drain, rinse in cold water and then drain again.
2 Cut the stems of the broccoli into 10 mm /½ in pieces and divide the heads into small florets. Cut the beans into 25 mm /1 in pieces. Slice the courgettes thinly.
3 Melt the butter in a large saucepan. Add the garlic, parsley and black pepper to taste and mix well. Add the broccoli stems and the sliced courgettes and cook over a low heat for 5 minutes, stirring constantly.
4 Add the remaining vegetables and the rest of the sauce to the pan. Stir the sauce over a medium heat for 5 minutes, then use immediately.

Tagliatelle with ham sauce

Bercy filling

🔪🔪🔪 making the bechamel sauce, then 25 minutes

Makes 1 L /1¾ pt filling
275 ml /10 fl oz bechamel sauce (see recipe)
225 g /8 oz sole, halibut or other white fish
4 shallots or ¼ large Spanish onion, finely chopped
275 ml /10 fl oz dry white wine
25 g /1 oz butter, softened
30 ml /2 tbls finely chopped fresh parsley
100 g /4 oz boiled, peeled prawns
100 g /4 oz cooked mussels
5–15 ml /1–3 tsp lemon juice
salt and freshly ground black pepper

1 Cover the fish with water in a pan with a lid and poach for 4–8 minutes, depending on the cut. Drain and keep warm.
2 Meanwhile, simmer the chopped shallots or onion with the wine until the liquid is reduced to about 30 ml /2 tbls.
3 Remove the pan from the heat and whisk the mixture while it cools slightly. Stand the pan in a larger one containing hot water and whisk in the softened butter until the mixture thickens slightly.
4 Add the wine sauce to the bechamel in the top pan of a double boiler. Cook over gently simmering water, stirring continuously, until heated through. Flake the fish, discarding any skin, and add with the parsley, prawns and mussels to the sauce. Season to taste with the lemon juice, salt and black pepper and use immediately.

Capricciosa filling

 making the bechamel sauce,
then 50 minutes

Makes 850 ml /1½ pt filling
275 ml /10 fl oz bechamel sauce (see recipe)
100 g /4 oz butter
100 g /4oz veal, finely chopped
salt and freshly ground black pepper
150 ml /5 fl oz dry white wine
225 g /8 oz frozen peas
100 g /4 oz mushrooms, sliced
1–2 slices Parma ham, cut into thin strips

1 Melt half the butter in a saucepan and
sauté the chopped veal until golden. Add the
salt, pepper and white wine, and simmer
gently for 5–10 minutes.
2 Add the veal mixture to the bechamel
sauce in the top pan of a double boiler. Cover
and cook gently for 30 minutes.
3 Meanwhile, cook the peas in boiling
salted water until tender, then drain. Sauté
the mushrooms and ham in the remaining
butter for 2–3 minutes. Add the peas,
mushrooms and ham to the sauce and use.

Chicken breasts with tarragon cream

 45 minutes

Serves 4
4 large chicken breasts, skinned and boned
salt and freshly ground black pepper
75 g /3 oz butter
45 ml /3 tbls flour
*275 ml /10 fl oz chicken stock, home-made
or from a cube*
*15 ml /1 tbls chopped, fresh tarragon,
or 7.5 ml /1½ tsp dried tarragon*
75–100 ml /3–4 fl oz soured cream
15 g /½ oz Gruyère cheese, grated
30 ml /2 tbls freshly grated Parmesan cheese
For the garnish
*15 ml /1 tbls finely chopped fresh tarragon or
parsley*

1 Rub the chicken breasts all over with salt
and freshly ground black pepper. Melt 50 g /
2 oz of the butter in a large frying pan and
sauté the chicken breasts for 5–8 minutes
until they are lightly browned on all sides.
Remove them from the pan with a slotted
spoon and keep on one side.
2 Melt the remaining butter in the pan.
Remove the pan from the heat, stir in the
flour and cook gently for 2–3 minutes.
Gradually stir in the chicken stock, then add
the tarragon. Return the pan to the heat and
bring slowly to the boil, stirring continuously. Simmer for 2–3 minutes.
3 Return the chicken breasts to the pan,
reduce the heat and simmer gently for 20–30
minutes, until the chicken is just cooked and
the liquids run clear when the chicken is
pierced with the point of a knife.
4 Using a slotted spoon, transfer the
cooked chicken breasts to a heated serving
dish and keep them warm.

5 Stir the soured cream and the Gruyère
and Parmesan cheese into the sauce and stir
over a gentle heat until the cheese has
melted. Pour the sauce over the chicken
breasts, sprinkle the tarragon or parsley over
the top and serve immediately.

Creamed finnan haddie

soaking the fish for 2 hours,
then 1 hour

Serves 4–6
1 kg /2 lb smoked haddock
275 ml /10 fl oz milk
40 g /1½ oz butter
45 ml /3 tbls flour
2.5 ml /½ tsp turmeric
425 ml /15 fl oz thick cream
freshly ground black pepper
a pinch of grated nutmeg
3 slices of white bread, crusts removed
50 g /2 oz butter
*melted butter and finely chopped fresh
parsley, to garnish*

1 Soak the haddock in cold water for 2
hours, in order to reduce its salt content.
2 Drain the fish and put it in a saucepan
with the milk and 275 ml /10 fl oz water.
Bring to a fast boil, then remove from the
heat and leave to stand for 15 minutes. Drain
the haddock, reserving the liquid.
3 Meanwhile, put the top pan of a double
boiler over direct heat and melt the butter in
it. Stir in the flour and cook over a low heat
for 2–3 minutes, stirring continuously. Off
the heat, gradually stir in 275 ml /10 fl oz
of the reserved cooking liquid. Return to
the heat and bring the sauce slowly to the
boil, still stirring. Simmer for 2–3 minutes.
4 Add the turmeric and the cream, then
cook the sauce over gently simmering water.
Bring to a simmer and season with pepper
and grated nutmeg. Flake the fish, removing
the skin and bones. Fold the fish into the
sauce. Cover the pan and simmer.

Creamed finnan haddie

5 Quarter the bread slices diagonally. Melt
the butter in a frying-pan and sauté the bread
until golden. To garnish, dip the top corner
of the triangular croûtons in melted butter
and then into the finely chopped parsley.
6 Transfer the finnan haddie to a shallow
serving dish and garnish with the croûtons.
Serve immediately.

Creamed ham piquante

1¼ hours

Serves 4
1 medium-sized onion, finely chopped
*150 ml /5 fl oz Chablis or other dry white
wine*
*150 ml /5 fl oz chicken stock, made with ½
chicken stock cube*
30–60 ml /2–4 tbls tomato purée
*4 thick gammon steaks 10 mm /½ in thick,
175 g /6 oz each*
oil, for brushing
225 ml /8 fl oz thick cream
25 g /1 oz butter

1 Put the finely chopped onion in a pan
with the wine and boil until the mixture has
reduced to half its original quantity. Add the
stock and tomato purée, cover the pan and
simmer very gently for 1 hour.
2 Remove any rind from the gammon
steaks and snip the fat at 12 mm /½ in
intervals. Heat the grill to hot.
3 About 15 minutes before you wish to
serve the dish, brush the gammon steaks with
oil and grill for 7–10 minutes. Turn the
gammon over, brush with more oil and grill
for a further 7 minutes.
4 Meanwhile, add the cream to the sauce
and simmer for a further 10 minutes.
5 Pass the sauce through a fine sieve, and
whisk in the butter. Pour the sauce over the
gammon and serve.

VELOUTE, CREAM & BUTTER SAUCES

A sauce should enhance and not mask the good points of any dish. For sauces to work in this way they must be made well and in this chapter I explain the secrets of making velouté, cream and butter-enriched sauces.

Velouté sauce — literally velvety sauce — is one of the three *sauces mères* (mother sauces) of classic French cooking, from which so many other sauces are derived. The other two mother sauces are the brown Sauce espagnole (see page 23) and the smooth and versatile white Bechamel sauce (see page 7).

Making a velouté sauce: a velouté sauce is made by the same method as a bechamel sauce, but with slightly different ingredients. White stock — chicken, veal or fish stock — is the main ingredient of the sauce (rather than milk) and it uses a pale rather than a white *roux*.

A pale roux is made by melting butter over a low heat and then stirring in an equal volume of flour and cooking it gently for 4–5 minutes, until it begins to change colour. Cook the roux in a pan directly over the heat, but make sure you keep the heat very low and be ready to take the pan quickly off the heat when the roux begins to colour.

Hot chicken, veal or fish stock is then gradually stirred or whisked into the pale roux. This is where velouté sauce has an advantage over bechamel; it can be closely linked to the food it accompanies by using a corresponding stock as its main ingredient: a chicken stock when it is to accompany chicken, a fish stock when it is to be served with fish.

After the stock has been stirred in and the mixture has been brought to the boil, mushroom trimmings are added to give the velouté sauce its characteristic flavouring. The sauce is then cooked in a double boiler over very gently simmering water — until it is reduced to the right consistency. This slow reduction gives the sauce a smooth texture and allows the flavours to blend and strengthen, so that the finished sauce has a marvellous, richly concentrated flavour.

You may find it easier to reduce the sauce in a heatproof measuring jug. Do this by standing the jug in a saucepan of gently bubbling water. This enables you to see at a glance when the sauce has reduced to the desired quantity. It does, however, take longer to reduce in a jug than in a double boiler.

In addition to the classic recipe, I have included one for Velouté sauce with trout in lettuce packets — an unusual dish which will show off your sauce-making skills to full effect. The sauce is based on fish stock and then the flavour is enriched by adding the juices from cooking the trout.

Embellishing the flavour: wine and stock, once they have been reduced down to a table-spoonful or two, can be stirred into the sauce to add depth of flavour. A squeeze of lemon juice or a dash of Tabasco will brighten the flavour, while a teaspoonful of dry Madeira or cognac will soften and darken it. Finely chopped fresh herbs such as tarragon and chives add a very delicate flavour; shrimps

(potted or plain, boiled) give extra body and richness to a fish-stock based creamy sauce.

Velouté variations: velouté sauce is the foundation for a number of the best white sauces in French cooking. With the basic recipe I give you a number of the simplest variations ranging from Andalouse sauce to Hongroise sauce, and suggestions for how to serve them. I have also included a full recipe for the most famous variation, Sauce suprême.

Enriching the sauce: a velouté sauce is sometimes enriched with egg yolks and cream. These are beaten together lightly, a little hot sauce is stirred in and then the mixture is stirred into the sauce. The sauce is returned to the heat for a few minutes to warm through and thicken, but it must not boil or it will curdle.

Extra butter is sometimes added to a finished velouté to make an even more luxurious sauce. The butter should first be finely diced, then whisked into the sauce after it has been removed from the heat, just before serving. Do not return the pan to the heat after this addition of butter, or the butter will separate out again.

To keep the sauce warm: cover the saucepan and stand it in a larger pan containing hot, but not boiling, water. If your sauce is fairly thick, it is a good idea to run a spoonful of liquid over the top — stock, milk, water or melted butter — then whisk it into the sauce just before serving.

Cream sauce

Rich but subtle, cream sauces are the perfect accompaniment to serve with delicately flavoured food, such as hot mousses of fish or vegetables, poached vegetables (particularly salsify, asparagus and sea kale), steamed young marrow, veal or poached chicken.

In this chapter I give you a recipe for Easy cream sauce, a rich and quick roux-based sauce which can be made within 15 minutes. I use Easy cream sauce as an alternative to bechamel sauce when there is not enough time to make a bechamel. It does not have

the wonderful blend of flavours that a bechamel has, but it is deliciously rich and luxurious. The sauce can be kept warm by covering the pan and standing it in a larger pan of hot (not boiling) water. To prevent a skin from forming, run a spoonful of melted butter over the sauce, then beat it into the sauce just before serving.

Butter-enriched sauces

These rich but light-textured sauces are part of the world of *nouvelle cuisine*. These two words — not to be confused with *cuisine minceur*, a calorie-counted cuisine unique to Michel Guérard — are simply a term used to describe the revolutionized gourmet cooking of France. Fernand Point, who is involved in the *nouvelle cuisine* movement, believes that sauces should be lighter than they have been, though not necessarily less rich. Sauces of *nouvelle cuisine* are thickened by reduction and by the addition of butter or cream, but never with flour.

Here I give you the renowned White butter sauce (*sauce beurre blanc*) which begins with a reduction of white wine vinegar and dry shallots. The mixture is then thickened by the addition of finely diced, unsalted butter which is whisked into the sauce, a little at a time. As this emulsifies, it adds

the body and texture which make the sauce.

Butter-enriched sauces require particular care in their preparation to avoid curdling. When the finely diced, unsalted butter is whisked into the sauce it must not melt, but merely soften, or the sauce will curdle.

To avoid curdling, the heat must be very gentle. You may use either a double boiler or a non-aluminium saucepan. If you are a beginner, it is best to use a double boiler. With the water in the bottom pan gently simmering, you can whisk the butter into the sauce without fear of it melting. Once you have got the knack of making this type of sauce, you may prefer to make them in a saucepan. Don't use an aluminium pan or the acid in the sauce will react with the metal and taint the flavour. Stand the pan over a very gentle heat and take if off the heat when the butter looks as if it might melt.

Don't be too disheartened if it takes you a couple of tries to master the art of butter-enriched sauces. They do require the right touch, but once you have acquired it, you have something to be proud of, and the ability to make the perfect, light accompaniments for lobster, fish, chicken or veal.

Fresh ingredients are needed to make perfect velouté, cream and butter-enriched sauces

Making a velouté sauce

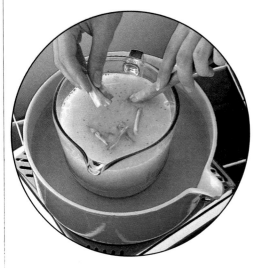

Put the sauce in a measuring jug in a pan of simmering water to reduce the quantity. Flavour with mushroom trimmings.

When reduced, the consistency will be correct. Highlight the flavour with a squeeze of lemon juice and check the seasoning.

Remove the finished sauce from the heat and enrich it by whisking in extra butter, diced into small pieces.

Classic velouté sauce

🍴 20 minutes initial cooking,
45 minutes reducing

Makes 300 ml /10 fl oz
600 ml /1 pt hot chicken, veal or fish stock
25 g /1 oz butter
30 ml /2 tbls flour
salt and freshly ground white pepper
stems from 6 mushrooms
lemon juice

1 Pour the stock into a saucepan, bring it to the boil and then continue to boil it until it has reduced to 450 ml /16 fl oz.
2 Make the roux in the top pan of a double boiler, placed directly over the heat. Melt the butter in the pan, add the flour and cook, stirring, for 4–5 minutes to form a pale roux. Remove the pan from the heat and gradually stir or whisk in the hot stock. Return the pan to the heat and bring the sauce slowly to the boil, stirring or whisking constantly to prevent lumps from forming.
3 Add a pinch each of salt and freshly ground white pepper and add the mushroom stems. Stand the pan of sauce over gently simmering water and cook for about 45 minutes, stirring occasionally and skimming the surface from time to time, if necessary, until the sauce is reduced to 300 ml /10 fl oz and is thick, light and creamy. Sieve the sauce and then discard the mushroom stems.
4 Flavour with more salt and freshly ground white pepper, if necessary, and a squeeze of lemon juice.

● If you are using stock made from a cube, do not add salt to the sauce in step 3.
● Instead of reducing the sauce in a double boiler, you can pour it into a heatproof measuring jug and stand it in a saucepan of gently bubbling water. This enables you to see at a glance when the sauce has reduced to 300 ml /10 fl oz, but it does take a little longer than in a double boiler. If you do reduce the sauce in a jug, and make the roux in a heavy-based saucepan, you will not need a double boiler at all.

Variations on velouté sauce
● Allemande sauce can be made with a chicken, veal or fish-based velouté. Beat 2 egg yolks with 60 ml /4 tbls thin or thick cream, stir in a little of the hot sauce, then stir the mixture back into the sauce. Stir over a gentle heat until the sauce has thickened. Do not allow it to boil. Made with a chicken or veal stock, Allemande sauce is good served with poached chicken, vegetables, eggs or offal. Made with a fish stock, it should be served with white fish.
● Andalouse sauce: skin and chop 2 or 3 large tomatoes and cook them in a little olive oil, with a crushed clove of garlic, until they have reduced to a purée. Finely chop 2

Velouté sauce with trout in lettuce packets

pimentos and then add them to the sauce with the tomato mixture and some finely chopped fresh parsley. Make it with chicken stock to serve with poached chicken or eggs, or with fish stock to serve with fish.
● Hongroise sauce is a paprika, onion and wine-flavoured sauce best served with sautéed chops or steaks, eggs, fish or poultry. To make it, sauté 60 ml /4 tbls finely chopped onion in butter until it is soft but not coloured. Season with a good pinch of paprika, then add about 100 ml /4 fl oz white wine and a small bouquet garni. Boil the liquid until it has reduced by two-thirds. Stir in the velouté sauce (based on veal, chicken or fish stock, depending on what you intend to serve the sauce with) and simmer it over a medium heat for 6 minutes. Sieve the sauce to remove any lumps and then whisk in 40 g /1½ oz diced butter.
● Normandy sauce is always made with a fish velouté. Beat 3 egg yolks with 125 ml /4 fl oz thick cream, a squeeze of lemon juice and 50–125 ml /2–4 fl oz oyster or mussel juice. Stir this mixture into the warm, fish-based velouté and heat without boiling, whisking in 50 g /2 oz diced, unsalted butter. Before serving, stir in another 50 ml /2 fl oz thick cream and 50 g /2 oz diced butter. Season with salt, pepper and more lemon juice. This sauce is a classic accompaniment to poached sole fillets, oysters and prawns.
● Poulette sauce can be served with eel, mussels, offal, or vegetables, particularly salsify. To make it, beat 2 egg yolks with 60 ml /4 tbls thick cream, stir in a little of the hot sauce, then stir this mixture back into the sauce. Heat gently, without boiling, then flavour with lemon juice and chopped fresh parsley.

Velouté sauce with trout in lettuce packets

🍴 1 hour 10 minutes

Serves 8
16 large green lettuce leaves
salt and freshly ground black pepper
8 trout, 175 g /6 oz each,
  skinned and filleted
225 g /8 oz fresh white breadcrumbs
30 ml /2 tbls each finely chopped
  parsley, tarragon and chives
50 g /2 oz butter
300 ml /10 fl oz dry white wine
1 chicken stock cube, crumbled
60 ml /4 tbls finely chopped onion
60 ml /4 tbls finely chopped
  mushroom stalks
For the fish velouté sauce
25 g /1 oz butter
30 ml /2 tbls flour
1.1 L /2 pt fish stock, home-made or
  from a cube
salt and freshly ground black pepper
60 ml /4 tbls finely chopped onion
1 chicken stock cube, crumbled
30 ml /2 tbls tomato purée
275 ml /10 fl oz thick cream

1 Blanch the lettuce leaves in boiling salted water for a few seconds, then put them in cold water. Heat the oven to 190C /375F / gas 5.

2 Season the trout fillets on both sides with salt and freshly ground black pepper. Mix the breadcrumbs and herbs and set aside.

3 Melt the butter in a frying-pan and sauté the fillets for 1 minute each side, until they start to colour. Remove them from the pan. Cut a rectangle from each fillet 5–7.5 cm / 2–3 in long and save the trimmings.

4 Spread the lettuce leaves on a tea-towel to dry. Place 1 trout segment on a lettuce leaf; spread it with some of the herbed breadcrumb mixture. Top it with a second trout segment and make a packet by folding and tucking in the lettuce leaf so it holds together neatly. Make up the other lettuce leaf packets.

5 To make the sauce, melt the butter in the top of a double boiler over direct heat; blend in the flour and cook the mixture for a few minutes. Stir in the fish stock and season with salt and pepper to taste. Place the pan over hot water and cook, stirring continuously with a whisk, until the mixture is well blended. Add the finely chopped onion, chicken stock cube and tomato purée; reduce the heat and simmer gently, stirring occasionally until the sauce is reduced by half. Strain through a fine sieve. Stir in the cream, adjust the seasoning and keep the sauce warm.

6 Place the trout packets in a shallow flameproof dish large enough to contain them side by side without touching. Pour the wine over them and then sprinkle with the crumbled stock cube, chopped onion and mushroom stalks. Bake for 10 minutes; place on individual dishes and keep warm.

7 Add the trout trimmings to the juices in the dish and boil over a high heat for 3 minutes. Strain and stir into the sauce. Adjust the seasonings and pour a little sauce around the trout packets and serve.

Sauce suprême

20 minutes initial cooking, then about 50 minutes

Makes 450 ml /15 fl oz
600 ml /1 pt hot chicken stock, home-made or from a cube
40 g /1½ oz butter
30 ml /2 tbls flour
salt and freshly ground white pepper
8 button mushrooms, finely chopped
150 ml /5 fl oz thick cream
15 ml /1 tbls lemon juice
a small pinch of cayenne pepper

1 Pour the stock into a saucepan, bring it to the boil and continue boiling until it has reduced to 450 ml /15 fl oz.

2 Melt 25 g /1 oz of the butter in the top pan of a double boiler, directly over the heat. Add the flour and cook, stirring, for 4–5 minutes to form a pale roux. Remove the pan from the heat and gradually stir or whisk in the hot stock. Bring it slowly to the boil, stirring or whisking continuously.

3 Add a pinch of salt and freshly ground white pepper and stir in the finely chopped button mushrooms. Stand the pan of sauce over gently simmering water and cook for about 45 minutes, stirring occasionally and skimming the surface from time to time, until the sauce is reduced to 300 ml /10 fl oz.

4 Strain the sauce into a clean saucepan. Add the thick cream, the lemon juice and the cayenne pepper and season to taste with salt, if necessary. Stand the pan over a gentle heat and heat, stirring, until the sauce thickens. Do not boil. Remove pan from the heat. Cut the rest of the butter into pieces and whisk them into the sauce. Serve immediately.

Easy cream sauce

This easy-to-prepare, rich cream sauce is excellent with poached vegetables or chicken.

10–15 minutes

Makes about 300 ml /10 fl oz
10 ml /2 tsp softened butter
10 ml /2 tsp flour
¼ chicken stock cube, crumbled
300 ml /10 fl oz thick cream
salt and freshly ground white pepper

1 Melt the butter in a heavy pan. Blend in the flour and the crumbled stock cube with a wooden spoon and stir over a low heat for 2–3 minutes to make a white roux.

2 Remove the pan from the heat and gradually add the thick cream, stirring vigorously with the wooden spoon or a small wire whisk to prevent lumps from forming. Return the pan to the heat, bring the sauce to the boil, stirring all the time, then simmer the sauce for 5–10 minutes. Season to taste with salt and freshly ground white pepper.

Sauce suprême served with asparagus

White butter sauce

One of the most famous sauces of French *nouvelle cuisine, sauce beurre blanc* is perfect for grilled or poached fish, lobster or even poached chicken.

5–10 minutes

Makes about 225 ml /8 fl oz
2 shallots, very finely chopped
45 ml /3 tbls white wine vinegar
45 ml /3 tbls dry white wine
225 g /8 oz unsalted butter, cut into small dice
salt and freshly ground white pepper

1 In the top pan of a double boiler, combine the very finely chopped shallots with the white wine vinegar and the dry white wine. Place the pan directly over the heat and simmer until the liquid around the chopped shallots is reduced to 15 ml /1 tbls.

2 Stand the pan of reduced liquid over simmering water and gradually whisk in the diced butter, a few pieces at a time. The butter will soften and thicken the sauce.

3 Season the sauce with salt and freshly ground white pepper. Serve immediately.

● Once you have got the knack of making this sauce you will be able to make it in an ordinary, non-aluminium saucepan. After reducing the liquid, stand the pan over a very gentle heat and whisk in the butter, removing the pan from the heat from time to time so that the butter does not melt, merely softens.

HOLLANDAISE & BEARNAISE SAUCES

These egg yolk and butter sauces are in the same family as mayonnaise, but are served warm. As with mayonnaise, the basic technique is quite simple, but you do need to concentrate!

To the French, a sauce is the basis of all good cooking — without it fish is just fish, asparagus is just asparagus, steak is just steak. In this chapter we look at two of the classic French emulsion sauces, Hollandaise sauce and Bearnaise sauce, and their variations.

Hollandaise has little to do with modern Holland, but the French have the charming habit of naming some of their greatest sauces after the country which gave the creators their inspiration.

These cooked sauces use exactly the same emulsifying process as uncooked mayonnaise. The egg particles are separated during beating and held in suspension — in oil in a mayonnaise, in liquid butter in hollandaise and bearnaise.

Both these sauces use a combination of egg yolk and an acid emulsifying agent — lemon juice in the case of hollandaise, and a mixture of chopped fresh herbs, shallots, wine vinegar and dry white wine (sharper and stronger than lemon juice) in the case of bearnaise. Diced butter is whisked into the egg yolk and acid mixture over a low heat and a thick, rich sauce results. The amount of butter you add to the egg yolks will determine whether you have a rich or a mild-flavoured sauce.

These classic sauces add a touch of splendour to poached or grilled salmon, delicate hot mousses of vegetables or fish, thick grilled steaks, fresh, green asparagus and many more dinner party favourites.

Making hollandaise

You will need the ingredients at the correct temperature, a double boiler (or a bowl set over a saucepan) and a wire whisk. Besides following the recipe carefully, you need to take the following points into account.
● The sauce must never come to the boil or the egg will scramble.
● The water over which the sauce is cooking must never be allowed even to simmer, or the sauce will become too hot and then it will curdle.
● Add the butter little by little, as carefully as you add the olive oil when making mayonnaise. I suggest using cold butter instead of the more classic method of using melted butter (except in my Blender hollandaise recipe). This way, the diced cold butter melts gradually in the warmth of the egg yolks and acid. As the butter melts slowly, there is no danger of there being too much melted butter for the egg yolks to cope with at one time, which would make the sauce curdle.

If the sauce has curdled because the water was too hot or the butter added too quickly, don't despair. Just throw in an ice cube and whisk furiously, over the hot water, until the sauce emulsifies again. Remove the ice cube immediately.

Many cooks do not strain a hollandaise before serving it. Though it should be perfectly smooth when you have finished cooking it, my experience is that it is best strained. This removes any thread of egg white that may have clung on to the egg yolk and then set to form a lump in the sauce. It also gives the sauce an extra gloss. I suggest pressing the sauce through a fine nylon sieve into a sauceboat.

Serve the sauce with your chosen meat or vegetables — even something simple becomes a luxury dish with one of these golden sauces on top of it.

Classic hollandaise sauce

Hollandaise is a classic of the French kitchen. It is the egg yolks that make the sauce richly flavoured, but you can vary this by adjusting the amount of butter you add to the egg yolks. Add less butter for a rich sauce to serve with the strong flavours of asparagus, broccoli or cauliflower, or more butter for a milder sauce to complement the delicacy of veal, poached or grilled salmon, or hot mousses of vegetables or fish.

🕒 15 minutes

Makes about 175–275 ml /6–10 fl oz
5 ml /1 tsp lemon juice, plus a few drops to finish
salt and freshly ground white pepper
4 egg yolks
125–225 g /4–8 oz unsalted butter, diced into 10 mm /¹/₂ in cubes

1 Place 5 ml /1 tsp lemon juice in the top pan of a double boiler, or in a bowl set over a saucepan, with 15 ml /1 tbls cold water and a pinch each of salt and white pepper.
2 Add the egg yolks and one piece of the butter to the lemon juice mixture and, using a wire whisk, stir the mixture rapidly and constantly over hot but not simmering water, until the butter has melted and the mixture begins to thicken.
3 Add the second piece of butter and continue whisking. As the butter melts, add the third piece of butter, stirring from the bottom of the pan until the butter has melted.
4 Continue to add the remaining butter in the same way. Using the smaller quantity of butter will give you a richer tasting sauce, using more butter will give you a gentler tasting sauce.
5 Remove the pan or bowl of sauce from the hot water and beat for a further 2–3 minutes. Next, return the pan or bowl to the hot water and beat for 2 minutes more. By this time the emulsion should have formed

and the sauce will be thick and creamy.
6 Finish with a few drops of lemon juice and more salt and pepper, if needed. Strain and keep warm over warm (not hot) water.

● For Horseradish hollandaise, make the hollandaise with 225 g /8 oz butter, then whisk in 15 ml /1 tbls horseradish sauce after straining. Serve with grilled steak.
● For Mousseline-hollandaise sauce, make the hollandaise with 225 g /8 oz butter, then fold in 75 ml /5 tbls thick cream, whipped, just before serving. Serve with fish or boiled vegetables.
● Mustard hollandaise is particularly good with fried or poached fish. Make the hollandaise with 225 g /8 oz butter, then beat in 10 ml /2 tsp Dijon mustard after straining.

Blender hollandaise sauce

If you think the classic way of making a hollandaise sauce sounds complicated, try using an electric blender. For this method the butter is melted before it is added to the egg yolks. Add it very slowly and carefully to prevent curdling.

🕒 5–10 minutes

Makes 175–275 ml /6–10 fl oz
125–225 g /4–8 oz unsalted butter
4 egg yolks
5 ml /1 tsp lemon juice, plus a few drops to finish
salt and freshly ground white pepper

Sirloin steaks served with the perfect accompaniment of Bearnaise sauce

Making a hollandaise sauce

Using a double boiler containing hot but not simmering water, over a very gentle heat, stir together the lemon juice and seasoning, the egg yolks and the first cube of butter.

Add the second piece of cold butter to the mixture and continue whisking. As the butter melts into the egg yolks, the sauce will begin to thicken.

Add the remaining butter little by little, whisking all the time from the bottom of the pan. Adding the cold butter slowly like this should prevent the sauce from curdling.

To adjust the seasoning, add a few extra drops of lemon juice, a little salt and freshly ground white pepper. Finally, strain the sauce to make sure that it is absolutely smooth.

1 Melt the butter in a small, heavy pan over a gentle heat. Do not allow it to bubble or sizzle, as this will colour it.
2 Warm the goblet of the electric blender by pouring in hot water and letting it stand for a few minutes. Then empty and dry the goblet.
3 Place the egg yolks in the blender goblet with 5 ml /1 tsp lemon juice, 15 ml /1 tbls cold water and a pinch each of salt and freshly ground white pepper.
4 Switch on the blender to mix the ingredients in the goblet. Remove the inner cover of the goblet and, with the blender at a moderate speed, add the hot melted butter in a very thin stream. If the butter is added slowly enough, the sauce will thicken before your eyes. If the sauce remains too liquid, pour it into the top pan of a double boiler, or a bowl set over a saucepan, and stir over hot but not simmering water for a few seconds to thicken it. If you think that your sauce is over-stiff, thin it by beating in 15–30 ml /1–2 tbls very hot water.
5 Finish the sauce with a few drops of lemon juice and more salt and white pepper, if needed. Strain the sauce and keep it warm over warm (not hot) water.

Ingredients for sauce-making

● This sauce can be flavoured in the same way as Classic hollandaise sauce: with horse-radish, mousseline or mustard flavourings.

Sauce maltaise

Serve this lovely pink sauce with broccoli, asparagus and poached or steamed fish.

 20 minutes

Makes 175–275 ml /6–10 fl oz
finely grated zest of 1 blood orange and
  45–60 ml /3–4 tbls juice
4 egg yolks
125–225 g /4–8 oz unsalted butter, cut into
  10 mm /½ in cubes
15 ml /1 tbls lemon juice
salt and freshly ground white pepper

1 Place the finely grated orange zest in a small pan with 60 ml /4 tbls water. Bring to the boil and simmer gently for 2 minutes. Drain the liquid through a muslin-lined

sieve; pat the rind dry in absorbent paper.
2 Place the blanched orange zest in the top pan of a double boiler, or in a bowl set over a saucepan, with the egg yolks, one piece of the butter, 15 ml /1 tbls each orange and lemon juice and a pinch each of salt and freshly ground white pepper.
3 Using a whisk, stir the mixture rapidly and constantly over hot but not simmering water, until the butter has melted and the mixture begins to thicken.
4 Add the second piece of butter and continue whisking. As the butter melts and the mixture thickens, add the third piece of butter, stirring from the bottom of the pan until the butter has melted. Continue to add the remaining butter in exactly the same way. Less butter gives a richer tasting sauce, more butter gives a much gentler tasting sauce.
5 Remove the pan or bowl of sauce from the heat and flavour it with the remaining orange juice and some more salt and pepper, if it is needed. Strain the sauce carefully and then keep it warm over warm (not hot) water until ready to serve.

● If blood oranges are unavailable, use an ordinary orange, flavour the sauce with a few more drops of lemon juice and then tint it with a spot of red food colouring.

Eggs in pastry with curried hollandaise sauce

making and chilling shortcrust pastry, then 1 hour

Serves 4
1 × My favourite shortcrust
  pastry (page 28)
40 g /1½ oz butter
flour, for dusting
4 eggs
60 ml /4 tbls white wine vinegar
salt and freshly ground black pepper
For the curried hollandaise
5 ml /1 tsp lemon juice
salt and freshly ground white pepper
75 g /3 oz softened butter
3 egg yolks
5–10 ml /1–2 tsp curry powder
flat-leafed parsley, to garnish

1 Grease 4 individual 10 cm /4 in loose-bottomed fluted tartlet tins, brioche or individual Yorkshire pudding tins.
2 Roll out the pastry thinly on a lightly floured surface and cut 4 circles 15 mm /½ in larger than the tins. Line the tins, easing the pastry into the flutes with your fingertips. Trim off the tops with a knife. Chill for 30 minutes. Heat the oven to 200C /400F /gas 6.
3 Line the chilled pastry shells with foil and fill with dried beans. Bake for 10 minutes, then remove the beans and foil. Turn down the oven to 180C /350F /gas 4. Bake for a further 8–10 minutes, or until set and golden. Remove from the oven, let the pastry cases set for 2 minutes, then remove from the tins. Keep warm.
4 Meanwhile, make the hollandaise sauce:

out 5 ml /1 tsp lemon juice with 15 ml / 1 tbls cold water, salt and white pepper in the top pan of a double boiler. Divide the butter in four. Add the egg yolks and ¼ of the butter to the pan. Whisk rapidly over simmering water until the butter melts and the mixture starts to thicken.

5 Being careful that the water never boils, whisk in the remaining 3 portions of butter in turn. Remove the top pan from the heat and whisk for 2–3 minutes. Next, return to the heat and whisk for 2 minutes more. Whisk in the curry powder. Strain and keep the sauce warm over warm water.

6 Poach the eggs. Fill a large saucepan with water, add the white wine vinegar and bring to the boil, then reduce the heat to a gentle simmer. Break an egg into a cup and slip it into the water. Repeat, quickly and carefully, with the remaining eggs. Raise the heat so that the water bubbles and simmer gently for about 3 minutes. Remove the eggs from the pan with a slotted spoon in the order in which they were added. Drain them on absorbent paper.

7 Place 1 poached egg in each pastry case. Season to taste with salt and freshly ground black pepper and dot with a little butter. Top each egg with 30 ml /2 tbls curried hollandaise, garnish and serve.

Bearnaise sauce

This sauce was invented by a Bearnaise chef working in the Pavilion Henri IV, a restaurant outside Paris, in the first half of the 19th century. He named the sauce to honour King Henri IV, who was also a native of Béarn. This sauce is the perfect accompaniment to grilled fillet or sirloin steak.

🕗 30 minutes

Makes about 275 ml /10 fl oz
4–6 sprigs of fresh tarragon, coarsely chopped
4–6 sprigs of fresh chervil, coarsely chopped
15 ml /1 tbls chopped shallot
2 black peppercorns, crushed
30 ml /2 tbls tarragon vinegar
150 ml /5 fl oz dry white wine
3 egg yolks
225 g /8 oz unsalted butter, diced into 10 mm / ½ in cubes
salt
lemon juice
cayenne pepper

1 Place half of the coarsely chopped tarragon and chervil in a saucepan with the chopped shallot, crushed black peppercorns, tarragon vinegar and white wine. Bring to the boil and cook over high heat until the liquid has reduced to 30 ml /2 tbls. Remove the pan from the heat and set on one side.
2 Beat the egg yolks with 15 ml /1 tbls cold water, then place them in the top pan of a double boiler, or a bowl set over a saucepan. Strain in the reduced liquid. Using a wire whisk, stir briskly and constantly over hot but not simmering water until the mixture is light and fluffy.
3 Whisk in the first piece of butter. When it has melted and has been incorporated, add

the second piece. Wait until each piece of butter has been incorporated before adding the next.
4 When the mixture begins to thicken, start adding a few pieces of butter at a time. Whisk thoroughly all the time, stirring from the bottom of the pan until the butter has melted.
5 Remove the pan or bowl of sauce from the hot water. Season to taste with salt, lemon juice and cayenne pepper. Strain the sauce through a fine sieve to give it a good gloss and stir in the remaining chopped herbs. Keep the sauce warm over warm (not hot) water until it is served.

● For Sauce Choron, to serve with roast saddle of lamb, grilled or sautéed meat, poached or fried fish, mix 15–30 ml /1–2 tbls tomato purée with the reduced wine and herb liquid before adding it to the egg yolks, then continue as for the basic recipe.
● For Sauce Foyot, to serve with grilled meat, add 5 ml /2 tsp Quick meat glaze (made by boiling a good quality canned consommé until it is reduced to a syrupy glaze — it will take about 20 minutes) to the reduced wine and herb mixture and stir until it is dissolved before adding it to the egg yolks.

Eggs in pastry with curried hollandaise sauce

CLASSIC FRENCH BROWN SAUCES

Sauces, no matter how simple, are of vital importance to the cook. They add flavour, moisture and colour to food, sometimes adding the touch that transforms it from an everyday dish to something special.

In French cooking the word sauce means any liquid, or semi-liquid, that complements a dish. This includes glamorous emulsified sauces, tomato-based and butter-enriched sauces and the lightly thickened gravy that inevitably accompanies the Sunday roast. It also includes the time-consuming classics of French cuisine — brown sauces.

Most sauces are thickened either with flour and butter (a *roux*) or by reduction, or by a combination of these methods. But don't necessarily think that sauces need always be thick and rich — the modern thought in France is to use as little flour as possible in sauce cooking, so that the sauces are smoother in texture, more delicate in flavour and more digestible.

Reduction is a key word in French sauce cooking terminology. It is important because this very simple process — boiling sauces over heat to reduce them to a half, or even a third or a quarter of their original quantity — concentrates the flavour and quality of the sauce wonderfully.

Making a roux

Many classic sauce recipes start with instructions to 'make a roux'. A roux is simply a mixture of butter and flour combined over a low heat. Many cooks use equal weights — I prefer a little more butter.

The technical explanation of what happens when you make a roux is that the starch cells contained in the flour burst and the starch combines completely with the melted butter to form a paste capable of absorbing many times its own weight. To bring this about, all you need do is to melt the butter in a saucepan, stir in an equal volume of flour and then cook the mixture over a low heat for a few minutes, until the taste of raw flour has gone. Your roux is then ready for the liquid to be added to it. There are three kinds of roux — white, pale and brown.

Brown roux is used for making all brown sauces. It is cooked in a heavy-bottomed saucepan over direct heat and it must be cooked enough to give it a good colour and a fine, nutty flavour. Cook the roux, stirring constantly with a wire whisk or a wooden spoon, for 6–7 minutes. It should be a light-brown colour and it should have a light, nutty aroma. Do not let the roux become too brown or it will taste bitter.

Making stock

Your stock will be only as good as the ingredients you put in it, so don't be tempted to treat it as a way of using up old and tired ingredients. However, you may vary the ingredients according to what is available.

When making a brown stock, the bones and vegetables are first roasted for a while so that they add a rich colour to the stock. The roasted ingredients are then put into the stock pot. The roasting tin is 'deglazed' by adding water to it and stirring over the heat to dislodge all the sediment and bits stuck to the sides and base. This is then added to the stock-pot as well.

Using stock cubes

Stock cubes are indispensable in the modern kitchen but they need to be used with discrimination. They are excellent for quick sauces and as a base for soups. Stocks made with cubes are unsuitable for any recipe in which they are to be simmered and reduced to a small quantity. This is because the flavour is heightened with monosodium glutamate and salt which become too strong and overpowering once reduced.

A final word about stock cubes — experiment with all the different brands available. You will find a difference between them.

Adding liquid to the roux

First remove the pan from the heat. Next add the liquid to the pan, a little at a time, stirring constantly with a wire whisk or a wooden spoon so that it is incorporated smoothly. After the liquid has been added and the pan returned to the heat, the sauce needs to be stirred constantly until it comes to the boil or it will become lumpy. Remember, no sauce is ready as soon as it thickens. Even the simplest flour-thickened sauce must be simmered for at least 3 minutes after it thickens otherwise it will have a raw taste because the flour is not properly cooked. More complicated sauces should be cooked for much longer to allow the flavours to improve by careful reduction.

Thickening sauces by reduction

The heart of every sauce is its flavorsome stock or liquid ingredient. The quality and flavour of this liquid is concentrated by boiling the sauce to reduce it. French chefs usually use extra liquid in their sauces — almost twice as much as they actually need — and then cook the sauces for longer until they are reduced to the right consistency. This concentrates and blends the flavours, making their sauces smoother, more transparent and more delicious.

Brown sauces

Basic brown sauce is made with a brown roux and a brown stock. It is given a long simmering with sliced vegetables, then sieved before serving.

Sauce espagnole is known as a *sauce mère*, mother sauce, or a foundation sauce, in French cooking, as many other sauces are derived from it. Because the sauce has extra substance and flavour, the roux is not made in the usual way. Diced fat salt pork or bacon and diced carrots and onion are cooked in dripping until they begin to turn golden. The flour is then sprinkled into the pan to make the roux, which is then cooked over a very gentle heat, stirred constantly, until it is a golden brown colour. To intensify the colour and flavour even more, I sear 2 halved Spanish onions in a hot, ungreased frying-pan until the halves are a very dark brown — almost black — on the cut sides. The browned onions are added to the sauce along with stock.

Glace de viande

Professional cooks swirl Glace de viande — or meat glaze — into the pan juices of cooked meat to create a quick, delicious, translucent sauce. It is also added to sauces, soups and consommés that lack flavour and strength. Glace de viande is made by boiling meat stock until it is reduced to a toffee-like, sticky consistency. To make it you need a large pan and a safe overnight burner on which it can bubble away. Once made, it will keep for several weeks in stoppered jars in the refrigerator. Make sure the jars are wide enough to spoon out the glace with a teaspoon. I think it is well worth the time and trouble involved in making it.

A teaspoonful or two of Glace de viande, added to the pan juices of grilled or fried steaks, chops, poultry, liver or kidneys immediately creates a sauce; add a little lemon juice or cognac, Madeira or sherry, or whisk in a little thick cream or some diced butter and you have a deliciously subtle sauce. Also, I like to whisk a little Glace de viande into melted butter with almonds and pine nuts and then toss this simple sauce with cooked noodles or rice, to serve as an accompaniment to meat, fish or poultry.

I have included a recipe for a Quick meat glaze which is practical to make, but be sure to make it with the best quality canned consommé you can find. If you use a poor quality consommé, your glaze will taste inferior.

Adding the highlights

In professional kitchens we sometimes use a few chef's tricks to embellish a sauce. First, liquid flavourings are added. Both wine and stock are used. Each one is reduced to just a tablespoonful or two before stirring in.

Taste the sauce after these additions — if it seems bland, add just a squeeze of lemon or a dash of Tabasco. On the other hand, if it needs to be mellowed, a teaspoonful of Madeira or cognac will soften and darken the flavour.

French chefs often incorporate extra butter into a sauce to make it thicker and more flavorsome. The butter is finely diced and whisked in with a wire whisk after the sauce has been removed from the heat, just before serving. The pan must not be returned to the heat after this addition of butter or the sauce will separate and become fatty.

Keeping the sauce warm

To keep sauce warm, cover the saucepan to prevent a skin from forming, then stand it in a larger saucepan containing hot, but not boiling, water. This is called a *bain-marie*. With thicker sauces a spoonful of liquid —

Gravy

Gravy is easy to make badly! Try this recipe for successful gravy.

making the stock and roasting the meat, then 8–10 minutes

Makes about 425 ml /15 fl oz
roasted meat and the drippings from the roasting tin
20 g /¾ oz or 45 ml /3 tbls flour
425 ml /15 fl oz stock
salt
freshly ground black pepper
a pinch of chopped fresh herb, such as rosemary, thyme or sage
15–30 ml /1–2 tbls red wine, white wine, port or Madeira

1 Lift the roasted meat onto a heated platter and keep it warm while you make the gravy. (The meat will carve better for having been rested.)
2 Pour off all but 45 ml /3 tbls of the drippings from the roasting tin, leaving the crusty bits and the meat juices in the tin.
3 Add the flour to the roasting tin and blend it in with a wire whisk or a wooden spoon. Cook and stir over a very low heat until the roux is frothy. This will be sufficent for a light gravy but if you want a richer gravy, then you will need to cook the roux for 3–4 minutes.
4 Gradually add the stock to the tin, stirring all the time. Bring to the boil over a gentle heat, stirring thoroughly, and scraping the base and sides of the tin with a wooden spoon to dislodge all the sediment and crusty bits.
5 Season the gravy to taste with salt and freshly ground black pepper. Add a pinch of chopped fresh herbs, then simmer the gravy for about 5 minutes. Add the red or white wine, port or Madeira, strain the gravy into a sauce boat and serve immediately.

● For a darker colour gravy, half fill a metal spoon with sugar, hold it over a direct heat until the sugar melts and turns brown. Use immediately.

Quick meat glaze

You need to use the best quality consommé for this recipe or the result will be poor.

20 minutes

Makes 45 ml /3 tbls
425 g /15 oz good quality canned consommé

1 Place the consommé in a saucepan and boil it fast for about 20 minutes, until it is reduced to just 45 ml /3 tbls and is a syrupy glaze. Watch it carefully towards the end. Store it in a small jar in the refrigerator.

● To use your time efficiently, boil the contents of 4 cans simultaneously in 4 saucepans. Cool the results and freeze in ice cube trays until required for other sauces.

---

water, stock or milk — or melted butter may be run over the top. Just before serving, whisk in this protective covering.

Basic brown sauce

making the stock, then 1¼ hours

Makes about 300 ml /10 fl oz
25 g /1 oz butter
1 small onion, thinly sliced
15 g /1½ oz or 30 ml /2 tbls flour
700 ml /1¼ pt brown stock, home-made or from a cube
1 small carrot, sliced
1 small turnip, sliced
4 mushrooms, sliced
1 celery stick, sliced, or 1.5 ml /¼ tsp celery seeds
2–4 tomatoes, sliced, or 15–30 ml /1–2 tbls tomato purée
1 fresh bouquet garni (3 sprigs parsley, 1 sprig thyme, 1 bay leaf, tied with string)
2 cloves
12 black peppercorns
salt

Gravy with roast beef and potatoes

1 Heat the butter in a heavy-bottomed saucepan. Add the thinly sliced onion and cook, stirring constantly, until golden. Stir in the flour and cook over a low heat for 1–2 minutes, stirring constantly, until the roux is a good golden brown colour but not burnt.
2 Remove the pan from the heat and gradually stir in the brown stock. Return the pan to the heat and bring the stock to the boil, stirring all the while. Boil for 5 minutes, carefully skimming off the scum with a slotted spoon.
3 Add the sliced carrot, turnip and mushrooms, sliced celery or celery seeds, sliced tomatoes or tomato purée, bouquet garni, cloves and black peppercorns to the pan. Simmer the sauce gently for 1 hour, stirring it occasionally and skimming the top very carefully when it is necessary.
4 Strain the sauce through a fine sieve and into a clean pan. Leave it to stand for a few minutes to allow the fat to rise to the surface, then carefully skim off the fat. Add salt to taste and reheat the sauce before serving. The sauce can be kept in a refrigerator for a few days.

Glace de viande

Here, for the record, is the classic French meat glaze. It is invaluable for adding to sauces, soups and consommés that lack flavour and strength. Once made, it can quickly be turned into a sauce for cooked meat by swirling it around in the hot cooking pan.

You need a 10 L /2¼ gal heavy-bottomed stock-pot and a completely safe overnight burner to simmer it on. The alternative is to divide the ingredients between two 5 L /1 gal pans — this will reduce the liquid much more quickly. Simmer the contents until they are reduced to about 1 L /1¾ pt in each — this will take 7–8 hours. Combine the stock and proceed with the recipe.

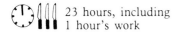 23 hours, including 1 hour's work

Makes 1 L /1¾ pt
3.5 kg /8 lb beef or veal bones with some meat, chopped into 10–15 cm /4–6 in pieces
1–2 chicken carcasses
1 large Spanish onion, cut in half
250 g /8 oz carrots, cut into 5 cm /2 in pieces
250 g /8 oz celery sticks and leaves, cut into 5 cm /2 in pieces
500 g /1 lb onions, cut into quarters
75–100 g /3–4 oz beef dripping
800 g /1 lb 12 oz canned tomatoes with their juice
bouquet garni
12 black peppercorns

1 Heat the oven to the highest temperature. Place the Spanish onion halves, cut sides down, in a hot, ungreased frying-pan or on an electric hot plate; sear over a high heat until the surfaces are dark brown, but not burnt.
2 Divide the bones, chicken carcasses, carrots, celery, onion quarters and beef dripping between 2 roasting tins. Cook them in the oven for about 1 hour, or until the bones and vegetables are well browned.
3 Using a slotted spoon, transfer the bones to a very large 10 L /2¼ gal, heavy-bottomed stock-pot. Pour in 6.7 L /12 pt water. Bring to the boil, lower the heat and skim off the scum, then continue to simmer and skim until all the scum has been removed.
4 Using a slotted spoon, transfer all the vegetables from the roasting tin to the stock-pot. Add the browned onion halves, canned tomatoes and juice, bouquet garni and black peppercorns, and simmer over the lowest possible heat for 18 hours, or until the stock is reduced to 4.5 L /8 pt. Skim when necessary.
5 Strain off the liquid, then pour it through a fine sieve into a clean stock-pot. Leave it to stand for a few minutes to allow the fat to rise to the surface, then skim off all the fat. Boil the stock for 2 hours, or until it has reduced to about 1 L /1¾ pt of syrupy glaze and the entire surface is covered with bubbles. Watch it carefully, so it does not over-reduce, burn and so become bitter.
6 Strain the hot Glace de viande through a muslin-lined sieve, then pour it into jars and

leave it to cool. Keep in the refrigerator until it is needed.

● Glace de viande will keep for several weeks in the refrigerator if it is boiled weekly. If a thin layer of fat rises to the surface while it is cooling, do not worry, it will make a seal and preserve the sauce for 2 weeks.
● Why not divide the Glace between two stoppered jars (wide enough to take a teaspoon) and share it with one of your 'cooking friends'? Next time it will be his or her turn to make the Glace de viande.
● Freeze Glace de viande in an ice cube tray. These cubes will be a handy size to use in sauces like Short-cut sauce espagnole and Sauce demi-glace.

Short-cut sauce espagnole

Sauce espagnole was introduced to France by the chefs of the Infanta of Spain when she married Louis XIV of France. It is the basis of a whole family of brown sauces. Make the Quick meat glaze ahead of the time when you are anticipating using this quick version of the classic espagnole sauce.

making the meat glaze (and stock, if used) then 45 minutes

Makes 425 ml /15 fl oz
25 g /1 oz butter
50 g /2 oz fat salt pork, finely diced
1½ Spanish onions, coarsely chopped
2 medium-sized carrots, coarsely chopped
1 celery stick, coarsely chopped
1 bay leaf
1.5 ml /¼ tsp dried thyme
45 ml /3 tbls flour
10 ml /2 tsp tomato purée
425 ml /15 fl oz beef stock, home-made or from a cube
75–90 ml /5–6 tbls dry white wine
45 ml /3 tbls Quick meat glaze (see recipe)
freshly ground black pepper

1 Melt the butter in a heavy saucepan and sauté the finely diced fat salt pork until it is transparent. Add the vegetables, the bay leaf and the thyme; continue to sauté until they are browned.
2 Sprinkle the flour into the pan, lower the heat and continue to sauté, stirring, for 2–3 minutes until the flour is golden.
3 Dilute the tomato purée with a little of the beef stock and stir it into the pan. Slowly stir in the remaining stock and the wine then bring to the boil, stirring constantly.
4 Stir in the meat glaze and simmer for 20 minutes, stirring occasionally.
5 Press the sauce through a fine sieve. Season to taste and use immediately, or allow it to cool, stirring occasionally, then store it in the refrigerator. Use within a week.

English devil sauce

making the basic sauce, then 15 minutes

Makes about 150 ml /5 fl oz
150 ml /5 fl oz Short-cut sauce espagnole or Basic brown sauce (see recipes)
50 ml /2 fl oz white wine
1 shallot, finely chopped
15 ml /1 tbls tomato ketchup
5 ml /1 tsp anchovy essence
5 ml /1 tsp Dijon mustard
5 ml /1 tsp vinegar
2.5 ml /½ tsp curry powder
a pinch of cayenne pepper

1 Place the Short-cut sauce espagnole or Basic brown sauce in a large saucepan with the white wine, finely chopped shallot, tomato ketchup, anchovy essence, Dijon mustard, vinegar, curry powder and cayenne pepper and simmer gently for 5–10 minutes.
2 Strain the sauce before using it. Serve it with roast or grilled meats or chicken.

● This sauce can also be flavoured with redcurrant jelly, or 15–30 ml /1–2 tbls of dry sherry.

1 Melt the butter in a saucepan and sauté the finely chopped shallot until it is golden. Add the red wine. Cook over a high heat to reduce the liquid to half the original quantity. Stir in the Short-cut sauce espagnole or Basic brown sauce and parsley; cook for 10–15 minutes.
2 Reduce the raw chicken livers to a purée in a blender or rub them through a fine sieve. Add the purée to the sauce and reheat thoroughly, without allowing the sauce to boil. Season to taste with salt and freshly ground black pepper. Serve the sauce with game or poultry.

Sauce bordelaise

making the basic sauce,
then 45 minutes

Makes about 300 ml /10 fl oz
425 ml /15 fl oz Short-cut sauce espagnole or
*   Basic brown sauce (see recipes)*
2 shallots, finely chopped
1 garlic clove, finely chopped
225 ml /8 fl oz red bordeaux
1 bay leaf
30 ml /2 tbls finely sliced beef marrow, taken
*   from the bone centre*
salt
5 ml /1 tsp finely chopped fresh parsley
a squeeze of lemon juice
freshly ground black pepper

1 Place the finely chopped shallots and the garlic in a small saucepan with the wine and the bay leaf and simmer until the wine is reduced to half its original quantity. Add the Short-cut sauce espagnole or Basic brown sauce and simmer for 20 minutes, carefully removing any scum that rises to the surface. Strain the sauce into a clean saucepan.
2 Poach the finely sliced beef marrow in gently simmering salted water for 5 minutes. Drain the marrow and add it to the sauce with the finely chopped parsley, a squeeze of lemon juice, and salt and freshly ground black pepper to taste. Serve the sauce with roast beef or steaks.

Sauce demi-glace

This sauce will set to a jelly-like consistency when it is cold.

making the basic sauce,
then 40 minutes

Makes about 300 ml /10 fl oz
600 ml /1 pt Short-cut sauce espagnole or
*   Basic brown sauce (see recipes)*
peelings and chopped stems of 6 mushrooms
90 ml /6 tbls dry sherry or Madeira
15–30 ml /1–2 tbls Quick meat glaze or
*   Glace de viande (see recipes)*

1 Boil the Short-cut sauce espagnole or Basic brown sauce until it is reduced to 300 ml /10 fl oz — this will take about 20 minutes.
2 Simmer the mushroom peelings and the chopped stems in the dry sherry or Madeira until the liquid is reduced to 45 ml /3 tbls.

Preparing Short-cut sauce espagnole

Add this, with the Quick meat glaze or Glace de viande, to the reduced sauce. Simmer over a low heat for 15 minutes.
3 Strain the sauce before serving it with baked ham, roast beef fillet or leg of lamb.

Sauce rouennaise

making the basic sauce,
then 30 minutes

Makes about 300 ml /10 fl oz
300 ml /10 fl oz Short-cut sauce espagnole or
*   Basic brown sauce (see recipes)*
15 g /½ oz butter
1 shallot, finely chopped
60–90 ml /4–6 tbls red wine
5 ml /1 tsp finely chopped fresh parsley
2 chicken livers, trimmed
salt
freshly ground black pepper

Sauce lyonnaise

making the basic sauce,
then 30 minutes

Makes about 300 ml /10 fl oz
300 ml /10 fl oz Short-cut sauce espagnole or
*   Basic brown sauce (see recipes)*
40 g /1½ oz butter
2 medium-sized onions, finely chopped
175 ml /6 fl oz dry white wine
10 ml /2 tsp freshly chopped parsley

1 Melt 25 g /1 oz of the butter in a saucepan and sauté the finely chopped onion until it is golden brown. Add the dry wine and simmer until it has reduced to half.
2 Add the Short-cut sauce espagnole or Basic brown sauce to the pan and cook gently for 15 minutes. Add the chopped parsley, then 'finish' the sauce by swirling in the remaining butter. Do not return the pan to the heat. Serve with lamb or vegetables.

MAYONNAISE

Mayonnaise, the rich, thick, golden sauce that springs, as if by magic, from the combination of olive oil, egg yolks and seasonings, is the basis of so many sauces. This is how to make it — and some variations.

There seem to be almost as many theories on the origin of the word mayonnaise as there are ways to serve this delicious sauce. The first theory has it that the word was created to celebrate a sauce brought back from the wars by the chef of the Duc de Richelieu when his master captured Port Mahon in 1756. Islanders used to dress cold meat and fish with a sauce made of raw egg yolk, garlic and olive oil. Richelieu's cook copied the sauce, leaving out the garlic, and *mahonnaise* — or *mayonnaise* as we know it today — was discovered. Some claim that the word was really *moyeunaise*, as in old French *moyeu* which meant the yolk of an egg.

Another school of thought claims that this golden sauce should really be called *magnonaise* as it comes from the verb *manier* (to stir). Others are of the opinion that it was originally called *bayonnaise*, as it was first known in the region of Bayonne in south-west France.

Whatever the origin of the word, we would lose a lot without mayonnaise. It is a delicious and useful accompaniment to cold beef, veal, chicken, cod, lobster, crab and pike. It can be served mixed with pieces of lobster, chicken, ham, turkey or assorted vegetables. It is lovely with the addition of fresh herbs, mustard, freshly grated horseradish, tomato purée, saffron, capers, or finely chopped gherkins or cucumber. It is the perfect accompaniment to hard-boiled eggs and a 'must' with chilled prawns. With the addition of dry white wine, vinegar, lemon juice or milk, mayonnaise is perfect for potato salad and, with liquid aspic added to it, it becomes a coating for cold chicken.

I use a rotary whisk to mix my mayonnaise. This is heresy to the teachers of my youth, who only used a wooden spoon and a plate, but I find the whisk is an almost foolproof method, which results in a mayonnaise with an excellent flavour and texture. On the other hand, you can use a blender and get quick, quite satisfactory results (see next page).

Mayonnaise should always be thick enough to cut with a knife — no wishy-washy emulsions for me! — and for this a considerable amount of olive oil must be used.

How to make perfect mayonnaise

Take two eggs out of the refrigerator ahead of time so that they come up to room temperature. Next, separate the eggs and place the yolks in a small mixing bowl or pudding bowl, carefully removing the gelatinous coiled thread that attaches the yolk to the white. Add 2.5 ml /½ tsp Dijon mustard and salt and freshly ground black pepper to taste to the yolks. Wring out a cloth in very cold water and twist it around the bottom of the bowl to keep it steady and cool. Now use a rotary whisk (or a wire whisk or fork) to beat the yolk mixture to a smooth paste.

Add a little lemon juice (the acid helps to form the emulsion), then beat in about 50 ml

Golden mayonnaise with salad

/2 fl oz olive oil, adding it drop by drop. Add a little more lemon juice, then add more oil, this time in a thin stream, beating all the time. Continue adding oil and beating until the sauce is a good, thick consistency — you will need about 275 ml /10 fl oz olive oil in all. Adjust the seasoning with more salt, pepper and lemon juice, if necessary. This will take you 5 minutes to make, and you will have 275 ml /10 fl oz of basic mayonnaise.

If your mayonnaise curdles, break another egg yolk into a clean bowl and gradually beat the curdled mayonnaise into it. Your mayonnaise will emulsify again immediately.

When the mayonnaise is to be used to dress a fish or potato salad, thin it down considerably with dry white wine, good vinegar, lemon juice or milk. If it is to be used for coating meat, poultry or fish, add a little liquid aspic to stiffen it.

If you are keeping mayonnaise for a day before using it, stir in 15 ml /1 tbls boiling water. This will keep it from turning or separating. Cover the bowl with a cool, damp cloth to prevent a skin from forming.

If you decide to save time and make your mayonnaise in a blender, then it will take you only a couple of minutes. Place the two egg yolks in the blender, add the wine vinegar or lemon juice, 2.5 ml /½ tsp of mustard powder, salt, freshly ground black pepper and 30 ml /2 tbls of cold water. Blend at maximum speed for 5 seconds.

Now remove the centre of the lid of the blender and, with the motor turned to maximum, add the olive oil in a thin, steady trickle. When all the oil has been incorporated, taste and adjust the seasoning.

Variations with mayonnaise
● If you add some saffron to your mayonnaise, it will give a very delicate and special flavour. This is good with turbot, or gull and duck eggs.
● Add 7.5 cm /3 in of cucumber, finely chopped, and 15 ml /1 tbls finely chopped parsley to 275 ml /10 fl oz plain mayonnaise to make a different accompaniment for fish (particularly salmon) and watercress.
● Russian mayonnaise is perfect with eggs and cooked salads and sea food. To 275 ml / 10 fl oz of plain mayonnaise add 30 ml / 2 tbls tomato ketchup, a dash of Tabasco and 5 ml /1 tsp each of chopped chives and canned pimentos.
● Horseradish mayonnaise is made by adding a little extra lemon juice, salt and some grated horseradish to the basic mayonnaise recipe.

Sauce verte

🍶 15 minutes

Makes 275 ml /10 fl oz
25 g /1 oz each fresh watercress, parsley and chervil sprigs
salt
275 ml /10 fl oz mayonnaise
15 ml /1 tbls each finely chopped fresh watercress, parsley, chervil and tarragon
15 ml /1 tbls lemon juice
freshly ground black pepper

Making perfect mayonnaise

Twist a cold wet cloth around the bottom of a bowl to keep it cool and steady. Beat 2 egg yolks, mustard and seasoning to a paste; use a rotary or wire whisk or a fork.

Add more olive oil, in a thin stream, beating all the time. Continue adding oil and beating until you have a good, thick emulsion. You will need about 275 ml /10 fl oz olive oil.

Add a little lemon juice to help form an emulsion. Now add 50 ml /2 fl oz good quality olive oil, drop by drop, beating all the time. Add some more lemon juice.

If your mayonnaise curdles, place another egg yolk in a clean bowl and gradually beat in the curdled mayonnaise. Your mayonnaise will emulsify again immediately.

1 Wash the sprigs of watercress, parsley and chervil carefully and plunge them into a small pan of boiling salted water. Bring back to the boil and simmer for 5–6 minutes. Drain thoroughly, put them between the folds of a tea-cloth and press dry.
2 Pound the blanched herbs to a paste in a mortar (or purée in a blender). Add the herb paste to the mayonnaise and mix well.
3 Stir in the finely chopped herbs and lemon juice and season to taste with salt and freshly ground black pepper. Chill the sauce before serving.

● Try this green mayonnaise with veal chops, ham, poached chicken, cold duck or on open sandwiches of tomato and avocado.

Sauce tartare

🍶 hard-boiling the eggs, then 10 minutes

Makes about 425 ml /15 fl oz
4 hard-boiled egg yolks
1 raw egg yolk
10 ml /2 tsp French mustard
10 ml /2 tsp lemon juice or wine vinegar
275 ml /10 fl oz olive oil
10 ml /2 tsp chopped capers
10 ml /2 tsp chopped gherkins
15 ml /1 tbls finely chopped fresh parsley
1.5 ml /¼ tsp finely chopped fresh tarragon
salt and freshly ground black pepper

1 Press the hard-boiled egg yolks through a fine sieve into a bowl. Add the raw egg yolk and mix with a spoon until blended.
2 Beat in the mustard and 5 ml /1 tsp each of lemon juice or wine vinegar and water.
3 Add the olive oil first a few drops at a time, then in a trickle, beating constantly.
4 Mix in the capers, gherkins, parsley and tarragon into the emulsion.
5 Season, and add the remaining lemon juice or wine vinegar.

SAVING THE SAUCE

A good sauce makes a memorable dish while a bad one spoils it. The same ingredients may result in either, but a little know-how can ensure success. Follow these easy tips and create beautiful sauces.

Sauces cause more bother to the inexperienced cook than almost anything else, except perhaps baking. With a cake you must get it right first time, with a sauce, you do have a second chance.

The first rule, if a sauce goes wrong, is don't panic! The second rule is, read these helpful hints and see what you can do to save your sauce if it is lumpy, thin, cold, greasy or scummy. There are also suggestions here, to enliven the flavour if the sauce tastes flat and uninteresting.

Is the sauce lumpy?

● If a roux-based sauce contains uncooked flour, you did not melt the butter and cook the flour correctly at the beginning.
● If the sauce contains uneven, thick patches, you probably hurried one stage too much. Did you add the liquid away from the heat? Did you warm the liquid (this helps it to thicken more quickly and evenly)? Did you stir continuously while it was thickening? All these precautions avoid lumps.
● Did you let it boil too long? This causes lumps to form.
● Reheating a cold sauce too rapidly may also cause lumps.
● To remove lumps, whisk with an electric beater. Alternatively, sieve it into a clean pan and whisk during reheating.

Is there too much liquid?

● If the flavour is adequate but the quantity excessive, simply ladle off some liquid and reserve it for making soup or another sauce.
● If there is a lot of liquid, but the flavour is poor — which is much more likely — concentrate the flavour of the sauce by reducing the liquid.
● To reduce the liquid a little, spoon off the excess sauce into a wide pan and boil it fiercely until it reduces to just a few tablespoons. Return this to the rest of the sauce and blend together.
● To reduce a large quantity of sauce to a small one, remove the solid ingredients with a slotted spoon to a serving plate and keep them warm. Now measure the liquid and decide how much you want; 300 ml /10 fl oz is plenty for 4 people. Return the sauce to the casserole, or a pan, and boil fiercely until you have the right quantity (measure again). Complete the thickening of the sauce and then combine it again with the rest of the ingredients.
● When making a casserole, if you are adding more liquid than you need for the sauce for the number to be served, remember to be sparing with the seasoning. For example, if you use several chicken cubes to make 1.1 L /2 pt chicken stock, in order to cover your chicken, this cannot be reduced to 300 ml /10 fl oz, as it will be grossly over-flavoured; use fewer cubes initially. Do not season the liquid heavily with salt and pepper before cooking; season after the final reduction.

Does the sauce taste boring?

● The addition of 1/8–1/4 chicken stock cube will help any sauce (even for fish) because it contains monosodium glutamate, which stimulates the taste buds.
● Add 60 ml /4 tbls wine, boiled to reduce it by half, to any non-alcoholic sauce. Dry white vermouth can be used, or 5 ml /1 tsp vinegar. A tablespoon of Marsala or Madeira will enrich any sauce.
● For a brown sauce, try adding a few drops of Tabasco, Worcestershire sauce, mushroom ketchup or some Dijon mustard. Try 15 ml /1 tbls anchovy essence.
● For a sweeter accent to a brown sauce, try adding 15 ml /1 tbls redcurrant jelly, the grated zest and juice of an orange or 15 ml / 1 tbls brown sugar plus 5 ml /1 tsp vinegar. Tomato purée — 30 ml /2 tbls — improves the appearance as well.
● White sauce is improved by adding some reduced white wine, a pinch of nutmeg or cayenne pepper and, of course, chopped fresh herbs.
● For extra gloss and richness, beat in small pieces of butter just before serving, but do not reheat the sauce, or it may separate and become fatty.

Is the sauce too thin?

● If the sauce is a chunky one, thicken it by adding a few more ingredients which cook quickly. To 300 ml /10 fl oz thin liquid add 15 g /1/2 oz rice or small pasta shapes or a small potato, thinly sliced.
● Alternatively, half the ingredients (for example vegetables) may be removed from the sauce, puréed and then returned. The remainder will add the chunky texture.
● For the majority of sauces, where adding extra fat is no problem, thicken with *beurre manié*. Mash to a very smooth paste, equal weights of flour and butter. Cut this into pea-sized pieces and drop it into the hot liquid. This will then thicken without lumps. Whisk over a low heat, but do not boil vigorously.
● For a good white sauce, thicken with egg. Use 1 egg yolk, stirring it into 60–75 ml /4–5 tbls thick cream, for 300 ml /10 fl oz liquid. Blend in a little hot sauce and return to the pan. Simmer over a low heat, without boiling.
● An unusual thickening, used in Mexican dishes, is melted chocolate. Added to a turkey or chicken recipe it does not taste sweet but imparts a richness to the sauce.

Is the sauce cold?

● Modern vacuum flasks, especially the squat ones with wide necks, are ideal for keeping sauces warm once they have been made.
● Another successful method of keeping a sauce warm is to put it over a pan of simmering water or in the top of a double boiler until you are ready to use it.

Is the sauce greasy or scummy?

● When frying or casseroling, check for fat on the meat before cooking it. Chickens have fat lumps near the vent. Remove these and also any visible fat from beef, lamb or pork. Often this fat can be rendered down and used for frying the dish.
● If fat floats on top of the liquid during cooking, skim it off carefully. When making stews or casseroles with meat that is likely to produce a fatty gravy, if possible it is best to prepare and cook the dish the previous day and then allow it to stand and cool overnight. Not only will the flavour generally be improved but the fat will solidify and can easily be removed.
● At the end of cooking, an ice cube dropped into the sauce will make the fat rise. Skim with a large metal spoon, or use a piece of bread or absorbent paper to soak up the floating fat.
● If there is a thick layer of excess fat (as in turkey gravy), remove the solid ingredients, then pour the sauce into a tall jug. Let it settle, then use a bulb baster to transfer the liquid back to the casserole, drawing it from the bottom of the jug. Leave behind several centimetres of juice and all the fat.
● To avoid a skin forming on top of a hot sauce while it waits, spread a dampened piece of greaseproof paper or a buttered paper, butter side down, on the surface.

● If you want an instant thickener but do not want to cook the sauce again, use potato flour or anything sold as *fécule*. Instant potato, used discreetly, has the same virtue. This will dissolve in the hot liquid without needing to be boiled (unlike flour additions). It is a very convenient way of thickening sauces which already contain egg yolks or cream, since they may curdle if cooked further.
● If you do not want to add any more fat, use cornflour. Use up to 15 ml /1 tbls cornflour for 300 ml /10 fl oz liquid to give a sauce of coating consistency. Blend the powder with 30 ml /2 tbls cold water, add a little sauce to the paste to raise the temperature and stir back into the hot sauce. Bring to the boil and cook until the consistency changes.
● For a sauce which is clear in appearance, use arrowroot. Use up to 12.5 ml /2 1/2 tsp arrowroot to thicken 300 ml /10 fl oz liquid. Make a paste and stir in the hot liquid, as for cornflour. Stir this into the sauce and bring it to the boil. Do not prolong the boiling or the sauce will thin again.

Pastry-making

SHORTCRUST PASTRY

If pastry-making is not your strong point, why not take a new look at shortcrust pastry. Use these easy-to-follow instructions to make delicious pastry dishes for every occasion.

Once you acquire the knack of handling shortcrust pastry, trickier ones like flaky and puff pastry will seem far less daunting. Like most other pastries, shortcrust is just a combination of flour and fat with a drop or two of liquid — iced water, milk or beaten egg yolk — to help hold it together.

Dry ingredients: for most pastries I use a good-quality plain flour, sometimes 'weakened' with a little cornflour to give a finer texture. Never use self-raising flour unless a recipe specially calls for it — the very nature of your pastry will alter radically.

Make sure your flour is quite dry. If it is damp, the carefully balanced moisture content of the pastry will be changed and your pastry will be tough. Always sift the flour with any other dry ingredients before rubbing in the fat. This ensures that they are thoroughly blended and free of lumps and it also helps to make the pastry lighter. Salt is added to bring out the flavour, and you may be surprised to know that I use a little icing sugar in my pastry, even for savoury flans. I assure you it is wonderfully successful!

Fat: the ratio of fat to flour is the crucial factor that decides the richness and flavour of a shortcrust pastry. Some shortcrust recipes suggest various combinations of butter, lard, margarine, etc. For me, there is nothing like the flavour of pure butter shortcrust, even though whipped vegetable fats in particular give a shorter texture. Use the butter at its coldest, straight from the refrigerator.

Liquid for binding: a pastry that is very rich in fat (like a shortbread, for example) can be kneaded together without the help of liquid but most pastries will need a sprinkling of water to bind them together. Once you have added the amount specified in the recipe, however, be careful about adding any more and if you do, keep it to a bare teaspoon at a time. Using too much liquid is the most common cause of tough pastry.

An egg yolk, which makes your pastry shorter and richer, also helps to keep the water content down, being largely composed of fat in a liquid form. Remember, too, that a pastry that has been resting in the refrigerator is noticeably moister when it comes out.

Handling a shortcrust pastry

Dice the butter into small pieces straight into the flour and toss them about to coat them. Next, use a pastry blender or two knives to chop the butter into smaller pieces.

The standard method of combining the fat and flour is known as 'rubbing in'. The objective is to distribute the fat as finely as possible throughout the flour. Obviously, you will have to work very quickly and lightly if all the fat and flour is to be reduced to fine breadcrumbs without the mixture turning oily, and this is what is meant by the expression 'having a light hand with pastry'.

Using just your fingertips, first break the

fat down into smaller pieces, making sure there is always a barrier of flour between the fat and the warmth of your fingers. Next, start rubbing the flakes of floury fat between your fingers and thumbs to make a crumb-like mixture. Do not attempt to work with all the mixture at once. Cup your hands slightly, scoop a portion of the mixture up into the air and let it run through your fingers and thumbs, rubbing out the little lumps of fat with a quick, light movement. The higher the floury crumbs have to fall, and therefore the more air you incorporate with them, the lighter your pastry will be.

Binding the pastry: when you come to add the liquid, sprinkle it over as large a surface as possible so that the actual mixing will be cut down to a minimum. I prefer to use a fork or knife blade to do the mixing — bits of dough are bound to stick to your fingers unless you are very careful. Handle the pastry as little as possible! As soon as you see that the pastry is holding together in lumps, stop mixing. Cup one hand and gently coax the mixture into a ball, rolling it around the bottom and sides of the bowl to pick up all the crumbs until it is almost clean.

Chilling: it is a good idea to chill pastry in the refrigerator for about 30 minutes, or up to 24 hours, before you roll it out ready for use. This is because it relaxes the gluten in the flour (which, when moistened, gives the elastic quality to the shortcrust) and makes the pastry lighter and more manageable.

Before you put the pastry in the refrigerator, wrap it tightly in greaseproof paper and a damp cloth or in foil or cling film. This prevents it from drying out and cracking.

Sweet shortcrust pastry

Shortcrust pastry is perfect for both sweet and savoury dishes, but there are those who have a particularly sweet tooth. For them use My favourite shortcrust pastry recipe, but substitute 5 ml /1 tsp icing sugar with 30 ml / 2 tbls icing sugar for an extra special result.

My favourite shortcrust pastry

🕙 20 minutes,
plus 1 hour resting

Makes 1 pastry case (plus spare pastry)
250 g /8 oz plain flour
5 ml /1 tsp icing sugar
2.5 ml /½ tsp salt
150 g /5 oz cold butter
1 egg yolk
5 ml /1 tsp lemon juice
30 ml /2 tbls iced water

1 Sift the flour, the icing sugar and the salt into a large bowl. Cut the cold butter directly

from the refrigerator into 5 mm /¼ in dice. Add these to the bowl.
2 Cut the diced butter into the flour mixture, using a pastry blender or two knives held one in each hand and cutting across each other like scissor blades. Continue until the mixture resembles coarse breadcrumbs.
3 Put aside the blender or knives. Scoop up some of the mixture with the fingers of both hands. Hold your hands high, just above the bowl rim. Lightly press out the lumps of fat between your thumbs and fingertips, letting the crumbs shower back into the bowl. You should only need to do this 6–7 times for the mixture to be reduced to the consistency of fine breadcrumbs.
4 Beat the egg yolk with a fork. Add the lemon juice and 15 ml / 1 tbls iced water and beat until the ingredients are well mixed.
5 Sprinkle this over the flour mixture, tossing and mixing with a fork. Rinse out the bowl or cup with another 15 ml /1 tbls of iced water and then mix this into the pastry in the same way as before. Continue tossing and mixing with the fork until about three-quarters of the pastry holds together. Next, use one hand, cupped, to press the

Crisp shortcrust pastry cases complement sweet and savoury fillings

pastry lightly and quickly into one piece.
6 Shape the pastry into a ball. Wrap it in a sheet of greaseproof paper, followed by a dampened tea towel, and chill for at least 1 hour before using. The pastry can be kept like this for 24 hours if you find this more convenient.

● To save time later, it is a good idea to make twice as much pastry as you need, then freeze it, wrapped in foil, for up to 3 months.

Making the pastry case
If, as a result of chilling, the pastry is too firm to roll out without breaking, leave it at room temperature for a little while to soften slightly. Knead the pastry lightly a few times to make it smooth and free of cracks.
Rolling out: lightly dust your working surface and a rolling pin with flour. Flatten the ball of pastry with a few strokes of the rolling pin, then start rolling it out to the required size and thickness using short, light strokes. Try to keep the pressure even at both sides; your right hand — or, if you're left-handed, your left hand — will instinctively want to press harder.

From time to time, lightly push the sheet of pastry over the working surface to make sure it is not sticking. Use only a light

Making shortcrust pastry

Use two knives to cut in the butter.

Lift your hands high for rubbing in fat.

sprinkling of flour to keep the pastry from sticking to the board or rolling pin, shaking it through a sifter if you have one. For a pastry case, roll your pastry between 3–6 mm / ⅛–¼ in thick. When the rolling has been

completed, dust off any loose flour with a soft pastry brush.

Loose-bottomed tart tins are excellent to use as delicate pastry shells can be baked, filled and then baked again if necessary. The flan or tart need not be unmoulded until the last moment, minimizing the risk of damage.
Filling in the tart: to avoid the pastry breaking when transferring it from the floured surface to the tin, fold the rolled-out sheet of pastry loosely over your rolling pin and transfer it to the tart tin. With floured fingertips, press the pastry down over the base of the tin and loosely up the sides. Do not stretch it into shape or it will shrink back again when it is baked. If you are using a tart tin with a wavy edge, lightly press the sides of the pastry into each flute of the tin with your index finger. Run your rolling pin across the top of the tin to trim off the excess pastry. To finish, uniformly press the pastry into the flutes again.

Prick the base of the shell all over with a sharp-pronged fork held vertically so that you make tiny holes, not gashes. Then chill the case for 30 minutes to allow the pastry to relax after all the rolling and to minimize shrinkage.

Baking an unfilled pastry shell
A pastry shell that is baked without any filling is liable to collapse at the sides if it is not supported. Also, the base may bubble up, although this is less likely if the base has been pricked properly. To prevent this happening, the shell is baked 'blind' — that is, lined with greaseproof paper or foil and weighted down with dried beans (which can be re-used for this purpose indefinitely) and then baked.

First line the pastry shell with greaseproof paper or foil. Fill it with dried beans. Push the beans up against the sides of the shell to ensure that they are supported. Place the tin on a baking sheet and bake the shell in an oven heated to 200C /400F /gas 6 for 10 minutes. Remove it from the oven and carefully lift out the paper (or foil) and beans. Turn down the oven to 180C /350F /gas 4.
Half-baked and fully-baked cases: if the

tart case is to be baked further after it has been filled, return it to the oven on its baking sheet, minus the beans and the lining paper. Bake it for just 8–10 minutes longer to dry out the base without colouring it. If the tart case is to be cooked completely at this stage, return it to the oven for 10–15 minutes or until set and golden.

Preparing the case for a wet filling: if you are going to pour in a wet filling — for example, a custard filling for a quiche or flan — guard against soggy pastry by brushing the baked pastry case inside with a little beaten egg white to 'seal' the pastry before you add the filling. If the base bubbles up slightly once it is no longer weighted down, gently press it back into position with a clean cloth. Always cool pastry at room temperature — if it is cooled too quickly, it may be tough.

Preparing a pastry case

Roll away extra pastry with the rolling pin.

Blind bake the pastry case lined with foil.

Blind-baked pastry case

1 hour, including resting

My favourite shortcrust pastry (see recipe)

1 Roll the pastry 3–6 mm /⅛–¼ in thick. Lift it on the rolling pin over the tin.
2 Press the pastry into the tin from the base outwards. Do not stretch it or it will shrink back later. Trim away extra pastry by rolling it with the pin. Prick the base with a fork; chill for ½ hour.
3 Heat the oven and a baking sheet to 200C / 400F /gas 6. Line the pastry with foil and beans. Bake on the sheet for 10 minutes.
4 Turn down the oven to 180C /350F /gas 4. Bake without foil for 8–10 minutes for a half-baked case, 10–15 minutes for a fully-baked pastry case.

Pissaladière

blind baking a pastry case, then 1 hour

Serves 4–6
20–23 cm /8–9 in pastry case, half-baked
1 medium-sized egg white, beaten
For the filling
60 ml /4 tbls freshly grated Parmesan cheese
75–90 ml /5–6 tbls olive oil
500 g /1 lb ripe tomatoes, skinned and
*   chopped or 400 ml /14 oz canned peeled*
*   tomatoes, chopped*
30 ml /2 tbls tomato purée
2.5 ml /½ tsp dried oregano
2.5 ml /½ tsp sugar
salt and freshly ground black pepper
3 Spanish onions, peeled and chopped
2.5 ml /½ tsp dried thyme
50 g /2 oz butter
3 large sweet peppers, 1 yellow, 1 green, 1 red

1 Brush the half-baked pastry shell with beaten egg white and sprinkle it with 30 ml / 2 tbls freshly grated Parmesan cheese. Leave the pastry case in its tin on a baking sheet.
2 Heat 60 ml /4 tbls olive oil in a heavy pan. Add the chopped tomatoes and the tomato purée. Sprinkle them with the dried oregano and the sugar, and season to taste with salt and pepper. Cook over a low heat for about 15 minutes, or until the excess moisture has evaporated. Stir and mash the tomatoes with a wooden spoon to reduce them to a thick purée. Stir in the rest of the grated Parmesan cheese and cool.
3 Sauté the chopped onions and dried thyme in butter until they are transparent and very soft. Season with salt and freshly ground black pepper. Let them cool.
4 Heat the oven to 180C /350 F /gas 4; heat the grill, turned to its maximum setting.
5 When the grill is hot, lay the peppers in the grill pan and grill them as close to the heat as possible, turning them frequently, until their skins are charred and blistered all over. Rub off the skins under cold running water. Cut the peppers in half, remove the cores, wash out the seeds and pat the peppers dry with absorbent paper. Cut each half into three good strips.
6 Cover the prepared pastry case with the sautéed onions and spread the tomato purée over the top. Arrange the pepper strips on top, using their colours to best advantage.
7 Brush the top of the flan and the pepper strips with olive oil and bake for 30 minutes. Serve hot or warm.

Quiche Lorraine

blind baking a pastry case, then 45 minutes

Serves 4–6
20–23 cm /8–9 in pastry case, half-baked
1 medium-sized egg white, beaten
For the filling
3 thick slices of unsmoked fat bacon
75 g /3 oz Gruyère cheese, in one piece
3 egg yolks
275 ml /10 fl oz thin cream
salt and freshly ground black pepper
a pinch of freshly grated nutmeg

1 Brush the inside of the half-baked pastry shell with beaten egg white. Leave the prepared pastry case in its tin on a baking sheet. Heat the oven to 180C /350F /gas 4.
2 If the bacon slices are very salty, blanch them in boiling water for 3 minutes. Drain the slices, cut them into thin strips and place them in a cold frying-pan. Heat the bacon gently until the fat begins to run, then sauté them for about 5 minutes, or until they are golden. Drain the strips of absorbent paper.
3 Cut the Gruyère into very small dice. Combine the egg yolks and cream and beat them with a fork until thoroughly blended, adding salt, pepper and nutmeg to taste.
4 Sprinkle the bacon and Gruyère over the base of the pastry case. Three-quarters fill it with the cream mixture, gently pouring in the cream over the back of a tablespoon to

2 For the crème pâtissière, combine the sugar and cornflour. Stir them into the milk and bring to the boil over a medium heat, stirring constantly. Simmer for 3–4 minutes, stirring, until the mixture has thickened and no longer tastes floury.

3 In a large bowl, beat the egg yolks lightly with a whisk until well blended. Add the hot sauce in a thin stream, beating vigorously.

4 Strain the custard through a fine sieve into a bowl. Beat in the butter until completely melted. Cool to lukewarm.

5 Heat the oven to 170C /325F /gas 3. Flavour the custard to taste with 15 ml / 1 tbls apricot brandy and the vanilla essence.

6 Crush the macaroons coarsely. Sprinkle them with 30 ml /2 tbls apricot brandy. Once absorbed, scatter crumbs over the base of the pastry case. Pour the custard filling carefully over the crumbs, then bake for 30 minutes, or until the custard has set.

7 For the topping, drain the apricot halves thoroughly, reserving a little syrup, and pat them dry with absorbent paper. Arrange them in one tight layer, rounded sides up, on top of the custard filling.

8 Dissolve the sugar in 15 ml /1 tbls reserved apricot syrup over a low heat. Simmer to a light caramel — remove from the heat a second or two before the colour is deep enough, to prevent burning. Blend in the apricot jam and stir over a low heat for 2–3 minutes longer. Strain the glaze through a fine sieve. Cool a little and then flavour to taste with apricot brandy. Brush the top of the tart with apricot glaze. Serve cold.

Amaretti apricot tart

Pissaladière

avoid disturbing the bacon strips and cheese.

5 Transfer the pastry case on its baking sheet to the oven and carefully spoon in the remaining cream mixture.

6 Bake the quiche for 25–30 minutes until the filling is puffed and set and a rich golden colour on top. Serve immediately.

Amaretti apricot tart

血血血 blind baking a pastry case, then 40 minutes, plus cooking

Serves 6–8
20–23 cm /8–9 in pastry case, half-baked
1 medium-sized egg white, beaten
For the crème pâtissière
125 g /4 oz caster sugar
30 ml /2 tbls cornflour
600 ml /1 pt milk
4 egg yolks
50 g /2 oz butter, diced
45 ml /3 tbls apricot brandy
1.5–2.5 ml /¼–½ tsp vanilla essence
50 g /2 oz Italian macaroons (amaretti)
For the topping
825 g /1 lb 13 oz canned apricot halves
15 ml /1 tbls sugar
45 ml /3 tbls apricot jam
30 ml /2 tbls apricot brandy

1 Leave the half-baked pastry case on a baking sheet. Brush inside with egg white.

FLAKY PASTRY

Light and melt-in-the-mouth, flaky pastry is ideal for sweet and savoury pies, tarts and tartlets. Use it to make an elegant fish en croûte or a hearty chicken pie.

There is a certain technique involved in making flaky pastry, but once mastered, practice will make you swift in the preparation. Success depends on trapping air and fat between the layers of pastry so that as the pastry bakes it rises into crisp, even flakes.

The ingredients

As for all pastries, I use a good quality plain flour. If possible, I prefer to use a strong flour. Most commercial bakers use strong flour for their flaky and puff pastry as well as their bread because it is a high gluten flour and gives pastry a crisper flake, defining the structure of the layers more evenly. Always sift the flour carefully to remove any lumps and to add extra air to your pastry.

The fat used for flaky pastry is mostly butter. I have found, however, that other fats will improve the 'flake' of the pastry without interfering with its flavour. The proportion of fat to flour is 3:4, and of the fat, no more than one-third should be lard. (You can use white vegetable fat, or shortening, if you prefer.)

The amount of water needed depends on the flour that you are using; different brands absorb different amounts and the freshness of the flour also affects its absorbency. I usually find that 15 ml /1 tbls liquid to 25 g /1 oz of flour is about right and I like to include a little lemon juice with the water to add a touch of flavour. Chill a jug of water in the refrigerator before you start making the pastry so that it is well iced by the time you come to use it.

Making flaky pastry

As with all pastries, the dough should be kept cold while you are preparing it. The richer the pastry, the more important this is. Always work in a cool room, and use a marble slab to work the pastry on, if possible. Failing that, the modern acrylic pastry boards give a good, cool rolling surface. It helps to chill all the ingredients and the mixing bowl, too, before you start.

While you are working, put the pastry back in the refrigerator at the first sign of the fat starting to soften. If it is allowed to ooze out of the folds of the pastry while you are working, the pastry is ruined — so keep it chilled and firm the whole time.

Start making flaky pastry much as you would shortcrust, rubbing fat into the flour with your fingertips, but you only rub in a proportion of the fat in this way (see recipe). Next, bind it with iced water to make a dough. Start off with less than the full amount of water, only gradually adding more as needed. Too much water will give you tough, hard pastry.

Folding and turning: when you have made the basic dough, turn it out onto a lightly floured board and work it very lightly to ensure it is smooth. Roll the dough to a rectangle, being careful to keep the edges straight and the corners square. Add some of the remaining fat (see recipe) in chilled flakes dotted over two-thirds of the pastry. Fold up the clear third of the pastry (see pictures) and then fold the top third down. Seal the edges.

The dough is rolled and folded like this 4 times in all. Each time fat is dotted over two-thirds of the rectangle before it is folded in three and 'turned'.

Chill the dough each time you have rolled and folded it. Once you have mastered the technique of making flaky pastry you will probably find that you can work more quickly and that the fat stays firm enough to allow you to complete 2 'turns' at a time. In very hot weather you are well advised to chill it between each turn.

To chill the dough, wrap it in cling film, or in greaseproof paper and a damp tea-towel. This prevents the surface from drying out and forming a hard crust that will stop the pastry rising.

Finally, when all the fat is incorporated, leave the pastry to relax before you shape it.

Fish en croûte

To do this, wrap it in cling film again and put it in the refrigerator for at least an hour. If you can leave it overnight, so much the better. Flaky pastry also freezes well, so you can make it in large quantities and take out only a small batch at a time.

Shaping the pastry

Roll out the pastry on a lightly floured surface, using long, smooth, light strokes. Lift it occasionally to make sure it has not stuck to the surface but be careful that you do not break it. When cutting, use a sharp knife with short, quick strokes to avoid dragging the edges of the pastry — this will make it rise unevenly. Pastry can be scored in a diamond pattern to help it rise evenly.

If you are using the pastry for a pie topping, first cut a strip 15 mm /½ in wide from the rolled out pastry. Dampen the rim of the pie dish and press the strip of pastry on firmly, then dampen the strip with a little water or some egg glaze.

Carefully lift the pastry lid on a rolling pin and place it on top of the pie. Firmly press it onto the dampened pastry strip to seal the edges. To help the appearance of the finished pie, knock up and flute the edges. To knock up, use the back of a knife blade to make horizontal 'cuts' against the pastry edges all the way round the pie. Flute the edges by drawing the knife blade up across the edges at 5 mm /¼ in intervals.

Brush off any excess flour from the surface of the pastry and, if it is a pie, decorate it with pastry trimmings. Leave the shaped pie or pastry to relax again in the refrigerator for 30 minutes before cooking. This helps to stop it shrinking during cooking, which may spoil the look of the finished dish.

Cooking the pastry

While the shaped pastry is relaxing, heat the oven. Flaky pastry is cooked in a hot oven at 220C /425F /gas 7. Whether you are using a baking sheet or a pie tin, you will not need to grease it. The pastry has enough fat content in it to prevent it from sticking. Before cooking, brush the pastry with an egg glaze made from either a whole egg lightly beaten or an egg yolk beaten with a little water. Make sure that you brush it evenly over the pastry but do not put any of this mixture on the knocked up edges as this will prevent them from rising.

Bake in the oven until the pastry is a good, golden brown. If the filling needs longer in the oven, cover the pastry with crumpled foil to prevent it from burning and turn the temperature down to 190C /375F /gas 5 until the filling is cooked through.

Flaky pastry

2 hours making the pastry,
then resting it

For 500 g /1 lb pastry
500 g /1 lb strong flour
5 ml /1 tsp salt
225 g /8 oz butter
15 ml /1 tbls lemon juice
125 g /4 oz lard
flour, for rolling

1 Chill all the ingredients, plus about 250 ml /9 fl oz cold water and the mixing bowl.
2 Sift the flour and salt into the mixing bowl. Dice half the butter into the bowl and rub it into the flour with your fingertips until the mixture resembles fine breadcrumbs. Make a well in the centre.
3 Carefully measure 150 ml /5 fl oz iced water into the well, together with the lemon juice. Stir vigorously with a broad-bladed knife, gradually incorporating the flour from the sides of the well. Start mixing in the remaining flour, adding more iced water if necessary, a teaspoon at a time, until you have a ball of dough that is neither too sticky nor too dry. It should be of such a consistency that you can use it to wipe the bowl clean. It will be easier to judge this if, in the final stages, you use your hands to push the dough gently together. In all, you will probably need another 45–60 ml /3–4 tbls iced water, depending on the flour.
4 Turn the dough out onto a lightly floured surface. Work it with just a few turns (kneading would be too strong a word) to smooth out the texture.
5 Roll the dough out into a rectangle 40× 20 cm /16×8 in, pushing the sides straight and the corners square with a ruler. If the dough has been kneaded too vigorously, it will probably start resisting before it reaches the right dimensions, but keep rolling gently to get it to the right size.
6 With the back of a knife, make a light indentation across the width of the rectangle, marking off one-third of the length of the pastry from the bottom.
7 Use the tip of the knife to dot the upper two-thirds of the pastry with half the lard, in nut-sized flakes. Leave a border, 15 mm / ½ in wide, clear on the 3 outer sides — if the fat is put too close to the edge, it may ooze out during rolling.
8 Fold the rectangle in 3 as follows: fold the clear (free of fat) third of the dough up towards the centre. Next fold the remaining third down over the top of it. Now seal all the edges with either the rolling pin or your hand.
9 Wrap the pastry in cling film, or in greaseproof paper, and then in a damp cloth and chill it for 15 minutes.
10 Unwrap the pastry and lay it on a lightly floured surface so that the fold is on your left-hand side and the longest sealed edge on your right. Roll out the pastry again into a 40×20 cm /16×8 in rectangle, using firm, even strokes down towards you from the centre and upwards away from you — never roll the pastry sideways or on the diagonal.
11 Repeat the dotting and folding process, this time using half the remaining butter. Seal the edges and wrap the pastry, return it to the refrigerator for 15 minutes.
12 Give the pastry its third and fourth 'turns' using the remaining lard for the third, and remaining butter for the fourth and final 'turn', chilling the pastry for 15 minutes in between.
13 After the final folding, seal the edges of the pastry. Wrap the packet in cling film and leave it to rest in the refrigerator for at least 1 hour, or, even better, allow the pastry to rest overnight before using.

Making flaky pastry

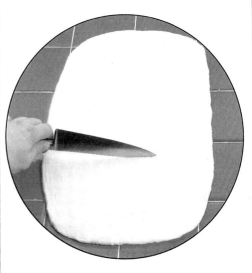

Roll the dough out to a rectangle 40×20 cm / 16×8 in. With the back of a knife, mark off one-third of the pastry length.

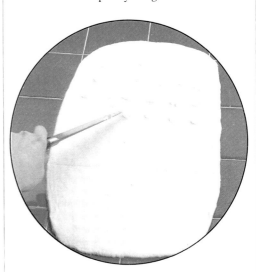

Use the tip of the knife to dot the upper two-thirds of the pastry with half the lard, covering the area with nut-sized flakes.

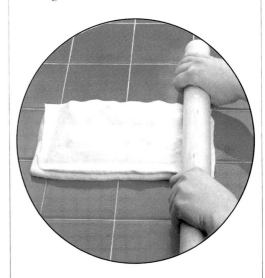

Fold the fat-free third of pastry up towards the centre. Fold the remaining third down over it. Seal the edges firmly.

33

Fish en croûte

making the pastry and sauce,
then 2 hours

Serves 6
500 g /1 lb frozen leaf spinach
salt and freshly ground black pepper
freshly grated nutmeg
½ × Flaky pastry (see recipe)
flour, for rolling
500 g /1 lb haddock or cod fillet, skinned
1 egg yolk, beaten with 15 ml /1 tbls water
White butter sauce (page 15)

1 Put the frozen spinach in a saucepan and cook over a low heat for 5 minutes, or until all the moisture has evaporated. Season to taste with salt, freshly ground black pepper and freshly grated nutmeg. Leave until it is completely cold.
2 On a lightly floured board, roll the pastry as thinly as possible. Transfer it to a baking sheet. Place half the fish down the centre of the pastry and then spread the cold spinach on top. Cover the spinach with the remaining fish.
3 Trim the pastry with a sharp knife and wrap it around the fish and spinach, sealing the edges with a little of the beaten egg and neatly tucking the ends underneath. Use the trimmings to cut decorations, such as leaves and plaits, and cover the seam with them. Refrigerate for 30 minutes.
4 Heat the oven to 220C /425F /gas 7.

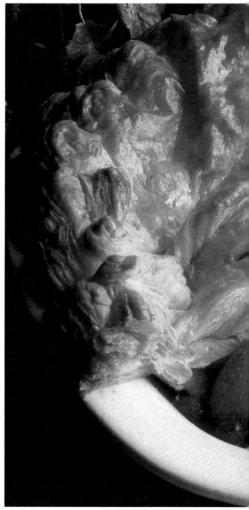

Stilton slice

making the pastry,
then 2¼ hours, plus chilling

Serves 10
½ × Flaky pastry (see recipe)
flour, for rolling
1 egg yolk, beaten with 15 ml /1 tbls water
paprika
For the filling
225 g /8 oz Stilton cheese
juice of 2 oranges
45 ml /3 tbls snipped chives
15 g /½ oz gelatine
300 ml /10 fl oz thick cream, whipped

1 On a lightly floured surface, roll the pastry as thinly as possible to approximately 25×25 cm /10×10 in and place it on a baking sheet. Prick the pastry all over and leave it in the refrigerator to relax for 30 minutes.
2 Meanwhile, heat the oven to 22C /425F / gas 7.
3 Brush the pastry with egg glaze. Cook the pastry in the oven for 15 minutes or until it is crisp and golden brown. Transfer it to a

Chicken pie with green olives

wire rack and leave it until it is quite cool.
4 Meanwhile in a blender or food processor, blend the Stilton with the orange juice and transfer it to a mixing bowl. Fold in the finely snipped chives.
5 In a small bowl, sprinkle the gelatine over 45 ml /3 tbls cold water and leave it to soften. Place the bowl in a saucepan of hot water and leave until the gelatine has dissolved. Leave to cool.
6 Pour the dissolved gelatine into the Stilton mixture and set the bowl over ice, stirring occasionally until the mixture is on the point of setting. Fold in the whipped cream and leave, again over ice, until it is on the point of setting. Stir occasionally.
7 Meanwhile, trim the edges of the flaky pastry with a sharp knife and cut it into 3 equal lengths. Place half the Stilton mixture on one of the pastry strips, spreading it evenly. Place another pastry strip on top, spread it with the remaining mixture and top it with the third pastry strip. Place the slice in the refrigerator.
8 To serve, sprinkle the top with a little paprika. Cut with a serrated knife into 10 slices. Serve as an after-dinner savoury or as an unusual cocktail snack.

5 Brush the pastry with the egg glaze and bake in the oven for 30 minutes or until the pastry is crisp and golden brown. Meanwhile make the White butter sauce. Serve immediately accompanied by the sauce.

Petites tartes aux pommes

🔪 making the pastry,
🔪🔪 then 1 hour 10 minutes

Serves 4
½ × Flaky pastry (see recipe)
4 large, tart eating apples
225 g /8 oz sugar
20 g /¾ oz butter
flour, for rolling

1 On a lightly floured board, roll out the pastry as thinly as possible, until it is almost transparent. Cut out four 18 cm /7 in pastry circles and place them on baking sheets. Prick the pastry and leave it in the refrigerator for 30 minutes.
2 Meanwhile, heat the oven to 220C /425F /gas 7.
3 Peel and core the apples and slice them very thinly. Place the slices, overlapping, on the pastry circles. Sprinkle with sugar and dot each tart with butter.
4 Cook in the oven for 15–20 minutes, or until the pastry is cooked. Serve immediately on individual flat plates.

Chicken pie with green olives

This chicken pie is unusual because the chicken pieces are left whole which makes a different and tasty dish.

🔪 making the pastry,
🔪🔪 then 2¾ hours, plus cooling

Serves 4–6
1.4 kg /3 lb chicken
30 ml /2 tbls flour
2.5 ml /½ tsp salt
freshly ground black pepper
15 g /½ oz butter
15 ml /1 tbls olive oil
125 g /4 oz unsmoked streaky bacon, diced
½ Spanish onion, finely chopped
8 large white button mushrooms, quartered
150 ml /5 fl oz dry white wine
45–60 ml /3–4 tbls chicken stock, home-made or from a cube
2 eggs, hard boiled and sliced
12 large green olives, stoned
flour, for rolling
½ × Flaky pastry (see recipe)
1 egg yolk, beaten with 15 ml /1 tbls water

1 Cut the chicken into 8 serving pieces; remove and discard the skin.
2 Season the flour with salt and freshly ground black pepper.
3 Heat the butter and olive oil in a flame-proof casserole and sauté the diced bacon for 10 minutes, or until it is golden. Remove with a slotted spoon and sauté the finely chopped onion for 15 minutes, or until golden. Remove with a slotted spoon.
4 Dust the chicken pieces with seasoned flour and cook a few pieces at a time, turning them until they are golden brown. Remove the chicken and toss the mushrooms in the remaining fat for 2 minutes or until they are lightly coloured.
5 Add the white wine and chicken stock and bring to the boil. Return the chicken and other cooked ingredients to the pan and season. Simmer, covered, for 15 minutes.
6 In a 1.7 L /3 pt pie dish layer this mixture with the sliced hard-boiled eggs and green olives. Leave to become cold.
7 Roll out the pastry on a lightly floured surface so that it is larger than the top of the pie dish. Cut four strips 15 mm /½ in wide, to go around the edge of the pie dish.
8 Brush the rim of the pie dish with water and press the strips of pastry onto it. Brush these with water or a little of the egg glaze. Cover the pie with the rolled out pastry, pressing lightly to seal the edges. Carefully brush off all the surface flour. Flute and knock up the edges. Cut a small hole in the centre of the pie to allow the steam to escape, and use the trimmings to make decorations. Attach the decorations and score the pastry lightly with a sharp knife. Refrigerate for 30 minutes.
9 Heat the oven to 220C /425F /gas 7.
10 Brush the pastry with egg glaze. Bake in the oven for 30–35 minutes or until the pastry is a golden colour. Serve the pie immediately.

Summer fruit pie

🔪 making the pastry,
🔪🔪 then 1½ hours

Serves 6–8
500 g /1 lb gooseberries, topped and tailed
500 g /1 lb strawberries, hulled
225 g /8 oz blackcurrants, topped and tailed
500 g /1 lb plums, stoned
75 g /3 oz sugar
flour, for rolling
½ × Flaky pastry (see recipe)
1 egg yolk, beaten with 15 ml /1 tbls water
thick cream, to serve

1 Place the prepared fruit in a 1.7 L /3 pt pie dish and sprinkle the sugar over it.
2 On a lightly floured board, roll the pastry as thinly as possible. Cut the pastry slightly larger than the top of the pie dish. Cut strips 15 mm /½ in wide from the pastry. Damp the edge of the pie dish and press on the strips firmly. Brush the strips with water and place the pastry lid on top. Make a hole in the lid to allow the steam to escape. Refrigerate for 30 minutes.
3 Heat the oven to 220C /425F /gas 7.
4 Brush the pie with the egg glaze. Bake in the oven for 30 minutes or until the pastry is crisp and golden brown. Serve it hot or lukewarm with thick cream.

Summer fruit pie

35

PUFF & ROUGH PUFF PASTRY

Rich, light layers of buttery pastry are the reward for mastering the art of making your own puff and rough puff pastry. Use your skills to make sweet and savoury delights that are always popular.

Puff and rough puff are formidable pastries, to be treated with respect. If you have never experienced any difficulty in turning out good puff pastry — each paper-thin layer separate, meltingly crisp and buttery — you are to be congratulated. You must indeed be a born pastry maker! For the rest of us, learning how to handle puff pastry, how to roll, fold and turn it so that the delicate layers build up, waiting for the moment when the intense heat of the oven will burst them apart again, is one of the great techniques of the kitchen. It is one to which you need to pay careful attention as making puff pastry does not lend itself to taking any short cuts.

The two techniques

The techniques involved in making these two pastries differ enormously. Of the two, rough puff is probably the less complex and the quicker to make. So if you are a beginner start with this one.

Rough puff: for rough puff the butter is cut into small pieces and mixed quickly with flour and liquid to make a rough dough. The lumps of butter are gradually eliminated from the dough by a series of rollings and foldings. The proportion of fat to flour can be as low as 1:2, rising to a maximum of 3:4.

Puff pastry: for puff pastry you start by making a basic flour and liquid dough which contains just a very little of the fat to be used. The dough is rolled into a rectangle and used to enclose a block of butter. This parcel is then rolled and folded 4 times in all, so that the butter is evenly distributed throughout.

The proportion of fat to flour is only slightly less than 1:1. We start off with an exact 500 g /1 lb flour to 500 g /1 lb butter, but extra flour gets incorporated with the dough during rolling.

The ingredients

Flour: good-quality, dry, plain flour should be used and never self-raising flour. Now that it is more readily available, I like to use strong flour. Its higher gluten content helps give puffed pastries a better, stronger structure. The flour, as when making other pastry, should be sifted even if there are no obvious lumps in it, to incorporate air and consequently lightness.

Fat: classic puff pastry recipes use only butter as the fat content and should be lightly salted only, if at all; otherwise you may find yourself with over-salty pastry.

However, other fats can be used along with butter, as long as they are kept proportionally low so they do not interfere with the flavour of the pastry which should be deliciously buttery. Lard and whipped white vegetable fats are the ones I prefer, using no more than 75 g /3 oz in 500 g /1 lb total weight of fat.

Keeping the butter at the right temperature and consistency is an important part of making good puff pastry. The butter must be chilled, but not so hard that you cannot work it. Initially it must be soft enough to shape to a wide, flat brick, then chilled again before adding it to the dough. About 30 minutes in the refrigerator is enough; if it is too cold and hard, the pastry is likely to crack.

Liquid: you will notice that the recipes all call for iced water. This is all part of the general aim of keeping everything as cold as possible, so that the butter is protected from

softening too much. Either drop a few ice cubes in a jug of water and leave for 10 minutes until the water is thoroughly iced, or put a jug of water in the refrigerator to chill with the other ingredients.

Lemon juice (or vinegar if you prefer) helps to develop the gluten in the flour, which means the structure of the pastry is strengthened. Egg yolk, apart from contributing moisture, can be added for richness of texture and flavour.

Helpful hints

Coolness: start everything as cold as possible. If you can work on a marble slab, so much the better — it really does make a difference. Brand new kitchen slabs are expensive to buy, but it is worth looking out for an old wash-stand at a bargain price. Take the top off, scrub it well and you have the perfect pastry slab.

Chill the pastry between rollings. Unless you work at lightning speed you are unlikely to be able to complete more than two rollings and foldings of the pastry at a time. The fat quickly starts to soften and become unmanageable. Indeed, if you are a novice, or if the weather is hot, be prepared to down tools at any stage if you feel the pastry start to soften under your rolling pin or if you notice a creaminess which indicates that the butter is about to start oozing through at any moment.

Rolling and handling: first of all make sure you have a really good rolling pin. It should be long so that the ends do not make lines on your rolled pastry. If you can find the type that spins on its handles, these are the easiest to use. Always roll the pastry in the same direction using long smooth strokes. The easiest way is to work from the centre, rolling one stroke away from you, then one stroke towards you. Try not to roll quite over the ends as this will make them thinner than the rest. Do not be tempted to push hard or

Making puff pastry

Sift the flour and salt into the mixing bowl. Add the finely diced butter and work it with your fingers until it is coated with flour.

Add the lemon juice and iced water and work with your hand to a moist but not sticky dough. Add more water if necessary.

Place the butter on a lightly floured board and knock it with your fist into a rectangle 15 × 12.5 cm /6 × 5 in.

stretch the pastry with the rolling pin as this will tear the layers of dough and butter that you have built up.

As you roll, lift the pastry occasionally to ensure it has not stuck to the work surface, but do this carefully to avoid breaking any layering with your fingers. As the rectangle begins to take shape, use a ruler or a knife with a long blade to knock the sides straight and keep the corners right angled. This is important — a rounded edge, falling short, means a loss in that area of so many layers and results in less flaky pastry.

When folding the pastry, brush off any loose flour which may be adhering to the underside, with a pastry brush, before folding the other side of the pastry over it. You want to incorporate as little extra flour into the pastry as possible. Seal the folded rectangle either by pressing gently but firmly against the seams with the rolling pin, or by using the side of your hand.

If in any doubt about the pastry's ability to take a further rolling and folding immediately, chill it for 15 minutes. When first starting, you may find it easier to roll a thick, folded packet of pastry if you press down on it several times with your rolling pin to flatten and spread it out slightly. The corrugated look will soon disappear when you start rolling in earnest.

Turning the pastry

This term refers to the quarter-turn you give the slab of pastry each time you re-roll it. The best way to remember the position the pastry should be in before you start to roll it, is to visualize the pastry as a closed book lying in front of you with the front facing upwards. In this way the long folded side will always be on the left-hand side before you start to roll it out. Then, once you have rolled it out to a rectangle again and folded it into three, you give the pastry a quarter-turn (anticlockwise 90°). It is then ready to roll again.

You should always keep a record of the number of turns completed, either in the classic way, by pressing light dents on the top of the pastry with the ball of a finger, or simply by making a note of them on a piece of paper. Otherwise, you will find that it is surprisingly easy to lose your place after the second or third turn.

The traditional way to fold pastry is to mark the rectangle into three, fold the bottom third up to the mark of the top third and the top third over this. Using this method, you roll and turn the pastry six times. An alternative method is to mark the pastry rectangle in half. Fold both the halves so the short edges meet in the middle and then fold the top half over the bottom half. I alternate these two methods and so only have to roll and turn the pastry four times to achieve the same number of layers. This also reduces the likelihood of the butter oozing out.

Both rough puff and puff pastry improve if left to relax in the refrigerator for at least 1 hour after the final folding and before shaping. Be sure to wrap the pastry up well in cling film, or in greaseproof paper and a damp tea-towel, to prevent a crust forming on the surface. Chilling not only allows the alternating layers of butter and dough to firm up so that they remain even more defined when baked, but also makes the pastry easier to roll and shape.

Shaping

To use the pastry, roll it out as thinly as possible, again rolling from the centre away and towards you. To cut it use a sharp knife that will not drag at the edge — this causes the pastry to rise unevenly. Shape the pastry as described in the recipe. I find that scoring the surface all over with a sharp knife helps to make the pastry rise evenly. Make a neat pattern of diagonals or a lattice without cutting right through — just lightly score the surface. If you are using the pastry to make a pie, knock up the edges with the back of a knife and flute them. This makes the edges of the pastry look more attractive and also makes it flake more evenly.

Resting: after shaping, leave the pastry to relax again in the refrigerator. This is particularly important for vol-au-vents where the finished shape is all important. Rolling the pastry stretches it and unless it is given time to relax before baking, the finished shape will be distorted. Half to one hour is enough for most shapes, although it is better to leave vol-au-vents overnight, but take them out of the refrigerator while the oven is heating just to take off the extreme chill.

Glazing: before baking, brush the pastry with egg glaze to give it a good rich gloss. Use either an egg yolk beaten with 15 ml / 1 tbls of water, or a whole, lightly beaten egg, whichever is more convenient. Take care not to let the glaze go over the edges of the pastry or they will not flake as they should.

Freezing

Puff pastry is quite time consuming to make and, as it freezes well, it is worth making a large quantity. To cut the dough, first flatten it lightly with a rolling pin, then cut it with a sharp knife and dip the cut edge in flour to seal the butter. Pack the dough in 500 g/1 lb or 250 g /8 oz packs and label them.

Baking

Bake all flaked pastries at a high temperature — 220C /425F /gas 7 is the most usual. If the pastry browns before the filling is ready, cover it loosely with crumpled foil and turn the temperature down.

Puff pastry

overnight chilling,
then 3 hours, plus chilling

Made weight of pastry is 1.2 kg /2¾ lb
500 g /1 lb strong flour, plus extra, for rolling
500 g /1 lb unsalted butter
2.5 ml /½ tsp salt
30 ml /2 tbls lemon juice or white wine vinegar

Place the brick of butter in the centre of the rectangle of pastry and fold over the four edges to make a parcel.

For the first turn, roll to 38 × 30 cm /15 × 12 in. Fold the bottom third up and fold the top third down over it. Seal the edges.

For the second turn, fold both the short edges to meet in the centre. Next fold one half on top of the other. Seal the edges.

1   Chill all the ingredients plus 250 ml /9 fl oz water and the mixing bowl you intend using in the refrigerator for several hours or, preferably, overnight.
2   Remove the ingredients from the refrigerator. Cut a 40 g /1½ oz block from the butter and dice it finely. Set the remaining butter aside.
3   Sift 500 g /1 lb flour and the salt into the chilled mixing bowl. Add the finely diced butter and work with your fingers until the pieces of butter are thoroughly coated with flour. Make a well in the centre.
4   Add the iced water and the lemon juice (or white wine vinegar) to the centre of the well and work the ingredients with your hand to a moist, but not sticky dough. Add 15–30 ml /1–2 tbls more water to the dough if it is necessary.
5   Turn the dough out onto a floured board and knead it into a ball, adding flour to the board and dough, until the dough is no longer moist.
6   Flatten the dough ball to 25 mm /1 in thick, wrap the dough in cling film and refrigerate for 15 minutes.
7   Meanwhile, place the remaining butter on a lightly floured board and knock and shape it by hand into a rectangle approximately 15×12.5 cm /6×5 in. Wrap it in cling film and chill.
8   Remove the dough ball from the refrigerator then, with plenty of flour on the board, pat the pastry down a little with your hands and roll the dough ball into a rectangle. Always roll from the centre of the pastry away from you or towards you so the dough does not stretch. Push the sides and corners as straight as possible with the side of a ruler.
9   Brush the excess flour off the top of the pastry, place the 'brick' of butter in the centre of the rectangle and fold over the 4 edges to make a parcel. Seal the pastry joins by pressing them gently with your fingertips.
10   To make the first turn, roll the pastry to a rectangle 38×30 cm /15×12 in. Use your finger to mark the pastry across the width into 3 equal segments. Fold the bottom ⅓ over the centre to meet the second mark, then fold the top ⅓ down on top of it, making sure that the edges fit exactly. Seal the pastry joins by pressing gently with your fingertips or with the rolling pin. Turn the pastry 90°. (Make a note to remind yourself that the pastry has had 1 turn.)
11   To make the second turn, roll the pastry out to a rectangle 38×30 cm /15×12 in. Mark across the pastry in the middle with your fingertip. Next, fold both the short edges of the dough to meet in the centre at the mark. Now fold one half on top of the other. Seal the pastry joins by pressing gently with your fingertips and turn the pastry through 90° so the fold is on the left-hand side.
12   To rest the pastry for the first time, wrap it in cling film and leave it to relax in the refrigerator for at least 15 minutes.
13   Repeat both the 'turns' as described above.
14   To rest the pastry for the second time, wrap it in cling film and leave it to relax and chill in the refrigerator for at least 15 minutes, preferably 1 hour.

Hideaway turkey pie

15   The pastry is now ready for use. If using immediately, roll to the desired shape and leave to relax in the refrigerator for ½–1 hour before baking.

Rough puff pastry

chilling the ingredients, 40 minutes, plus 1 hour chilling

Made weight of pastry is 500 g /1 lb

250 g /8 oz strong flour, plus extra, for rolling
a pinch of salt
175 g /6 oz unsalted butter
5 ml /1 tsp lemon juice

1   Put all the ingredients, plus about 150 ml /5 fl oz water and the mixing bowl you intend using, into the refrigerator to chill.
2   Remove the ingredients from the refrigerator. Sift the flour and the salt into the chilled bowl.
3   Dice the butter into 15 mm /½ in cubes and drop them into the flour. Add the lemon juice and 125 ml /4 fl oz water and mix quickly to a light dough. Add 15–30 ml /1–2 tbls more water if necessary.
4   Turn the dough onto a lightly floured board and roll it out to a rectangle 30×15 cm /12×6 in, pushing the sides straight and the corners square with the side of a ruler.
5   Fold one-third of the pastry up towards the centre, then fold the top third down over this. Seal the edges with your hand or a rolling pin. Turn the pastry through 90°.
6   Roll, fold and turn the pastry twice more.
7   Wrap the pastry in cling film, or in greaseproof paper and a damp cloth and chill for 1 hour before shaping.

Mushroom chaussons

making the pastry, then 1¼ hours, plus cooling

Makes 8–10
15 g /½ oz butter
15 ml /1 tbls olive oil
½ Spanish onion, finely chopped
225 g /8 oz mushrooms, finely chopped
30 ml /2 tbls finely chopped fresh parsley
30 ml /2 tbls thick cream
5 ml /1 tsp Dijon mustard
salt and freshly ground black pepper
15 ml /1 tbls brandy
500 g /1 lb made-weight Rough puff pastry (see recipe)
1 egg yolk beaten with 15 ml /1 tbls water, for the egg glaze

1   In a frying-pan, heat the butter and the olive oil and sauté the finely chopped onion for 2–3 minutes until transparent. Add the finely chopped mushrooms and sauté them for 15 minutes. Add the parsley, the thick cream and the mustard. Season to taste with salt and freshly ground black pepper. Add the brandy and remove the pan from the heat. Leave the mixture until cold.
2   On a floured board, roll out the pastry very thinly and cut out eight or ten 12.5 cm / 5 in diameter circles. Place the mushroom mixture on half of each circle. Brush the edge with egg glaze, fold the circle in two and seal tightly. Brush off any excess flour.
3   Cut 2 or 3 small slits in the top of each chausson to allow the steam to escape. Arrange them on a baking sheet and leave them to relax in the refrigerator for 30 minutes.
4   Heat the oven to 220C /425F /gas 7.

5 Brush the chaussons with the egg glaze. Sprinkle the baking sheet with water and bake for 15 minutes. Serve piping hot.

Hideaway turkey pie

 1 hour

Serves 4–6
500 g /1 lb left-over cooked turkey
2 celery sticks, chopped in 15 mm /½ in lengths
250 g /8 oz left-over cooked vegetables
2 medium-sized onions, chopped
50 g /2 oz butter
50 g /2 oz flour
600 ml /1 pt stock
100 g /4 oz Cheddar cheese, grated
salt and freshly ground black pepper
375 g /12 oz made-weight puff pastry
milk, to glaze

1 Heat the oven to 230C /450F /gas 8. Place the meat, celery and left-over vegetables in a 1.7 L /3 pt pie dish with a pie funnel positioned in the centre.
2 Fry the onion in the butter for 2 minutes, then stir in the flour and cook for 1 minute over a moderate heat. Slowly add the stock and bring the sauce to the boil, stirring, until it is thickened. Add the grated cheese then adjust the seasoning. Pour the sauce into the pie dish.
3 Roll out the puff pastry and use it to cover the dish. Knock up the edges and use any left-over pastry to make decorative

Cream horns

leaves. Brush the pastry with milk and cook in the oven for 20 minutes.
4 Lower the heat to 170C /325F /gas 3 and cook for a further 20 minutes until the pie is golden.

Cream horns

 making the pastry, then 1¼ hours, plus cooling

Makes 10–12
flour, for rolling
500 g /1 lb made-weight puff pastry (see recipe)
1 egg yolk, beaten with 15 ml /1 tbls water, for the egg glaze
icing sugar
75–90 ml /5–6 tbls strawberry or raspberry jam
150 ml /5 fl oz thick cream
15–30 ml /1–2 tbls caster sugar

1 On a lightly floured board, roll out the dough 3 mm /⅛ in thick. Cut it into strips 25 mm /1 in wide and 23 cm /9 in long. Brush off any surface flour and then brush one side of each pastry strip with the egg glaze.
2 Wind a strip of pastry around each of 10 cm /4 in cream horn moulds, with the glazed side to the outside. Start by pressing the pastry firmly onto the pointed end, then start winding it round, overlapping each round a little. Trim the top level and place each horn on a baking sheet. Chill for 30 minutes.
3 Heat the oven to 220C /425F /gas 7.
4 Sprinkle the baking sheet with cold water and bake the horns in the oven for 10–12 minutes or until they are golden brown.
5 Sprinkle with sifted icing sugar and bake

for a further 3 minutes, or until glazed. Transfer the horns to a wire rack, carefully remove the moulds and leave to cool.
6 About 3–4 hours before serving, place the horns upright in a tall mould (e.g. a brioche mould) so that they are easy to fill. Put 7.5 ml /½ tbls of jam in the bottom of each horn.
7 Whip the thick cream to stiff peaks and fold in sugar to taste. Place the cream in a piping bag fitted with a star nozzle. Pipe the whipped cream into the horns.

Mille feuilles

 1½ hours

Serves 6
225 g /7½ oz made-weight puff pastry
For the crème chantilly
150 ml /5 fl oz thick cream
15 ml /1 tbls caster sugar
15 ml /1 tbls iced water
a few drops of vanilla essence
45 ml /3 tbls raspberry jam
For the glacé icing
100 g /4 oz icing sugar
red food colouring

1 Heat the oven to 220C /425F /gas 7. Roll out the pastry as thinly as possible to cover a 30×40 cm /12×16 in dampened baking sheet. Prick the pastry well with a fork. Chill it for 10 minutes.
2 Cook the pastry in the oven for 7–10 minutes until it is golden brown and risen. Trim the edges of the pastry with a sharp knife, cut it into 3 equal lengthways strips. Turn each strip over carefully and return to the oven for 2–3 minutes to allow the underside to cook. Remove the strips from the oven; transfer to a wire rack and cool.
3 To make the crème chantilly, whisk the thick cream in a bowl until it forms soft peaks. Add the caster sugar and beat until it is stiff. Add the iced water and vanilla essence and beat until the cream is smooth.
4 To assemble the mille feuilles spread one strip of pastry with half the jam and half the crème chantilly; lay the second strip of pastry on top, pressing down very lightly and spread it with the remaining jam and crème chantilly and carefully place the third strip on top. With a palette knife scrape away any cream which overhangs the edges.
5 To make the glacé icing, sift the icing sugar into the top pan of a double boiler. Add 25 ml /1½ tbls plus ½ tsp water and a few drops of food colouring and stir over a low heat. As the sugar melts the icing becomes softer and when ready it should coat the back of a spoon.
6 Coat the top of the mille feuilles with glacé icing. Thin the remaining icing with a little water and add a few more drops of food colouring. Put the icing into a small piping bag and pipe parallel lines across the mille feuilles, 15–20 mm /½–¾ in apart. Quickly draw a skewer at right angles to the piping, again at 15–20 mm /½–¾ in intervals. Draw the skewer in alternate directions to give a feathered effect.
7 To serve, cut the mille feuilles into 6 portions with a very sharp, fine-bladed knife.

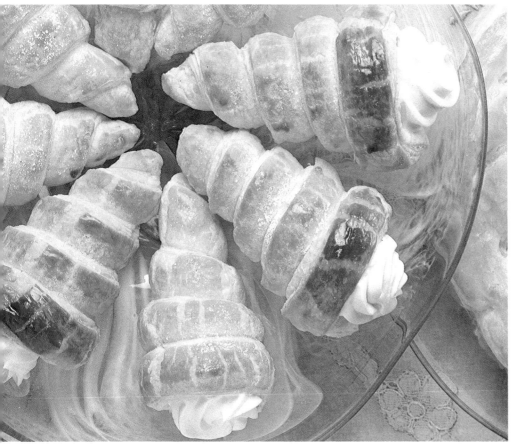

SWEET & SAVOURY CHOUX PASTRY

Making choux pastry is a very simple technique which will give you impressive results. Make savoury nibbles — which you can conveniently prepare ahead and freeze for a party — or mouth-watering desserts.

Choux pastry is familiar to most of us because of family favourites like chocolate éclairs and profiteroles. Because many of the recipes which use choux paste are considered delicacies, it is easy to imagine that the technique involved is complicated, and become defeated even before you start. The opposite is actually true and the method of making choux paste is really very simple because the paste does not need to be handled in any way. Follow my easy step-by-step instructions for making the paste and then choose from a selection of recipes that demonstrate how versatile it is. For savoury nibbles, try Cocktail cheese puffs or for a delectable dessert serve Beignets with hot raspberry sauce — these are deep-fried soufflé fritters which are masked in a hot fruit sauce.

Making a choux paste
Choux pastry is something of a culinary phenomenon at first sight. Uncooked, it is a thick, close-textured paste — really a sauce — of flour, water and eggs, which puffs up when cooked to become a crisp, delicate, hollow case about twice its original size. Choux paste can be cooked in the oven or deep-fried.

The paste itself is not difficult to make, provided you follow the recipe. Measure the ingredients accurately, as for all pastries, and follow the instructions carefully (see pictures). After adding the flour you must carry on beating, with a wooden spoon, until the mixture attaches itself around the spoon in a smooth, shiny ball, leaving the surface of the pan quite clean.

Some people add the eggs directly into the hot flour mixture. I prefer to let the mixture cool a little first — this way it seems to take more egg, which means it is easier to shape, and the cooked pastry puffs up better. After adding the eggs, carry on beating until the pastry develops a definite gloss or sheen and acquires a flexible consistency which can easily be shaped.

Shaping the choux: I always bake my choux on a dampened baking sheet (this helps them to rise), so prepare this first. The choux can be piped or shaped with spoons. Piping, with a plain nozzle, is probably the easiest. Use a knife dipped in water to smooth the choux shapes. The traditional shapes vary from tiny rounds for petits fours, larger ones for profiteroles, through to strips for éclairs and large rings for gateaux — but remember to leave room for expansion.

Cooking the choux
The secret of baking choux is an initial burst of high, steamy heat that forces the maximum of air into the paste, making it rise. Next, I lower the temperature so that the choux can dry out without colouring too darkly. To test whether the choux is cooked, take it out of the oven and lift it off the baking sheet, then tap the base. If it is firm, the pastry is cooked. Make a small slit in the side of each puff or éclair with a sharp knife to allow the steam inside to escape. Put the pastries on a wire rack to cool. If there seems to be some uncooked paste inside, scrape it out carefully with a teaspoon.

To deep-fry choux pastry, heat the oil in a deep-fat frier to 180C /350F and drop spoonfuls of the paste into the hot fat. Fry for 6–8 minutes or until the choux puffs are firm and golden. Only fry a few spoonfuls at a time as they will swell during cooking. Drain the puffs on absorbent paper to soak up any excess fat.

Using choux pastry
Although the well-known choux recipes tend to be sweet, it can be used to make some delicious savouries; make a cheese choux paste, as for Gougère or Cocktail cheese puffs (see recipes). For simple deep-fried choux, just roll them in caster sugar and serve as a sweet.

Always use choux pastries the day they are made as they lose their crispness if kept. They do, however, freeze well, excellent if you are preparing for a party and want to get ahead with your cooking. A tip, though: never fill them with a soft mixture until shortly before serving as they will go soggy — two hours is about the maximum length of time.

One of the easiest and yet most effective desserts to make are little choux puffs — baked in the oven for 15–20 minutes, then split and filled with plain whipped cream. Serve with chocolate sauce for an extra touch of glamour. Crème pâtissière or ice cream is also delicious if you fancy a change. By contrast, hot, bit-sized choux puffs and éclairs make wonderful appetizers. Fill them with creamed fish, curried chicken or creamed ham. Or serve cold miniature éclairs, like my Crab and watercress éclairs (see recipe).

Making choux paste

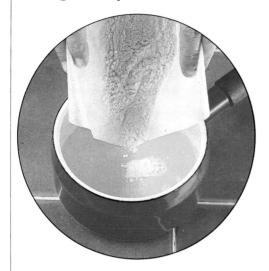

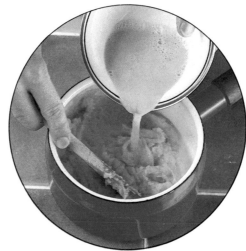

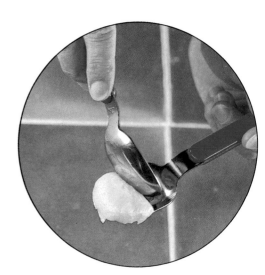

Measure the correct amount of water into a heavy-based saucepan and add the butter, and sugar if using. Bring the water slowly to the boil. As soon as the water boils and the butter is melted, remove the pan from the heat and shoot in the sifted flour.

Beat vigorously with a wooden spoon until the paste attaches itself around the spoon in a smooth ball. Remove the pan from the heat and allow the paste to cool. Start adding the beaten egg, a little at a time, beating vigorously between each addition.

Each time you add some egg the mixture will thin out, but as you beat it 'comes together' again. When all the egg is incorporated, the paste should be shiny and of a gentle 'dropping' consistency ready to shape or to pipe.

Basic choux paste

If you wish to make a dish as part of a meal, this recipe will make enough for four.

25 minutes

65 g /2½ oz flour
50 g /2 oz butter, diced
5 ml /1 tsp caster sugar (if making sweet
  choux)
2 large eggs, beaten
salt and freshly ground black pepper (if
  making savoury choux)

1 Sift the flour onto greaseproof paper.
2 In a heavy-based, medium-sized saucepan, combine the diced butter and sugar (if making sweet choux) with 150 ml /5 fl oz cold water. Slowly bring to the boil to give the butter time to melt.
3 As soon as the liquid is boiling briskly, remove the pan from the heat. Quickly shoot in the sifted flour all at once and immediately start beating vigorously with a wooden spoon.
4 Return the pan to a low heat and continue to beat the paste until it attaches itself around the spoon in a smooth ball, leaving the bottom and the sides of the pan clean — this takes about 2 minutes. Then remove the pan from the heat.

5 Allow the contents to cool a little and then add the beaten eggs a little at a time, beating vigorously with the spoon. Continue to beat until the paste is glossy.
6 If the paste is to be savoury, season with salt and freshly ground black pepper.

Crab and watercress éclairs

making the choux paste, then 1 hour, plus cooling

Makes 16
savoury Basic choux paste (see recipe)
1 egg, beaten
150 ml /5 fl oz mayonnaise
30 ml /2 tbls thick cream
salt and freshly ground black pepper
5 ml /1 tsp lemon juice
a few drops of Tabasco sauce
200 g /7 oz crabmeat
½ bunch watercress
paprika (optional)

1 Heat the oven to 220C /425F /gas 7.
2 Fit a piping bag with a 15 mm /½ in plain nozzle. Spoon choux paste into the bag. Lightly dampen a baking sheet. Pipe out 6.5–7.5 cm /2½–3 in lengths about 25 mm / 1 in apart on the baking sheet. Hold the nozzle of the piping bag slightly above the

Crab and watercress éclairs

surface of the baking sheet so that the lengths remain rounded. Cut off each length with a knife dipped in water, or give the nozzle a slight pull upwards to free it, then pat the point of the éclair smooth. Brush the éclairs with beaten egg to glaze.
3 Bake them in the oven for 10 minutes, then reduce the heat to 170C /325F /gas 3 and continue to bake them for 20 minutes longer, or until the éclairs are crisp, light and golden.
4 As soon as the éclairs are ready, remove them from the oven, slit them along one side to let the steam escape and, if necessary, remove any uncooked paste from the inside with a teaspoon. Leave the éclairs to cool on a wire rack.
5 Make the filling: in a bowl combine the mayonnaise with the cream and season with salt and freshly ground black pepper, lemon juice and a few drops of Tabasco to taste.
6 Cut the cold éclairs in half and spread a little of the mayonnaise on the top half of each éclair.
7 Combine the crab meat with the remaining mayonnaise.
8 Cut the stalks from the watercress and put a sprig of watercress on each choux base. Spread a little of the crab mayonnaise on top of the watercress and replace the lid. Sprinkle with paprika, if wished, garnish with watercress and serve.

41

Almond apples

🍴🍴🍴 making the choux paste and almond paste, then 2¼ hours, plus chilling

Makes 20

½ × sweet Basic choux paste (see recipe)
350 g /12 oz good-quality marzipan
green food colouring
20 small apple leaves
For the crème pâtissière
200 ml /7 fl oz milk
a piece of vanilla pod, 5 cm /2 in long, split
2 egg yolks
25 g /1 oz caster sugar
15 ml /1 tbls flour
7.5 ml /½ tbls cornflour
7.5 g /¼ oz butter
7.5 ml /½ tbls kirsch
butter, for greasing

1 Heat the oven to 220C /425F /gas 7. Lightly dampen a baking sheet.
2 Spoon the choux paste into a piping bag fitted with a 15 mm /½ in plain nozzle. Holding the piping bag vertically in one hand, pipe out the paste into rounds, about 25 mm /1 in in diameter, onto the damp baking sheet. Do not twist the bag, either pull it up sharply to disengage it from the piped paste, or cut the paste free with a knife dipped in cold water. Smooth down any sharp points with the damp knife, otherwise they will burn. Space the puffs about 25 mm / 1 in apart on the baking sheet.
3 Bake in the oven for 10 minutes, then reduce the heat to 170C /325F /gas 3 and continue to bake for 15–20 minutes, until the puffs are crisp, light and golden. Remove from the oven and make a small slit in the sides of the choux puffs with a sharp knife to allow the steam to escape. If necessary, scrape any uncooked paste out of the puffs with a teaspoon. Leave to cool on a wire rack.
4 Meanwhile, make the crème pâtissière: put the milk and split vanilla pod in a saucepan and place over a low heat. Bring slowly to boiling point, then remove from the heat, cover and set aside to infuse.
5 In a large bowl, whisk the egg yolks and sugar until thick and light. Gradually whisk in the flour and cornflour.
6 Remove the vanilla pod from the milk and gradually pour the milk onto the egg yolk mixture, whisking until blended.
7 Return the mixture to the saucepan and bring to the boil over a moderate heat, stirring constantly. Simmer for 3 minutes, beating vigorously with a wooden spoon, until the cream is thick enough to coat the back of a spoon.
8 Remove from the heat and add the butter. Beat for 1–2 minutes longer to cool the cream, then beat in the kirsch. Pass the cream through a fine sieve into a clean bowl, cover with a sheet of lightly buttered greaseproof paper and set aside to cool. When cold, chill until required.
9 When the choux puffs are cold, fit a piping bag with a small plain nozzle. Spoon crème pâtissière into the bag; pipe the custard cream into the puffs through the slits made in the sides.
10 Knead the marzipan lightly to soften it, then colour it faintly with a few drops of green food colouring. Knead thoroughly to disperse the colour evenly. Divide the marzipan into 20 balls and roll out each ball between sheets of cling film to a round large enough to enclose a choux puff.
11 Place a choux puff in the centre of a round of marzipan. Draw up the sides of the round to enclose the puff and seal it firmly, then mould the marzipan into an apple shape. Make a marzipan stalk and decorate it with a leaf. Repeat with the remaining puffs.

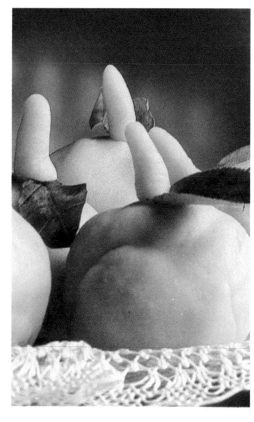

Almond apples

Cheese and salmon puffs

🍴🍴 making the choux paste, then 1 hour 40 minutes, plus cooling

Makes 35–40

savoury Basic choux paste (see recipe)
50 g /2 oz Gruyère cheese, grated
1 egg, beaten
sprigs of parsley, to garnish
For the cheese filling
125 g /4 oz full fat cream cheese
30 ml /2 tbls thick cream
30 ml /2 tbls finely snipped chives
freshly ground black pepper
For the salmon filling
125 g /4 oz smoked salmon trimmings
50 ml /2 fl oz soured cream
5 ml /1 tsp lemon juice
freshly ground black pepper

1 Heat the oven to 220C /425F /gas 7. Lightly dampen a baking sheet.
2 Beat the grated Gruyère cheese into the choux paste while it is still warm. Fit a piping bag with a 15 mm /½ in plain nozzle and fill the bag with the cheese choux paste. Holding the bag vertically, pipe out small bun shapes, about 15 ml /1 tbls in size, onto the dampened sheet, 25 mm /1 in apart. Brush the puffs with the beaten egg to glaze.
3 Bake the choux puffs for 10 minutes, then reduce the heat to 170C /325F /gas 3 and cook for a further 15–20 minutes.
4 Remove the puffs from the oven and make very small slits in their sides to allow the steam to escape, then cool completely on wire racks.
5 Meanwhile, make the 2 fillings. Beat the cream cheese until it is light and fluffy, then beat in the thick cream. Add the chives and season to taste with freshly ground black pepper.
6 Pound the smoked salmon trimmings to a smooth paste using a pestle and mortar and stir in the soured cream. Add the lemon juice and season to taste with freshly ground black pepper.
7 Just before serving, fit 2 piping bags with small plain nozzles and fill the puffs through the slits with the 2 fillings. Fill half the puffs with the cream cheese and half with the smoked salmon filling. Place on a serving dish and garnish with sprigs of parsley.

Beignets with hot raspberry sauce

🍴🍴🍴 making the choux paste, then 1 hour

Serves 4

sweet Basic choux paste (see recipe)
caster sugar
oil, for deep frying
For the raspberry sauce
350 g /12 oz raspberries
60 ml /4 tbls icing sugar, sifted
30 ml /2 tbls crème de cassis
15 ml /1 tbls lemon juice

1 First make the raspberry sauce; place the raspberries in a blender and purée them. Press the raspberries through a sieve into a heavy-based saucepan to remove the pips. Stir in the sifted icing sugar, crème de cassis and lemon juice.
2 Put the sauce over a very low heat to heat through while you cook the beignets. Do not let the sauce boil or it will change colour. Heat the oil in a deep-fat frier to 180C / 350F.
3 Dip a palette knife into the hot oil and use this to lift 5 ml /1 tsp of the choux paste at a time and place it in the hot oil. Cook only a few beignets at a time as they will swell during cooking. Cook for 6–8 minutes until they are golden brown and firm — they should turn themselves during cooking. Remove them with a slotted spoon and drain them on absorbent paper. Dust well with caster sugar while still hot. Keep warm. Cook further batches of beignets until all the paste is used.
4 Pour the raspberry sauce into a heated sauce-boat. Serve the beignets immediately with the hot sauce served separately.

Beignets with hot raspberry sauce

Raspberry choux ring

50 minutes, plus chilling

Serves 6
75 ml /5 tbls flour
a pinch of salt
50 g /2 oz butter, diced
5 ml /1 tsp sugar
2 eggs, beaten
butter, for greasing
30 ml /2 tbls chopped almonds
icing sugar, to serve
For the crème pâtissière
425 ml /15 fl oz milk
5 cm /2 in piece vanilla pod, split
5 egg yolks
100 g /4 oz caster sugar
30 ml /2 tbls flour
15 ml /1 tbls cornflour
15 g /½ oz butter
350 g /12 oz raspberries

1 Heat the oven to 220C /425F /gas 7.
2 Sift the flour and salt onto a sheet of greaseproof paper. In a small, heavy saucepan slowly bring to the boil 150 ml /5 fl oz water with the diced butter and sugar. Quickly remove from the heat and pour in all the flour, beating vigorously with a wooden spoon. Return to a low heat and beat the paste for 2 minutes, or until it forms itself around the spoon in a smooth ball, leaving the bottom and sides of the pan clean. Remove from the heat.
3 Gradually add the beaten eggs, beating vigorously. Continue to beat until the paste is glossy. Fit a piping bag with a 12 mm /½ in plain nozzle and spoon the paste into it. Lightly butter a heavy-duty baking sheet. Mark a circle, 15 cm /6 in in diameter, and pipe a thick ring, using all the paste. Sprinkle with the chopped almonds.
4 Bake for 15 minutes. Remove from the oven and reduce the heat to 190C /375 F /gas 5. With a skewer, pierce the ring at intervals in the side. Continue to bake for 15 minutes or until firm and dry. Cool on a wire rack.
5 Make the crème pâtissière. Add the vanilla pod to the milk and bring to the boil over a low heat. Remove from the heat, cover and leave until needed.
6 In a bowl, whisk the egg yolks with the sugar until thick and light. Gradually whisk in the flour and cornflour. Remove the vanilla pod and pour the milk onto the egg yolk mixture in a thin stream, whisking until well blended. Return to the pan and bring to the boil over medium heat, stirring constantly. Simmer for 3 minutes, beating vigorously with a wooden spoon to disperse the thickened parts of the mixture. Remove the mixture from the heat, beat in the butter and cool.
7 Reserving some raspberries for decoration if wished, stir the raspberries into the crème pâtissière and chill.
8 Cut the ring in half horizontally. Place the bottom half on a serving platter and fill it with raspberry crème pâtissière. Place the other half on top. Sift icing sugar over the top, decorate with the reserved raspberries and serve immediately.

Gougère with chicken livers

making the choux paste, then 1¼ hours

Serves 4
savoury Basic choux paste (see recipe)
50 g /2 oz Cheddar cheese, grated
butter, for greasing
For the filling
225 g /8 oz chicken livers
25 g /1 oz butter
1 Spanish onion, finely chopped
75 g /3 oz mushrooms, sliced
15 ml /1 tbls flour
300 ml /10 fl oz chicken stock, home-made or from a cube
salt and freshly ground black pepper
1 tomato, skinned, seeded and coarsely chopped
30–45 ml /2–3 tbls freshly grated Parmesan cheese

1 Beat the grated Cheddar cheese into the choux paste mixture while it is still warm. Heat the oven to 190C /375F /gas 5.
2 To make the filling, check the chicken livers and discard any green bits, rinse the livers and dry them well on absorbent paper. Melt the butter in a frying-pan and sauté the

Raspberry choux ring

livers until they are golden on the outside but still pink on the inside. Remove them from the pan with a slotted spoon and set them aside.
3 Add the finely chopped onion to the frying-pan and sauté for 3–4 minutes, stirring occasionally, until the onion is softened but not coloured. Add the sliced mushrooms and sauté for a further 2 minutes. Remove the finely chopped onion and mushrooms to a plate with a slotted spoon and set aside.
4 Stir the flour into the fat remaining in the pan and cook for 2–3 minutes to form a pale roux. In a separate saucepan, bring the chicken stock to the boil. Pour it onto the roux, stirring constantly with a wire whisk to prevent lumps forming. Season with salt and freshly ground black pepper to taste. Simmer for 15 minutes, stirring occasionally, or until the sauce is reduced to half its original quantity. Take the pan off the heat.
5 Add the sautéed chicken livers, onions, mushrooms and the coarsely chopped tomato. Adjust the seasoning.
6 Grease a 1.7 L /3 pt round ovenproof dish. Spoon the choux paste around the edges of the dish, leaving a hollow in the centre. Pour the filling into the hollow and dust the surface with grated Parmesan cheese. Bake for 30–40 minutes or until the gougère is well risen and brown. Serve immediately, straight from the dish.

Cakes & Breads

ALL ABOUT SPONGE CAKES

A light and airy sponge cake, attractive to look at, makes a luxury of tea time. Many dessert gateaux are made with sponge and their simple or elaborate fillings and decorations are then chosen to suit the occasion.

Successful cake-making is a skill demanding a greater degree of accuracy and self-discipline than most other branches of cooking. Some people seem to be able to turn out light cakes right from the word go. For others, the knack comes with practice.

Although it is perfectly true that our grand-mothers baked good cakes without accurate weights and measures or thermostatically controlled ovens, that is no reason for us to deprive ourselves of these modern aids. So, if you want to be a successful cake-maker, I urge you to start by investing in reliable measuring equipment.

Measuring equipment
First, it is essential to choose whether you are working in metric or imperial measures, and then stick to that system. Never mix grams with ounces — the proportions will be slightly different and may ruin your recipe. Of the measuring equipment you will need for making cakes, the most important is a set of good scales. You will also need a set of standard spoons and a measuring jug.

Most scales have dual markings but if you use the balance type, you will have to choose between metric or imperial weights. Measuring jugs are usually marked with both pints or fluid ounces and litres or millilitres. Measuring spoons come in a set that includes either 1 tbls, 1 tsp, ½ tsp and ¼ tsp or 15 ml, 10 ml, 5 ml and 2.5 ml.

To measure a dry ingredient such as flour or spice in a spoon, scoop up a generous amount in the appropriate spoon, then level off the top with a knife. When measuring liquid in a jug, check the measure at eye level to be sure you are reading it correctly.

Checking your oven
Next, check your oven thermostat and find out what are its eccentricities, if any. Use an oven thermometer, or try the following test.

Make up a portion of Victoria sandwich batter (see recipe). Divide it between two 19 cm /7½ in sandwich tins and place them, side by side, in the centre of an oven that has been preheated to 180C /350F /gas 4. To pass the test, the cakes should be perfectly risen and cooked, exactly 25 minutes later, with the tops a rich, even, golden brown. If they fail, check the following oven faults.

Too hot: the cakes may have risen in a cone in the centre. This happens because the sides harden into a crust before the batter has finished rising; sometimes the tops will crack badly as well. Or you may find the cakes have browned too fast; they are unlikely to actually burn in 25 minutes, but the look and flavour of the sponges will be spoilt. With a delicate sponge-type cake a too-hot oven often causes a hard crust over the top which completely spoils the texture.

Try the same test with the oven one setting lower — if it works this time, remember in

future to adjust the temperature every time you are baking. If your oven is wildly out, call in the service engineers who should be able to adjust the thermostat.

Too cool: the test sponges may have sunk in the middle. They may also be coarse or too close-textured or too dry and crumbly. If you were baking a fruit cake, the fruit would tend to drop to the bottom. Test the sponge again, with the oven one setting higher.

Uneven heat: if the tops of the sponges have cracked and are overbrowned, but still level, this probably means that the oven is much hotter at the top than at the bottom. In future you will need to bake on a lower shelf.

Occasionally a cake rises lopsidedly and the likelihood is that the oven is hotter on the side that has risen higher. Correct this by turning the cake tin a little from time to time during baking.

Baking tins
Good baking tins that do not warp or buckle are a sound investment as they should last you a lifetime. I have never been particularly impressed by the non-stick type, possibly because I don't really trust them completely and usually end up either greasing or lining them 'just in case'. However, I am a great believer in loose-bottomed tins which make it that little bit easier to cope with a cake that has stuck despite your precautions.

If a recipe calls for a tin or tins of a certain diameter, that size should be used. If you change the size, then the baking time — even the temperature — or the total amount of mixture will have to be adjusted accordingly.

The following range of tins is a comprehensive selection which will cover most requirements when you are baking sponges.

Sandwich tins: round tins about 4 cm /1½ in deep and 19 cm /7½ in in diameter and a 22.5 cm /8½ in diameter tin.

Layer tins: these are shallower than sandwich tins, about 20–25 mm /¾–1 in deep and 18 cm /7 in diameter.

Sponge flan tins: these have deep sides and

a raised centre. Choose one 20 cm /8 in in diameter.
Swiss roll tin: this is a shallow oblong tin about the same depth as a layer tin. I use one measuring 30 × 20 cm /12 × 8 in.
Plain or fluted ring tin for angel cakes: 23 cm /9 in in diameter.

Preparing cake tins
The next job after turning on the oven should always be the choosing and preparing of the correct size tin (or tins). For light sponges and layer cakes that cook comparatively rapidly, there are two ways of doing this. For complete safety, brush the base and sides of the tin with melted butter. Next, line the base with a neat circle of greaseproof paper and brush that with melted butter as well. Finally, dust the base and sides of the tin lightly with flour, knocking the tin to shake off the surplus. Alternatively, omit the paper and just brush with melted butter and then coat with flour.

The basic ingredients
Flour: all my recipes have been tested with good-quality plain flour. When necessary I have softened this by adding cornflour to

All-in-one sandwich cake

make the cake as light and delicate as possible. Keep flour dry in a tightly stoppered jar. For lightness always sift it before use even if it doesn't look lumpy because sifting helps to incorporate air.
Self-raising flour: many people prefer to use self-raising flour when a recipe specifies plain flour and baking powder. This is acceptable, providing that the proportion of baking powder to flour in the recipe is approximately 5 ml /½ tsp baking powder per 100 g /4 oz flour.
Eggs: my recipes are tested with large eggs, EEC size 2 (67–70 g). Take the eggs out of the refrigerator well before you intend to use them as they should be at room temperature before whisking or mixing them with the other ingredients.
Flavourings: vanilla and grated lemon or orange zest are the most common flavourings for sponge cakes. To convert a plain sponge to a chocolate one, replace up to 25 g /1 oz flour with cocoa powder.
A word of warning — always use vanilla or almond essence, or extract, rather than the cheaper, synthetic 'flavouring' for best results.

Creamed batter cakes
The simplest traditional sponge starts with a creamed batter (see Victoria sandwich). First beat, or cream, the butter and sugar together until they are light and fluffy. Next beat the eggs until frothy and beat them, a few spoonfuls at a time, into the mixture.
Sift the flour with the baking powder and fold it into the batter with a metal spoon.
People tend to be over-enthusiastic when it comes to creaming, believing wrongly that the harder they beat, the better the cake will be. In fact it is all too easy to over-cream. Tell-tale signs are air-bubbles just under the top crust of the baked cake and crumbly edges. The texture should be fairly fine, the crust thin and smooth, and the cake generally of a uniform colour and thickness.
The All-in-one sandwich cake (see recipe) is an even simpler version of this method in which all the ingredients are beaten together at the same time. But you do need an electric mixer for this recipe — it will not be successful if beaten by hand.

Whisked sponges
Basically a whisked sponge is a mixture of eggs and sugar with flour folded in. The eggs, whisked to include as much air as possible, are the only raising agent and you must take every care not to deflate the whisked mixture when adding the flour.
For the Basic whisked sponge (see recipe), the eggs are separated. The yolks are whisked with the sugar and the flour added. The whites are whisked independently and are then folded into the batter.
Examine the consistency of the batter into which you are folding the whites. If it seems very thick and heavy, fold in a little of the egg white to lighten it. Up to one-third can be used initially to lighten the batter. Next, fold together the batter and the egg whites using a large metal spoon.
Use the side of the spoon like a knife to cut down through the egg whites, then just roll the egg whites over with the spoon. Make a figure-of-eight motion down into the bowl,

round the bottom and back to the top. Do not stir with the flat of the spoon, or this will break up the air bubbles which are going to supply the lift for your cake. You can fold the egg whites into the batter, or the other way round, as you choose.
A fatless sponge is another type of whisked sponge. The eggs and sugar are whisked in a bowl over hot water to encourage them to hold the maximum of air bubbles. The mixture will change colour from yellow to white and will increase to about four times the original volume. A hand-held electric mixer is best for this continual beating — it will take about 10 minutes. (With a hand whisk it will take twice as long.)
Occasionally an additional raising agent is used. Some recipes call for baking powder as well as eggs to lighten the cake.
Finally, always plan to make your whisked sponge on the day you wish to eat it as it will go stale very quickly.

Genoise sponge
This French cake is made by the whisking method, but melted butter is folded in at the end for extra taste and richness. Another advantage is that this cake will keep for a couple of days. The genoise cake can also be used to make the sponge base of a flan.

Baking a cake
● First turn on the oven.
● Prepare the tins before you start mixing — a cake batter that is kept waiting will not rise properly.
● Place the baking tin(s) in the centre of the oven (unless the recipe states otherwise). If you have to use two shelves, you may need to switch the tins over two-thirds of the way through, or once the cakes have set.
● Don't open the oven door unless absolutely necessary, and then close it carefully, without slamming.
Is it cooked? A light, sponge-type cake is ready when it shrinks away slightly from the sides of the tin and springs back into shape when you press it lightly with a finger.
Turning out a cake: all cakes should be left to settle before being turned out of their tins. Leave sponge cakes for 1–2 minutes in the tin. Turn the sponge out onto greaseproof paper and then invert it onto a wire rack so that it cools resting right side up, otherwise you will have the marks of the rack on the top of your sponge.

Serving a cake
All these sponges can be filled simply with jam and whipped cream and decorated by sprinkling icing sugar over the top. For a pretty pattern, put a doily on top of the cake, sprinkle the sugar over it, then remove the doily. Flavoured butter creams and frostings can also make good fillings and toppings.

Storing cakes
Butter-rich cakes can be stored for 2–3 days in an air-tight tin, although they are better eaten fresh. Whisked sponges, which contain no fat, tend to dry out very quickly, so they should be eaten fresh. Put in a cream filling as close to serving as possible, because it hastens the staling process to put a cake in the refrigerator.

Making a whisked sponge

Put the egg yolks, caster sugar, lemon juice and salt in a bowl and whisk for about 5 minutes, until the mixture is light and fluffy and leaves a trail when the whisk is lifted.

Sift the flour and cornflour a little at a time over the surface of the egg yolk mixture and fold it in with a cutting motion to disperse the flour.

Whisk the egg whites until soft peaks form, tip them onto the sponge batter and fold in gently but thoroughly, cutting with the side of a large metal spoon.

Basic whisked sponge

⏳ 45 minutes (or 1 hour if using a hand whisk), plus cooling time

Makes 6 slices
melted butter and flour, for sandwich tins
50 g /2 oz flour
25 g /1 oz cornflour
4 eggs, separated
175 g /6 oz caster sugar
22.5 ml /1½ tbls lemon juice (or water)
a generous pinch of salt
jam and whipped cream, for filling
icing sugar, for decorating

1 Heat the oven to 180C /350F /gas 4.
2 Brush the bases and sides of two 19 cm / 7½ in sandwich tins with melted butter. Line the base of each tin with a neat circle of greaseproof paper and brush that with melted butter as well. Lightly dust the bases and sides of the tins with flour, knocking the tins to shake off the surplus.
3 Sift the flour and cornflour together 3 times onto greaseproof paper.
4 Put the egg yolks, caster sugar, lemon juice (or water) and salt into a mixing bowl. Whisk with an electric mixer at high speed for 5 minutes. If whisking by hand, whisk steadily until the mixture is light and fluffy.
5 Put the egg whites in another bowl which must be spotlessly clean and dry. Wash and dry the whisk carefully and whisk the egg whites until soft peaks form.
6 Resift the flour and cornflour a little at a time over the surface of the egg yolk mixture, at the same time folding it in lightly but thoroughly with a large metal spoon. Do not mix or beat, just cut deep into the mixture with the edge of the spoon and turn it over gently until the flour is evenly dispersed through the egg mixture.
7 Fold in the whisked egg whites, using the same gentle cutting and folding action.
8 Divide the batter evenly between the prepared sandwich tins. If necessary, level the tops lightly with a spatula. Place the tins in the hot oven and bake for 20–25 minutes. The cakes are cooked when they shrink away slightly from the sides of the tins and spring back into shape when lightly pressed.
9 Remove the cakes from the oven and leave for 1–2 minutes to settle. Now turn them out onto a clean tea-towel. Peel off the greaseproof paper and invert the cakes onto a wire rack to cool, right side up.
10 When the cakes are cold, sandwich the layers with jam and whipped cream and dust the top with icing sugar.

All-in-one sandwich cake

This easy sponge is made by the all-in-one method — the ingredients are beaten all together with an electric mixer.

⏳ 35 minutes, plus cooling

Makes 6 slices
melted butter and flour, for sandwich tins
100 g /4 oz self-raising flour
5 ml /1 tsp baking powder
100 g /4 oz soft margarine
100 g /4 oz caster sugar
2 eggs
a few drops of vanilla essence
jam, for filling
icing sugar, to decorate

1 Heat the oven to 170C /325F /gas 3.
2 Brush the bases and sides of two 19 cm / 7½ in sandwich tins with melted butter. Line the base of each tin with a neat circle of greaseproof paper and brush that with melted butter as well. Lightly dust the bases and sides of the tins with flour, knocking the tins against the side of the table to shake off the surplus.
3 Sift the flour with the baking powder into the mixing bowl of your electric mixer and add the remaining ingredients. Whisk until well mixed (1–2 minutes). Divide the mixture between the prepared sandwich tins. Place them in the hot oven and bake for 25–30 minutes. The cakes are cooked when they shrink away slightly from the sides of the tins and spring back into shape when pressed lightly with a finger.
4 Remove the cakes from the oven and leave for 1–2 minutes to settle. Next, turn them out onto a clean tea-towel. Peel off the greaseproof paper and invert the cakes onto a wire rack to cool right side up.
5 When the cakes are cold, sandwich the layers with slightly warmed jam and dust the top with icing sugar.

Fatless sponge

⏳ 1 hour (or 1½ hours if using a hand whisk), plus cooling

Makes 6 slices
melted butter and flour, for layer tins
3 eggs
75 g /3 oz caster sugar
75 g /3 oz flour
a few drops of vanilla essence
jam and whipped cream, for filling
icing sugar, to decorate

1 Heat the oven to 180C /350F /gas 4.
2 Brush the bases and sides of two 18 cm / 7 in layer tins with melted butter. Line the base of each tin with a neat circle of greaseproof paper and brush that with melted butter as well. Lightly dust the bases and sides of the tins with flour, knocking the tins against the side of the table to shake off the surplus.
3 Choose a heatproof bowl with a capacity of 1.5 L /2½ pt or larger in which to whisk up the cake, and select a large saucepan over which it will fit firmly. Pour 5 cm /2 in water into the pan and bring it to the boil. Reduce the heat until the water in the pan is barely simmering.
4 Put the eggs, sugar and vanilla in the bowl. Set it over the simmering water and whisk continuously until very thick, light and lukewarm. (This will take 10 minutes if using a hand-held electric mixer at high

speed.) The mixture should increase to about four times its original volume.

5 Remove the bowl from the heat. Stand it on a cool surface and continue to whisk until the mixture leaves a distinct trail on the surface when the beaters are lifted and the mixture has cooled (5 minutes with an electric mixer at high speed).

6 Sift the flour a little at a time over the egg mixture, folding it in lightly but thoroughly with a large metal spoon.

7 Divide the batter between the prepared layer tins. Place the tins in the hot oven and bake for 20–25 minutes. The cakes are cooked when they shrink away slightly from the sides of the baking tins and spring back into shape when lightly pressed.

8 Remove the cakes from the oven and leave for 1–2 minutes to settle, then turn them out onto a clean tea-towel. Peel off the greaseproof paper and invert the cakes onto a rack so that they cool right side up.

9 When the cakes are cold, sandwich the layers together with jam and whipped cream and dust the top with icing sugar.

To make a Swiss roll
Cook the mixture in a 30 × 20 cm /12 × 8 in Swiss roll tin for 20–25 minutes. While the cake is in the oven, lay a sheet of greaseproof paper on a table and sprinkle with 5 ml /1 tsp caster sugar.

Turn the cake out onto the sugared paper and carefully peel off the lining paper and trim off the crusty edges of the cake with a

Basic whisked sponge

sharp knife. Lay a fresh sheet of greaseproof paper on top of the cake. Starting at one of the shorter sides, carefully roll up the cake with the paper inside. Leave the cake to cool on a rack.

When it is cold, carefully unroll it and remove the top paper. Spread the cake evenly with jam and whipped cream and roll it up again, this time without the paper. Dust the top with icing sugar to finish.

It may help to keep the cake flexible if you lay a damp tea-towel underneath the sugared greaseproof paper. When you roll up the cake, roll both the paper and the damp tea-towel together.

Making a Swiss roll

Turn the cake out onto sugared greaseproof paper, peel off the lining paper and trim the crusty edges of the cake with a sharp knife.

Lay a sheet of greaseproof paper on top and, while the cake is still warm, roll it up carefully, with the paper inside.

When it is cold, unroll the cake, spread it evenly with jam and whipped cream. Roll it up carefully. Dust the top with icing sugar.

Victoria sandwich sponge

 50 minutes, plus cooling

Makes 6 slices
melted butter and flour, for sandwich tins
225 g /8 oz softened butter
225 g /8 oz caster sugar
2.5 ml /½ tsp vanilla essence
2.5 ml /½ tsp finely grated lemon zest
4 eggs
225 g /8 oz flour
10 ml /2 tsp baking powder
jam and whipped cream, for filling
icing sugar, to decorate

1 Heat the oven to 180C /350 F /gas 4.
2 Brush the bases and sides of two 19 cm / 7½ in sandwich tins with melted butter. Line the base of each tin with a neat circle of greaseproof paper and brush that with melted butter as well. Lightly dust the bases and sides of the tins with flour, knocking the tins to shake off the surplus.

3 In a large mixing bowl, combine the butter with the caster sugar, vanilla essence and finely grated lemon zest. Cream them together with a whisk until light and fluffy.
4 In another bowl, whisk the eggs until they are light and frothy.
5 Whisk the eggs, a few spoonfuls at a time, into the creamed butter and sugar mixture. Do not add the eggs too quickly, as this might make the mixture curdle.
6 Sift the flour and baking powder over the creamed mixture a little at a time, folding it in lightly but thoroughly with a large metal spoon.
7 Divide the batter evenly between the pre-pared sandwich tins and level the tops lightly with a spatula. Place the tins in the hot oven and bake for 25 minutes or until they are a good golden brown. The cakes are cooked when they shrink away slightly from the sides of the tins and spring back into shape when pressed lightly with a finger.
8 Remove the cakes from the oven and leave for 1–2 minutes to settle, then turn them out onto a clean tea-towel. Peel off the greaseproof paper and invert the cakes onto a wire rack to cool, so that they are resting right side up.

Chocolate Victoria sandwich sponge

9 When the layers are cold, sandwich them together with slightly warm jam and whipped cream and top the cake with a sprinkling of icing sugar.

● To make a chocolate Victoria sandwich, you can replace 25 g /1 oz flour with cocoa powder or drinking chocolate.

Basic genoise sponge cake

 1 hour 10 minutes (or 1½ hours if using a hand whisk), plus cooling

Makes 8 slices
melted butter and flour, for sandwich tin
100 g /4 oz flour
3 eggs
2 egg yolks
100 g /4 oz caster sugar
5 ml /1 tsp vanilla essence
50 g /2 oz butter
lemon cream frosting, to decorate

1 Heat the oven to 180C /350F /gas 4.
2 Brush the base and sides of a 22 cm /8½ in sandwich tin with melted butter. Line the base of the tin with a neat circle of grease-proof paper and brush that with melted butter as well. Lightly dust the base and sides of the tin with flour, knocking the tin to shake off the surplus.
3 Clarify the butter: put it in a small, thick-bottomed saucepan and melt it over a very low heat. When the butter foams, allow the foam to fall gently to the bottom of the pan, then pour off the clear oil from the top into a small bowl, being careful not to disturb the white sediment.
4 Sift the flour 3 times onto greaseproof paper.
5 Choose a bowl of 1.5 L /2½ pt or larger capacity in which to whisk up the cake, then select a large saucepan over which it will fit firmly. Pour 5 cm /2 in water into the pan and bring it to the boil. Reduce the heat until the water is barely simmering.
6 Add the eggs and egg yolks, caster sugar and vanilla essence to the selected bowl and set it over the simmering water and whisk until very thick, light and lukewarm (10 minutes if using an electric mixer at high speed, longer with a hand whisk).

7 Remove the bowl from the heat. Stand it on a cool surface and continue to whisk until the mixture leaves a distinct trail on the surface when the beaters are lifted and the mixture has cooled (5 minutes if using an electric mixer at high speed; it will take longer with a hand whisk).
8 Resift the flour a little at a time over the surface of the egg mixture, folding it in lightly but thoroughly with a large metal spoon, and cutting with the spoon edge.
9 Add the cool clarified butter to the batter a spoonful at a time, continuing with the folding motion until it has been completely absorbed. This may take slightly longer than you expect, so work as lightly as you can to avoid deflating the mixture.
10 Pour the batter into the prepared tin. Place the tin in the hot oven and bake for 25–30 minutes. The cake is cooked when it shrinks away slightly from the sides of the tin and springs back into shape when pressed.
11 Remove the cake from the oven and leave it for 1–2 minutes to settle, then turn it out onto a clean tea-towel. Peel off the greaseproof paper and invert the cake onto a wire rack so that it cools resting right side up.
12 When the cake is cold, decorate it with lemon cream frosting.

Genoise flan

 1½ hours, plus cooling

Makes 6–8 slices
melted butter and flour, for the flan tin
50 g /2 oz flour
25 g /1 oz butter
2 eggs
1 egg yolk
50 g /2 oz caster sugar
2.5 ml /½ tsp vanilla essence
whipped cream and fresh fruit, for filling

1 Prepare a 20 cm /8 in flan tin — obviously you cannot use a paper lining, so take great care to butter and flour the flan tin well.
2 Make the batter following the method for Basic genoise sponge cake (see previous page). Fill the flan tin with batter and bake for 20–25 minutes.
3 When the flan is completely cold, fill it with chilled whipped cream and decorate the top with any seasonable fresh fruit.

Genoise flan

BRIOCHE

Deliciously rich in butter and eggs, yet airy and light, brioches will be a revelation if you have never tasted them. They are equally good eaten plain with butter and jam or filled with a savoury or a sweet mixture.

I find it puzzling that croissants are so popular and well-known and yet at the same time we have almost ignored one of the finest of all French breads — the brioche. It tastes of butter, yet is marvellously light, not at all flaky, but with a golden, airy crumb; it is certainly one of my favourites. Traditionally brioche dough is baked in a special tin which is twice as wide at the rim as it is at the base and has heavily fluted sides. (Brioche tins make admirable jelly moulds.) You may use one large tin or tiny ones for individual brioches. The tins are brushed with oil or melted butter to make the brioche crusty and golden brown on the outside when baked.

The dough is placed in the tin in a ball. For *brioche à tête*, characteristically French, the dough is divided into two. A larger ball is placed underneath and a smaller one (the little head or *tête*) secured on top.

If you do not have the right sort of tin don't despair — brioches will bake quite happily in a large, low ring mould, loaf tins, any tall, narrow tin, such as a Gugelhupf mould, or small individual tins, preferably ones with sloping sides.

A brioche dough can also be used as an alternative to puff pastry, to enclose a savoury filling, for example a salmon mixture for coulibiac. Try it wrapped around a fillet of beef *en croûte* — brioche dough is much easier to cut than pastry, which may crumble. Use brioche for wrapping up a length of spicy sausage (see recipe). Or make the breakfast treats loved by French school-children, by wrapping brioche around batons of plain chocolate to make buttery, chocolate-stuffed fingers (see recipe); warm from the oven they are quite irresistible.

Fresh brioches with plenty of butter and home-made jam can be served for breakfast, or with tea and coffee. But you can also scrape out the crumbs and use the brioche as a case for delicate fillings of pâté, meat, fish or shellfish in a rich creamy sauce, or fruits poached in syrup.

If you decide to have filled brioches, you will need brioches that are at least one day old: carefully remove the head or *tête* and set it aside; scoop out the soft crumbs of the brioche with a small, sharp spoon, leaving a firm case. Brush the inside of the brioche with a little melted butter or dust with caster sugar, and slip it into a low oven to crisp up. Fill the brioche, set the little heads back on top and serve. (For recipes, see Brioches farcies and Cherry brioches.)

Making brioche dough

All brioches are made from a slightly sweetened yeast dough enriched with butter and eggs, similar to the doughs used for Savarin and sweet yeast doughs. The rules for working with yeast are the same but as the dough gets richer, according to the recipe, the kneading and rising methods change. For my first Brioche recipe, which is the basic method, the problem is that the dough is rather wet and sticky. In fact, it is so wet that it is easiest to beat it by hand until it is smooth and shiny — use one hand only in a slapping, turning and pulling motion. Keep the other hand clear to help when clearing up — the dough really is very sticky!

After beating the dough, it is left to rise — the time will depend on the temperature of your room but it is ready when it has doubled in bulk. I generally find that at normal room temperature it takes about 1½ hours.

Next I beat the dough again — still by hand — and chill it overnight. I have found that this overnight chilling is the only thing that makes a brioche dough fit to handle;

Brioches farcies

Making brioche

Beat the dough with one hand. Lift the dough from the bottom of the bowl with a circular movement of your fingers — it will be floppy and sticky.

Slap the dough down into the bowl with a flick of your wrist. Repeat for 5–10 minutes until the dough is smooth and elastic, then chill overnight.

Make two balls, one one-third the size of the other. Put the larger ball in the mould and cut a cross on top of it. Press on the smaller ball, making sure it is secure.

without it it is simply too soft and gooey to manage. If at any time during the preparation the dough gets too warm and starts to ooze melting butter, put it in the refrigerator to firm up before carrying on. When the dough is thoroughly chilled, you can knead it again before shaping, proving and baking it.

Basic brioche

This basic dough gives brioche with a smooth, close texture. Use it to make individual brioches, as in this recipe, or to make one large brioche. The principles of putting it in the mould and fixing on the *tête* are the same.

⊕ 🍴 2½ hours, overnight chilling, then 1½ hours, plus cooling

Makes 12 individual brioches
25 g /1 oz fresh yeast
550 g /1¼ lb strong flour
60 ml /4 tbls caster sugar
2.5 ml /½ tsp salt
4 eggs
120 ml /8 tbls lukewarm milk
5 ml /1 tsp vanilla essence
125 g /4 oz butter, softened
flour, for kneading
melted butter, for moulds
1 egg yolk beaten with 15 ml /1 tbls
  water, to glaze

1 Put 120 ml /8 tbls lukewarm water in a small bowl, crumble the yeast over it and stir until it is dissolved.
2 Sift the flour, sugar and salt into a large, warmed bowl and make a well in the centre.
3 Beat the eggs with the lukewarm milk. Stir in the vanilla essence and add this to the flour, together with the yeast liquid. Mix well with one hand.
4 Add half the softened butter, in small pieces, and beat with one hand until the dough is smooth and elastic — 5–10 minutes.

The dough will be very soft at this stage.
5 Dot the surface with the remaining butter, cover the bowl with cling film and leave the dough in a warm place to rise until it is doubled in bulk — this will take about 1½ hours.
6 Punch the dough down again and beat vigorously with one hand for 5 minutes, or until it no longer sticks to the sides of the bowl (flour your hand from time to time while beating).
7 Cover the bowl tightly with cling film and refrigerate overnight. Brioche dough is very rich and sticky and chilling it overnight helps to make it easier to handle.
8 The following day, brush 12 individual 65 ml /2½ fl oz brioche moulds with melted butter.
9 Turn the dough out onto a lightly floured surface and knead a few times until smooth again. Weigh the dough and cut off a quarter, making two balls. Divide each ball into 12 pieces of equal size. Roll the 12 larger pieces into balls and place them in the prepared moulds. Roll each of the smaller pieces into a ball; snip the top of each large ball twice with scissors to form a cross, and set one of the smaller balls on top. Place the moulds on a baking sheet and leave the brioche in a warm place to rise again until doubled in bulk, about 30 minutes.
10 Heat the oven to 200C /400F /gas 6.
11 When the brioches have risen, brush the tops with the egg glaze. Bake them in the oven for 15–20 minutes, or until firm and well risen, and a rich golden colour.
12 Turn out and cool on a wire rack.

● To make one large brioche, brush a 1 L / 1¾ pt brioche mould with butter. Weigh the dough and then cut off one quarter. Roll the larger amount into a ball and place in the mould. Cut a cross in the top with a sharp knife. Roll the smaller quantity into a ball and place on top. Leave it to rise until doubled in bulk — 30–45 minutes — then glaze and bake for 30 minutes.

Cherry brioches

⊕ 🍴 making the brioche, then 1¼ hours, plus chilling

Serves 4
425 g /15 oz canned black cherries in syrup
45 ml /3 tbls caster sugar
30 ml /2 tbls kirsch
75 ml /5 tbls red wine
10 ml /2 tsp cornflour
a cinnamon stick
a piece of vanilla pod or 1.5 ml /¼ tsp
  vanilla essence
4 individual brioches, 1 day old
15–30 ml /1–2 tbls softened butter
1.5 ml /¼ tsp almond essence
25 g /1 oz flaked toasted almonds

1 Strain the cherry syrup into a saucepan. Add 30 ml /2 tbls caster sugar, the kirsch and the red wine. Stir over gentle heat until the sugar has dissolved.
2 In a small bowl, blend the cornflour with 10 ml /2 tsp water. Stir it into the cherry syrup and add the cinnamon stick and vanilla pod or essence. Bring to the boil, stirring, and boil until reduced to 120 ml /8 tbls, about 8–10 minutes, stirring frequently. Stone the cherries, if necessary.
3 Remove the cinnamon stick and the vanilla pod from the syrup and stir in the cherries. Leave to cool.
4 Heat the oven to 200C /400F /gas 6.
5 Remove the tops from each brioche. Then scoop out the crumbs, leaving a fairly thin but unbroken shell. Brush the inside of each brioche with softened butter and sprinkle with 15 ml /1 tbls caster sugar. Bake in the oven for 6–8 minutes to dry out the centres.
6 Pile the cherries into the brioches. Stir the almond essence into the remaining syrup and pour over the cherries. Decorate each brioche with a few flaked toasted almonds and chill until ready to serve.

Brioches farcies

⏱🍴🍴 making the brioche,
then 1¼ hours

Serves 4–6
4–6 individual brioches, 1 day old
175 g /6 oz calf's sweetbread, soaked in cold
water for one hour, changing the water
several times
175 g /6 oz raw white chicken meat
300 ml /10 fl oz chicken stock, home-made,
or from a cube
½ bay leaf
6 peppercorns
4–6 parsley stalks
beurre manié (made with 15 g /½ oz butter
and 15 ml /1 tbls flour)
300 ml /10 fl oz thick cream
salt
freshly ground black pepper
Madeira (optional)
lemon juice (optional)
40 g /1½ oz butter
125 g /4 oz button mushrooms, quartered

1 Place the sweetbread, chicken meat, chicken stock, bay leaf, peppercorns and parsley stalks in a saucepan and bring slowly to the boil, skimming off the scum that rises to the surface. Simmer for 12–15 minutes until the chicken meat and sweetbread are cooked. Remove the chicken meat and sweetbread with a slotted spoon. Carefully remove any membrane from the sweetbread.
2 Reduce the poaching liquid over a high heat to half its original quantity (this will take approximately 10 minutes), then whisk in the *beurre manié* a little at a time and boil until it is thickened. Add the thick cream, bring the sauce back to the boil, reduce the heat and simmer until it has the consistency of thick cream. Season to taste with salt, freshly ground black pepper, and, if wished, Madeira and lemon juice.
3 Meanwhile, heat the oven to 110C /225F / gas ¼. In a small saucepan, melt 25 g /1 oz butter.
4 Cut the top off each brioche. Scoop out the crumbs and brush the inside and outside of the crust (tops and bottoms) with melted butter. Place the brioches in the oven to heat through until lightly browned.
5 Dice the cooked chicken meat and calf's sweetbread into very small cubes.
6 Heat the remaining butter in a small frying-pan and sauté the button mushrooms until they are golden. Then add the diced chicken meat and calf's sweetbread and heat it all through very thoroughly. Strain the sauce through a fine sieve over the meat and mushrooms.
7 Fill the brioches with the mixture, replace the tops and then serve immediately.

Briochin de volaille

This brioche is unusual in that the dough is made, put into the mould and the filling added, then cooked through.

⏱🍴🍴 2¼ hours, overnight chilling,
then 1½ hours

Serves 6
7.5 g /¼ oz fresh yeast
225 g /8 oz strong flour
15 ml /1 tbls caster sugar
a generous pinch of salt
2 eggs
40 g /1½ oz very soft butter
600 ml /1 pt fresh tomato sauce, for serving
melted butter or oil, for brushing
For the filling
175 g /6 oz cooked chicken
salt
freshly ground black pepper
90–120 ml /6–8 tbls thick cream

1 The day before you intend to bake the brioche, prepare the dough. In a bowl, sprinkle the yeast over 30 ml /2 tbls luke-warm water and stir until it is dissolved. Sift in 60–90 ml /4–6 tbls flour and mix well. Cover the bowl with cling film and leave to rise until the dough has doubled in bulk and is full of air bubbles, about 20 minutes.
2 Sift the remaining flour into a large bowl with the sugar and salt. Make a well in the centre, add the yeast mixture and the eggs and incorporate into the flour gradually, beating vigorously with one hand.
3 When the dough is smooth, beat in the butter, which should be soft to the point of melting. Beat by hand until thoroughly incorporated — the dough should be soft and shiny.
4 Cover the bowl with cling film and leave the dough in a warm place until doubled in bulk, about 1½ hours. Next, place it in the refrigerator and chill overnight.
5 The following day, brush a plain 1.1 L / 2 pt ring mould with butter or oil and line the bottom and sides completely with half of the dough.
6 Cut the chicken into large slivers, mix with the thick cream and season to taste with salt and freshly ground black pepper.
7 Fill the brioche-lined mould with the chicken and cream mixture. Cover with the remaining dough; brush the base and top edges of the dough very lightly with water, and press together to seal in the chicken completely.
8 Cover the mould with cling film and leave to rise for 30 minutes in a warm place.
9 Meanwhile, heat the oven to 190C /375F / gas 5.
10 Bake the briochin for 30–35 minutes, or until golden brown and well risen. Turn out and serve hot with hot fresh tomato sauce handed separately.

● There are many quick and easy fresh tomato sauces that complement briochin de volaille. Canned tomatoes or tomato purée can be used with very good results, see French tomato sauce, page 90.

Chocolate brioches

These little pastries are sold, still warm from the oven, by French bakers, in time for breakfast. They are delicious dunked in a cup of milky coffee.

⏱🍴🍴 making the brioche dough,
then 1½ hours, plus cooling

Makes 40
75–125 g /3–4 oz thin plain chocolate squares
1 × Basic brioche dough, risen and chilled
overnight (see recipe)
butter, for greasing
beaten egg, to glaze

1 Prepare the chocolate. Divide the bar into double squares. Heat a sharp-bladed knife by dipping it in boiling water for a few minutes, then cut each double-square of chocolate in three lengthways to make long, thin fingers, using as little pressure as possible to avoid splintering the chocolate, and reheating the knife blade as it begins to cool.
2 Roll the brioche dough out 3 mm /⅛ in thick; cut it into 5 cm /2 in squares.
3 Place a rectangular piece of chocolate in the centre of each square. Roll the square of dough round it so that it is completely enclosed.
4 Place the rolls on a buttered baking sheet and leave them in a warm place until doubled in bulk, about 30 minutes.
5 Heat the oven to 200C /400F /gas 6.
6 Brush the brioche rolls lightly with beaten egg and bake in the oven for 12 minutes, or until golden. Cool on wire racks and serve very fresh.

Saucisson en brioche

⏱🍴🍴 making the brioche,
then 1¾ hours

Serves 6
flour, for dusting
½ × Basic brioche, risen and chilled
overnight (see recipe)
350 g /12 oz French garlic sausage in one
piece, skinned
oil, for greasing
beaten egg yolk, to glaze

1 Heat the oven to 190C /375F /gas 5.
2 Dust the pastry board and rolling pin lightly with flour, and roll out the dough into a rectangle large enough to envelop the sausage completely.
3 Wrap up the sausage in the dough, moistening the edges very lightly with water to make sure they are completely sealed. Brush a 1.4 L /2½ pt loaf tin with oil. Place the garlic sausage roll in it. Make 2 holes in the top of the brioche dough and place a length of rolled greaseproof paper in each, to let steam escape.
4 Leave to rise for 30 minutes or until the dough has doubled.
5 Brush with beaten egg yolk, then bake for about 40 minutes in the oven or until puffed and golden brown. Cover with foil after 20 minutes if the top of the brioche dough is browning too quickly.
6 Remove the brioche from the oven. Ease it out of the tin, then reverse it to stand right way up. Cut into thick slices and serve immediately, while hot.

● This tasty, filling recipe can be served with a crisp, green salad.

MAKING BREAD

The smell of home-made bread filling the kitchen, coupled with the delight of eating an oven-warm loaf — crisp on the outside, soft and melting on the inside — are pleasures often missed today. Here's how you make it.

People are said to have a 'light hand' with pastry and cakes; with yeast doughs, 'feel' would be a better word. Recipes can describe the consistency of a particular yeast dough, but only as you gain experience will you be able to judge whether it is soft or firm enough, whether it is pliable and elastic, or whether it requires more kneading. Your eye will learn to recognise the right sheen on a ball of dough that has had its full share of pummelling and kneading. I can only give you a rough guide as to how long it takes me, but you may work more vigorously or less quickly than I do. Also, only you can tell how long it will take for your dough to double in bulk, because I do not know the temperature of your kitchen.

The basic ingredients

Yeast is the most important ingredient in bread making. It is a living plant and if you can get fresh yeast, so much the better. There is something very pleasing about its soft, creamy-crumbly texture and strong aroma. I instinctively prefer it, although I can find little justification for this attitude, except for the fact that you can tell by its appearance when fresh yeast has gone stale and will not work.

Assuming that it is really fresh when you buy it, a lump of fresh yeast in a polythene bag can be stored for up to 5 days in a cool place, up to a month in the refrigerator in an airtight container and, tightly wrapped, up to a year in the deep freeze, although its strength may diminish.

Dried yeast is available in packets and drums and if stored correctly it will stay active for up to 6 months. 'Easy blend' dried yeast is a newer variety which is packed in vacuum-sealed sachets; follow the manufacturer's 'use by' dates.

When substituting dried yeast in a recipe that calls for fresh, use half the quantity specified; 25 g /1 oz fresh yeast = 15 g /½ oz or 15 ml /1 tbls dried yeast.

Flour: strong plain flour is best for most breads because of the high proportion of gluten it contains. It is the gluten which stretches the bread, making it light and airy. When you buy a fresh bag of flour, transfer it to a glass jar or an air-tight container and store it in a cool, dry place. If necessary you can substitute ordinary plain flour for strong, but never use self-raising flour. Often for wholemeal recipes I mix in some strong white flour, too, as this gives the bread a lighter texture.

Working with yeast

Dissolving fresh yeast: to dissolve or 'cream' fresh yeast, use some of the liquid specified in the recipe. Heat it to blood temperature (37C /98F) and crumble the yeast into it. Stir until dissolved; it is now ready to use.

Activating dried yeast: in a small bowl, dissolve a little sugar in a measured amount of the recipe liquid (individual recipes will specify the amount). Sprinkle the dried yeast over the top and beat it thoroughly with a fork. Now leave it for at least 10 minutes. The liquid should be very frothy with no trace of the hard little granules. If they are not thoroughly dissolved at this stage, they will still be in evidence when the bread comes out of the oven to be eaten.

Easy blend dried yeast: in appearance this yeast resembles sand grains and is easy to blend, as its name implies. Just mix the grains with the flour and then add the specified liquid directly to the mixture.

Quantities: in general terms, 15 g /½ oz fresh yeast (10 ml /2 tsp dried) will leaven 550 g /1 lb flour, but note that this proportion changes with larger quantities, so that 1.4 g /3 lb flour requires only 25 g /1 oz fresh yeast.

Making a bread dough

Sift the dry ingredients into a large mixing bowl as directed in the recipe. Make a well in the centre and add the tepid yeast liquid to this. (Other ingredients, such as beaten egg, lard or butter, may also be added to the

White bread plait

Kneading a bread dough

Turn the dough out onto a lightly floured surface. Push down and away with the heels of your hands until the dough is about 30 cm / 12 in long.

Fold the dough towards you to make a ball again. Give the dough a quarter turn so that this time it will be stretched in a different direction. Push the dough out and fold it.

Continue pushing and folding, developing a rocking rhythm as you do so. Gradually the texture of the dough changes from sticky to smooth and elastic, with a firm, springy feel to it. Kneading takes about 10 minutes.

dough at this stage.) Stir the ingredients together and then knead with your hand, in the bowl, to bring the dough together so that it leaves the sides of the bowl clean.

Kneading: turn the dough out onto a floured board and knead the dough for about 10 minutes or until it is shiny and elastic. Follow the step-by-step pictures on the left-hand side of the page, aiming to maintain a steady, even rhythm of pulling and pushing the dough together. Once the dough is kneaded, roll it into a ball, ready for the next process.

Rising: take a clean bowl and oil it lightly with flavourless oil. Put the ball of dough in the bowl and roll it around so that it is lightly coated with the oil. Slip the bowl into a large plastic bag and tie the ends, or cover the top of the bowl loosely with cling film (which allows you to see what is going on underneath). The bowl must be large enough and the covering loose enough for the dough to rise comfortably. The wrapping not only keeps the dough moist, it also helps to contain the heat that the dough generates of its own accord. This is quite noticeable when you take the covering off.

Put the dough in a warm place to rise. Remember that while cold only retards the growth of a yeast dough, excessive heat will kill it. For a steady, even rise that doesn't take too long, aim for an average-to-warm room temperature (21–22C /70–75F).

Shaping bread dough

It is essential to choose the right sized tin for a tinned loaf. For a small 850 ml /1½ pt tin cut off a piece of dough weighing 500 g /1 lb 2 oz. For a larger 1.5 L /3 pt tin use 1 kg / 2 lb 4 oz dough. Make sure the dough is well distributed in the tin or you will get a very domed loaf. A good method is shown in the diagrams on the next page.

The dough should fill two-thirds of the tin so that there is room for it to rise. If, on the other hand, the tin is too full, the dough will rise and spill over the edges.

To make rolls or buns, divide the dough into pieces of 50 g /2 oz each and follow the instructions and the diagrams overleaf.

● There is a special technique for forming simple rolls — first roll 50 g /2 oz dough into a ball shape, using a circular motion. Still using the circular motion, press down on the dough, then ease the hand up, cupping the fingers around the ball; this gives the roll a good rounded shape. Continue to roll until the dough has formed a perfect ball shape — there should be a whirl mark under the roll.

● For rolls which pull apart, place the pieces of rolled dough 12 mm /½ in apart on the baking sheet. They will join up as they rise. Space the rolls 25 mm /1 in apart on the sheet if you want them crisp all round.

● To make a classic bloomer loaf, roll the dough into a smooth oval about 25 cm /10 in long. With a sharp knife make 3 diagonal slashes across the top. Glaze with milk.

● For a cob, shape the dough into a ball and, using a sharp knife, cut a deep cross in the top.

● For a plait, divide the dough into 3 equal pieces and roll each into a strand about 30 cm /12 in long, tapering each end. Press the ends together at one end and plait the free strands (see picture page 58). When plaited, pinch the ends together. Place the loaf on a greased baking sheet, tucking the pinched ends under. Glaze with egg and sprinkle with poppy seeds or kibbled wheat.

● To make a crown, cut the dough into 2 pieces, then divide each piece into 6 equal-sized pieces, each weighing about 50 g /2 oz. Roll the pieces into smooth rounds. Using 2 greased 18 cm /7 in sandwich tins, place one round in the centre of each tin, then surround with the remaining rounds to form a crown shape (see picture overleaf). Glaze with milk.

● For a cottage loaf, cut off ⅓ of the dough and form into a round. Roll the remaining dough into a round. Place the small round on top of the larger one. Using the floured handle of a wooden spoon, make a hole through the middle, from top to bottom. Snip the dough edges with scissors to make notches (see picture on the next page). Glaze with milk.

Proving: the shaped loaf or rolls are left to 'prove'; that is, to rise a second time to their final shape. As before, you can time the rising to suit yourself by choosing a warm or cold place. However, this time the dough will rise more quickly — 30 minutes in a warm place for a loaf (less for rolls) and up to 2 hours in a cool place or 2–8 hours in the refrigerator.

For proving in a warm place, put the shaped dough in an oiled tin or baking tray and then in an oiled polythene bag which is large enough to allow the dough to rise without sticking to it. Tie the bag loosely.

If you are proving in the refrigerator, the loaf can wait for several hours before baking even after the dough has risen above the top of the tin. For proving in the refrigerator, brush the surface of the dough with oil and cover the top of the bowl with cling film. Let the dough stand for 15 minutes at room temperature before baking.

During proving, take care not to put the dough in a draught as it is rising and do not knock it, or it may collapse. If this happens, try kneading and reshaping; it may be saved.

Baking

Before it is baked the dough is glazed to give the finished bread a smooth, golden finish. The most usual glaze is an egg yolk beaten with several tablespoons of water but for some recipes, when a very crisp crust is required, just cold water is brushed over the bread. To make the crust even crisper, a pan of water can be put in the oven while the bread is baking. For added flavour, extra toppings may be sprinkled on the glazed dough: kibbled wheat, caraway seeds, poppy seeds and sesame seeds are a few ideas.

To create a soft, floury finish, the shaped dough is dusted with flour and then, when the bread is removed from the oven, it is covered with a clean cloth which traps the steam and prevents the outside from hardening. This finish is used in particular for soft rolls.

The oven temperature and cooking times for baking bread vary from recipe to recipe. They are dependent on the size of the loaf or rolls and the texture of the finished loaf. Nevertheless, the same test for seeing if the bread is done applies to all. When you think the bread is ready, remove it from the tin or baking sheet and tap the base with your knuckles — it should sound hollow. If not, return the bread to the oven and bake it for a further 10 minutes, turning the bread up the other way if it is not cooked in a tin. When it is cooked, remove it from the oven; if it is in a tin, take it out and cool it on a wire rack.

Freezing

After baking, bread and rolls can be kept in the freezer for up to 1 month. You can freeze dough immediately after mixing and before the yeast has begun to work. Thaw it out for a minimum of 24 hours in the refrigerator, when it will defrost and then rise in sequence. Most satisfactory results are obtained by freezing part-cooked loaves and rolls. These can then be quickly cooked from frozen to produce freshly baked bread and rolls.

White bread plait

about 2½ hours, plus cooling

Makes 1 small loaf
300 ml /10 fl oz milk
15 g /½ oz fresh yeast
500 g /1 lb strong flour
2.5 ml /½ tsp salt
25 g /1 oz butter, diced
1 egg, lightly beaten
flavourless oil, for greasing
1 egg yolk, beaten with 30 ml /2 tbls water

1 In a small saucepan, heat the milk to blood temperature. Crumble the fresh yeast into the milk and stir until it has dissolved.
2 Sift the flour and salt into a bowl. Rub in the butter with your fingertips until all the pieces of butter are coated with flour. Make a well in the centre.
3 Pour in the yeast liquid and the lightly beaten egg. Stir to mix, then knead vigorously until the dough comes away from the sides of the bowl.
4 Turn it out onto a floured board and knead for about 10 minutes until elastic (see diagrams).
5 Roll the dough into a ball and place it in a clean, lightly oiled bowl. Turn the ball of dough so that it is coated all over with oil. Cover the bowl with cling film and leave the dough to rise for about 1 hour in a warm place until it has doubled in bulk.
6 When the dough has risen, turn it out onto a lightly floured board and punch it down again. Knead vigorously for 10–15 minutes until the dough has regained its elasticity and has a deep sheen.
7 To plait the loaf, cut the dough into 3 equal portions, weighing them to make sure they are equal. Roll them into sausage shapes 32.5–35 cm /13–14 in long and plait them on a baking sheet. (You can do a 'five plait' if you are feeling ambitious.) Pinch the ends together and turn them under to seal. Brush lightly with oil and leave to rise for 30 minutes, covered with a damp tea-towel, until the loaf has risen again to double its bulk.
8 Heat the oven to 190C /375F /gas 5.
9 When the loaf has risen to the required

size, brush the top with the egg glaze and bake it in the oven for 35 minutes. The loaf should be a rich golden colour on the top and sound hollow when you rap on the base with your knuckles. Cool on a wire rack.

American rolls

1¾–2½ hours, shaping the rolls, then 1¼ hours

Makes about 24
25 g /1 oz fresh yeast
150 ml /5 fl oz milk
90 ml /6 tbls sugar
75 g /3 oz butter, plus melted butter
10 ml /2 tsp salt
700 g /1½ lb strong white flour, plus extra for kneading
2 eggs, lightly beaten
oil, for greasing
1 egg yolk, beaten with 30 ml /2 tbls water

1 In a small bowl, crumble the yeast over 65 ml /2½ fl oz lukewarm water and stir until it is dissolved.
2 In a saucepan, combine another 65 ml / 2½ fl oz water with the milk, sugar, butter and salt. Stir over a moderate heat until the butter and sugar have melted, then remove the pan from the heat and allow the liquid to cool to lukewarm.
3 Sift one-third of the flour into a large, warm mixing bowl. Add the milk mixture gradually, beating vigorously until smooth. Beat in the prepared yeast and beaten eggs.
4 Gradually sift in enough of the remaining flour to make a moderately stiff dough, kneading between additions until smooth.
5 Turn the dough out onto a floured surface and knead vigorously until smooth, shiny and elastic — about 5–8 minutes. Sift more flour over the dough if it still tends to stick to the board or your fingers.
6 Shape the dough into a ball and put it into a clean, lightly oiled bowl, turning it so that the entire surface is greased. Cover with cling film and leave to rise until the dough has doubled in bulk.
7 When the dough has risen, remove it from the bowl, punch it down and knead lightly until smooth and elastic again. Divide it into 3 equal-sized pieces. Knead each piece to a ball.
8 Shape the rolls (see below and on the following page).
9 Oil the surface of the rolls, cover them with cling film and leave them to rise again until doubled in bulk — about 1 hour.
10 Heat the oven to 200C /400F /gas 6.
11 Brush the rolls with the egg glaze and bake them in the oven for 15 minutes or until a rich golden brown. Serve hot.

● **Fantans.** Dust the board and rolling pin lightly with flour and roll one ball of dough into a rectangle 18 × 23 cm /7 × 9 in and 5 mm /¼ in thick. Cut it lengthways into 4 cm /1½ in strips. Brush each with melted butter and pile them on top of each other; cut into 4 cm /1½ in lengths. Arrange, sideways down, on a well-oiled baking sheet. Repeat with the rest of the dough. Each ball makes 6 fantans. Continue with steps 9–11.

Finishing a bread dough

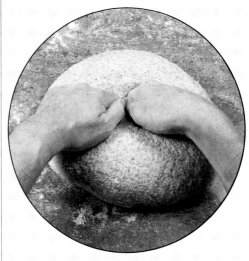

To knock back dough, plunge your knuckles into the centre of the dough to disperse any air bubbles, then knead the dough for 1–2 minutes to make it ready for shaping.

To shape the dough for a tin, flatten it into a rectangle 3 times the width of the tin; fold in 3. With the seam underneath, drop it into the tin. Press each corner with your knuckles.

To prove the loaf, put the shaped dough in its tin into an oiled polythene bag and tie loosely. Leave to prove — it should double in size when fully risen.

Shaping baking tray loaves and rolls

Plait: roll into 3 strands about 30 cm /12 in long; taper each end. Press the ends together at one end and plait the strands. Pinch the ends together and tuck under.

Crown: divide the dough into 12; roll into smooth rounds. Place one round in the centre of 2 sandwich tins, then surround with the remaining rounds to form a crown.

Cottage loaf: form ⅓ of the dough into a round. Roll the remainder into a round. Place the smaller one on top. Press a floured spoon handle through the middle. Snip edges.

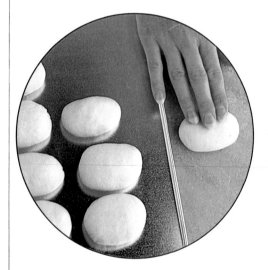

Oval rolls: divide the dough into 24 pieces. Form each piece into a smooth ball, then into an oval shape. Place about 15 mm /½ in apart so they join up, then glaze.

Baps: roll the dough out about 15 mm /½ in thick. Cut into 24 rounds, using a floured 7.5 cm /3 in cutter. Dust with flour and, for soft crust, cover with a cloth after baking.

Coils: divide the dough into 12 pieces. Roll each into a strand about 10–12 cm /4–5 in long. Curl up each strand firmly from one end to make a flat coil. Glaze with egg.

Cheese and onion rye bread

Try this unusual and very flavorsome loaf as a change for tea.

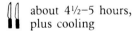 about 4½–5 hours, plus cooling

Makes 1 large loaf
225 ml /8 fl oz milk
25 g /1 oz lard
25 g /1 oz fresh yeast
500 g /1 lb strong white flour
15 ml /1 tbls salt
500 g /1 lb rye flour
15 g /½ oz butter
15 ml /1 tbls olive oil
½ Spanish onion, chopped
25–50 g /1–2 oz Cheddar cheese, grated

1 In a saucepan, heat the milk. Stir in the lard until it melts, then cool the mixture to blood temperature. Crumble the fresh yeast into the tepid liquid and stir until dissolved.
2 Sift the white flour and salt into a bowl and add the rye flour. Stir to mix well. Stir in the milk and yeast mixture.
3 Work into a dough and knead until smooth. (This is a very heavy dough — it is easier to use a dough hook or food processor.)
4 Form the dough into a ball and place it in a lightly oiled bowl; turn the ball of dough so that it is coated all over with oil. Cover with cling film. Leave the dough to rise in a warm place until it has doubled in size.
5 Knock down the dough and knead it a second time for 10 minutes. Clean the bowl and re-oil it. Place the dough in it, and turn to coat. Cover it again with cling film and leave the dough to rise for a second time.
6 Knead the dough for a third time and place it in a lightly oiled 23 cm /9 in spring-release cake tin. Oil the surface and leave the dough to rise again for 30 minutes covered with a damp tea-towel.
7 Heat the oven to 190C /375F /gas 5.
8 Heat the butter and olive oil in a frying-pan and sauté the chopped onion for 4–5 minutes or until softened.
9 Sprinkle the cooked onion and grated cheese over the bread and bake in the oven for 50 minutes or until the loaf sounds hollow when tapped. Cool on a wire rack.

● If using a machine for kneading, check its capacity in the manufacturer's booklet — it may only handle dough for one loaf. With a table-top mixer, beat the made dough with the dough hook at lowest speed for 1 minute. Increase to top speed and beat for 3 minutes.

With a food processor, make the dough in the bowl using the double-bladed knife. Cut the butter into the flour, then add the yeast through the tube. Process for 1 minute.

Wholemeal soda bread

| 50 minutes,
| plus 45 minutes cooling

Makes 2 small loaves
225 g /8 oz plain flour
225 g /8 oz wholemeal flour
7.5 ml /1½ tsp salt
5 ml /1 tsp bicarbonate of soda
300 ml /10 fl oz buttermilk
butter and flour, for baking sheets

1 Heat the oven to 220C /425F /gas 7.
2 Sift the plain flour, salt and bicarbonate of soda twice through a fine sieve into a large bowl. Add the wholemeal flour, stir to mix well and make a well in the centre.
3 Add the buttermilk and mix to a dough, adding a little warm water if the mixture is too dry.
4 Quickly divide the dough into 2 pieces, form them into well-shaped round buns as tall as you can make them and then place them on a buttered and floured baking sheet. The alternative method of shaping the loaves is to make them flatter, like a scone, and then make a deep cross cut so that each loaf, after it has been baked, will divide easily into 4 parts.
5 Cover each loaf with a deep 15 cm /6 in or 18 cm /7 in cake tin. Put them immediately on the shelf above the centre of the oven and bake for 15 minutes. Remove the

tins and leave the loaves for another 15–20 minutes, until they have formed brown but not overbaked crusts.
6 Cool on a wire rack. This bread is at its best when served just cooled.

Wholemeal rolls

Mix white flour with the wholemeal flour to give the rolls a lighter texture.

| about 2¾ hours,
| plus cooling

Makes 24
300 ml /10 fl oz milk
25 g /1 oz fresh yeast
400 g /14 oz strong white flour
salt
400 g /14 oz wholemeal flour
50 g /2 oz butter, softened
flavourless oil, for greasing
1 egg yolk, beaten with 30 ml /2 tbls water

1 In a small saucepan, warm the milk to blood temperature. Crumble in the fresh yeast and stir until dissolved. Add 300 ml / 10 fl oz lukewarm water.
2 Sift the white flour and salt into a large bowl and add the wholemeal flour. Stir to mix well.
3 Make a well in the centre of the flour and add the yeast liquid and the softened butter; mix all the ingredients together to make a dough. Turn this out onto a floured board

and knead for 10 minutes, until you have a smooth and moist, but not sticky, dough.
4 Form the dough into a ball. Put it into a clean, lightly oiled bowl and then turn the ball of dough so that it is coated all over with oil. Cover it with cling film and leave it to rise for 45 minutes in a warm place, or until it has doubled in size.
5 Turn the dough onto a lightly floured board and knead it again for 10 minutes.
6 Divide the dough into 4 even-sized pieces and shape each piece into 6 rolls. Put them on an oiled baking sheet. Brush with oil and leave them to rise in a warm place, covered with a tea-towel, until doubled in size.
7 Meanwhile, heat the oven to 220C /425F / gas 7. Brush the rolls with egg glaze and bake for 10–15 minutes or until they sound hollow when tapped. Cool the rolls on a wire rack before serving.

Crusty rolls

|| 1 hour plus rising,
|| then 20 minutes

Makes 12
300 ml /10 fl oz hand-hot milk
15 g /½ oz fresh yeast
5 ml /1 tsp caster sugar
500 g /18 oz strong white flour
10 ml /2 tsp salt
25 g /1 oz butter
beaten egg, to glaze

Wholemeal rolls and Wholemeal soda bread

● Use a sachet (7 g /¼ oz) 'easy blend' dried yeast instead of fresh yeast: stir the yeast into the flour before rubbing in the fat, then add the milk and water.

Pumpernickel

 about 4½–5 hours

Makes 2 loaves
350 g /12 oz strong white flour
7.5 ml /1½ tbls salt
350 g /12 oz rye flour
350 ml /12 fl oz lager
150 ml /5 fl oz light molasses
25 g /1 oz butter, diced
20 g /¾ oz fresh yeast
flavourless oil, for greasing

1 Sift the white flour and salt into a large bowl and add the rye flour. Stir to mix well and make a well in the centre.
2 In a medium-sized saucepan, heat the lager, molasses and butter to blood temperature. Crumble the fresh yeast into the tepid liquid and then stir until it has completely dissolved.
3 Gradually pour the yeast liquid into the dry ingredients. Mix in the flour by hand, gradually forming a sticky dough. Turn out onto a floured board and knead well, adding more flour as necessary. Knead for 10 minutes or until the dough is smooth and elastic.
4 Shape the dough into a ball. Place it in a lightly oiled bowl and turn the ball of dough so that it is covered with oil. Loosely cover it with cling film. Leave the dough to rise for 1–1½ hours in a warm place or until it has doubled in bulk.
5 Punch down the dough and knead it again lightly. Return it to the oiled bowl and turn it again so that it is coated. Cover with cling film and leave it to rise again until doubled in bulk.
6 Divide the dough into 2 equal portions. Form 2 balls and place them on an oiled baking sheet. Oil the loaves very lightly, cover with a damp tea-towel and leave them to rise in a warm place until they have doubled in size — about 1 hour.
7 Meanwhile, heat the oven to 180C /350F / gas 4.
8 Bake the loaves in the oven for 50 minutes or until the bottom sounds hollow when tapped. If they need a little more cooking, turn them over and cook for a further 10 minutes. Cool on wire racks.

● To keep, tightly wrap the bread in foil. Pumpernickel improves if it matures for several days before it is eaten.
● Yeast dough rises quite happily in the refrigerator — eventually — and the slower the rise, the stronger will be the gluten framework of the flour. But if it is too warm, the dough will rise too fast and have a coarse, open texture.

Pumpernickel

Crusty rolls

1 Heat the oven to 220C /425F /gas 7 with a shelf above the centre.
2 Put half the hand-hot milk into a small bowl and crumble in the fresh yeast.
3 Put the flour into a large bowl and add the salt and sugar. Rub in the butter.
4 Make a well in the centre of the flour mixture and pour in the yeast and the rest of the milk. Mix to a dough, then knead on a lightly floured surface for 10 minutes until smooth and pliable.
5 Put the dough into an oiled bowl, cover

with greased polythene or cling film and leave until doubled in bulk.
6 Knock back the dough, knead it briefly, then shape it into 12 rolls and place them 4 cm /1½ in apart on a greased baking tray. Brush well with beaten egg. Leave to rise again for 15–20 minutes until puffy looking.
7 Bake the rolls above the centre of the oven for 15–20 minutes, until they are golden brown and crisp. Cool them on a wire rack.

● Use 10 ml /2 tsp dried active baking yeast instead of fresh yeast: dissolve 5 ml /1 tsp sugar in the milk and water, whisk in the

Sophisticated Skills

MAKING PERFECT ASPIC

One of the most elegant dishes of classic French cookery — the aspic — is sadly neglected today. Yet anyone willing to make a little effort can master the simple tricks of the trade, and turn out masterpieces of jellied art.

Even when summer is over it's still pleasant to eat cooling and refreshing meals, if only as a reminder of the months gone by. It is then that jellied meat, poultry or vegetables provide the perfect answers for entertaining. These are dishes prepared in advance and then chilled in the refrigerator until the moment they are to be presented as the centrepiece of a buffet or as the first course of a party meal.

Aspic is basically a savoury jelly made from strong chicken, veal, beef or fish stock. So that the jelly is transparent and light, the stock is first clarified. Sometimes these clarified stocks are rich enough in gelatinous matter to set without the addition of gelatine. At other times, however, it is necessary to add gelatine.

Making the aspic

An amber-tinted aspic, shimmering and crystal clear, is simple to make. It can be a lengthy business but the techniques involved are uncomplicated.

Start off by making a good stock. This can be done by following a recipe or by using whatever items you have in the kitchen. Scraps of meat, giblets, poultry carcasses, fresh bones, vegetables, bouquet garni and herbs and flavourings are the essential elements. You need double the weight of water to solids and a meat stock should boil for at least five hours. Poultry (chicken and turkey) stock, generally needs only three hours cooking and fish stock needs to simmer for just 20 minutes.

Marrow bones, a knuckle of veal or the bone from a weekend joint are all good starting points for making your own stock. Fish bones, trimmings or a cod's head make a beautiful basic fish stock.

Although stock cubes are often indispensable in the kitchen, it is not advisable to use them when making stock for aspic since their concentrated flavour becomes too salty if simmered for any length of time. However, a quickly made aspic (see recipe) does sometimes use a stock cube — but the flavour is never so good.

Because it is used mainly for decorative purposes, aspic should be absolutely clear. For this reason stock has to be clarified by simmering it with minced meat or fish, chopped vegetables and the frothed whites and crushed shells of eggs (see individual recipes). The end result is consommé.

If the consommé is not strong enough in gelatinous matter to set by itself, gelatine is added — usually 30 ml /2 tbls powdered gelatine to 600 ml /1 pt consommé. First sprinkle the gelatine over 45 ml /3 tbls of cold consommé and leave it to soften for a few minutes. Now place the bowl in a saucepan of simmering water to allow the gelatine to dissolve very slowly. Carefully strain the dissolved gelatine mixture into the rest of the

consommé, which should be warm, and stir thoroughly.

In my recipe for Boeuf à la mode less gelatine is used. This is because the recipe includes a calf's or a pig's foot, which are, of course, principal sources of gelatine.

You can flavour your aspic with 15 ml /1 tbls Madeira, port or sherry per 600 ml /1 pt aspic, or add fresh tarragon to the stock before clarifying it (3 sprigs for every 600 ml /1 pt stock).

Using aspic

Freshly made aspic should be allowed to cool until it is syrupy — the consistency of un-beaten egg white. At this stage the aspic will be firm enough to hold any decorations in place or to form a coating, and will set very quickly when it is chilled.

If you are making a dish with layers of aspic so that it takes you several hours to complete, you can put as much aspic as you need at any one time in a bowl, stand it over a pan of hot water until it is melted and then you can cool it over a bowl of ice until it is the correct consistency. On the other hand, you can keep all the aspic liquid hot and ladle out and cool just as much as you need at that moment. But never heat and cool all your aspic time after time since this will cause it to go cloudy.

Lining a mould with aspic

If you intend to line a small mould with aspic, you should pour the syrupy aspic into the mould, swish it around and then stand the mould in a bowl containing crushed ice. As soon as a 3 mm /⅛ in layer of aspic appears to be set round the edges, pour the excess aspic back into the bowl. Try and get the thickness of aspic even all over the mould, but if, however, too much aspic sets at the bottom of your mould it can be removed with a spoon that has been dipped into hot water.

If you wish to line a larger mould, fill a large bowl with ice and stand your empty mould in it. Add the aspic to the mould, one tablespoonful at a time, and swirl it around so that the base is evenly coated. Then tip the mould onto its side on the ice and spoon in a little more aspic — gradually turning and coating the mould until the inside edges are completely covered.

Continue to add the aspic in this fashion until there is a 3 mm /⅛ in layer all over the inside of the mould. Chill the mould in the refrigerator. Dip your decorations into the aspic and arrange them on the set aspic and chill until set.

Coating and layering with aspic

Stand the food to be coated on a rack and set it over a baking tray. Any aspic drips can be poured off and used again.

Have the food well chilled before coating it

with the first layer of syrupy aspic, this way the aspic will begin to set on contact with the food and will stay in position. Chill the coated food, making sure that the first layer is thoroughly set before applying the next layer. Never pour hot aspic onto set aspic as it will melt the first layer. You can arrange aspic-dipped decorations on the food before coating it with a final layer of aspic — shapes cut from colourful vegetables and hard-boiled egg, pieces of black olive and leaves of fresh herbs can all be used to make very attractive decorations.

Take the same precautions when layering a mould with aspic, making sure that each layer is set before adding the next, and taking care that you do not pour hot aspic onto set aspic.

Chopped aspic

Chopped aspic makes an attractive border or bed for many cold dishes, particularly pâtés, cold mousses and food set in aspic.

Pour a 5–10 mm /¼–½ in layer of aspic into a shallow dish and leave it to set in the refrigerator. When it is set, turn it out and either cut it into dice or coarsely chop it. You can also cut out decorative shapes — diamonds, hearts and triangles — with fancy cutters.

Decorating with aspic

Sprays of tarragon and fennel are often used for decoration in aspic, as are pimentos, carrots, olives, truffles and yolks and whites of hard-boiled eggs. The decorations are dipped into syrupy aspic and laid in place on a layer of set aspic. This is chilled until set, then covered with another layer of aspic.

Remember that time is required when working with aspic. If the decoration is complicated, several coats may be required and this can take several hours. It is possible to put aspic in the freezer for a few minutes to speed up the setting process but if it is allowed to freeze, the aspic will crystallize, and even after defrosting it will not look smooth and clear.

Simple aspics

Aspics made by short-cut methods are simple to make but produce less rewarding results. Nevertheless, they are useful to know in case you ever want to make an aspic in a hurry. Instead of clarifying your own home-made stock, you can use a good quality canned consommé or packaged aspic granules or crystals, which are simply mixed with hot water.

A quick aspic can be made quite easily by sprinkling 15 ml /1 tbls powdered gelatine over 60 ml /4 tbls water and leaving it for a few minutes to soften without stirring. Next strain 425 ml /15 fl oz of chicken, beef or vegetable stock (which can be home-made or from a cube) through muslin. Heat the stock almost to boiling and then add the softened gelatine and stir until dissolved. When the stock is cool, add 30 ml /2 tbls each of Madeira and dry sherry. While this method has the advantage of speed, it is not such a satisfactory way of making aspic — the

Above, Boeuf à la mode; below, American vegetable aspic mould (recipes on page 66)

flavour is far less subtle than if you use the longer and more traditional recipes and methods.

Testing your aspic
It is very important that you test your aspic for setting power before you commit it to the mould. This little extra effort may prevent a disaster at the table!

Pour a 10 mm /½ in layer of aspic into a chilled cup or small bowl and chill it in the refrigerator for 10–15 minutes until it is set. Now remove it from the cup or bowl, cut it into pieces and leave it at room temperature for 10 minutes; it should remain set.

If the mixture is too weak, add some more powdered gelatine to strengthen it, softening and dissolving it in a little of the liquid in the same way as before. (Try about 2.5 ml /½ tsp powdered gelatine at first.) If the mixture is too stiff or rubbery, simply stir in some more liquid.

This density test also provides you with an opportunity to taste the set aspic and adjust the flavour of the bulk of the mixture.

When to use aspic
I like to use aspics in several ways:
● For lining moulds, to encase dice or slivers of meat or poultry or seafood or vegetables.
● For lining moulds of meat, poultry, game, seafood or vegetable mousse.
● For coating whole fish, chicken, duck or quail or for coating individual servings of meat, poultry, game or fish.
● For coating a galantine (white meat, poultry, game birds or fish, boned, stuffed and rolled, and coated with chaudfroid sauce) (see page 72) or a ballotine (stuffed, boned meat, poultry, game or fish, formed into a 'parcel' shape) (see page 70).
● For coating canapés for buffet food.
● For layering aspic with decorations or for layering aspic with a different flavouring added to each layer.
● For chopping, dicing or cutting into decorative shapes to use as a garnish.

Basic beef aspic

◖◖◖ making the beef stock,
◖◖◖ then about 3 hours, plus cooling

Makes about 1 L /2 pt
175 g /6 oz lean minced beef
2 leeks, trimmed and fairly finely chopped
2 celery sticks, fairly finely chopped
2 carrots, fairly finely chopped
½ Spanish onion, fairly finely chopped
2 soft, over-ripe tomatoes, coarsely chopped
frothed whites and crushed shells of 2 eggs
1.7 L /3 pt cold home-made beef stock, skimmed of all fat
45–60 ml /3–4 tbls powdered gelatine

1 In a large, heavy-bottomed saucepan, combine the minced beef, the chopped leeks, the celery sticks, the carrots, the onion, the tomatoes and the frothed whites and crushed shells of the eggs.
2 Place the stock in a separate pan and bring it slowly to the boil. Pour the stock onto the egg white mixture a little at a time,

stirring constantly with a balloon whisk or wooden spoon.
3 Stand the pan over a low heat and bring the mixture slowly to the boil, whisking all the time. When the mixture boils, stop stirring and reduce the heat. Allow the foam to rise to the surface, then simmer gently for 1 hour, uncovered and without stirring.
4 Line a large sieve or colander with muslin and stand it over a bowl. Gently draw back the scum from one-quarter of the clarified stock. Lower a ladle through this gap and, disturbing the scum as little as possible, ladle the clarified stock into the muslin-lined sieve. Measure 60 ml /4 tbls of the consommé into a small bowl and leave it to get cold.
5 Sprinkle the gelatine on the consommé in the small bowl. Allow it soften for a few minutes, then stand the bowl in a pan of simmering water until the gelatine has dissolved.
6 Strain the dissolved gelatine mixture into the remaining consommé and stir it thoroughly. Allow the mixture to cool until it is very syrupy (the consistency of unbeaten egg white) and on the point of setting. The aspic is now ready to use.

● You can flavour the aspic jelly with 30 ml /2 tbls Madeira, sherry or port, adding it to the consommé with the dissolved gelatine.

Basic fish aspic

◖◖ making the fish stock,
◖◖ then about 2 hours, plus cooling

Makes about 1 L /2 pt
3 egg whites, whisked until frothy
100 g /4 oz minced white fish
½ Spanish onion, finely chopped
1 carrot, finely chopped
white part of 1 leek, finely chopped
3 parsley stalks
3 or 4 mushroom stalks, finely chopped
10 white peppercorns
1 bay leaf
a pinch of dried thyme
1.5 ml /¼ tsp tomato purée
juice of 1 lemon
1.5 ml /¼ tsp salt
1.1 L /2 pt cold home-made fish stock, skimmed of any fat
45 ml /3 tbls powdered gelatine

1 Mix the frothy egg whites in a large, heavy-based saucepan with the fish, the onion, the carrot, the leek, the parsley, the mushroom stalks, the peppercorns, the bay leaf, the thyme, the tomato purée, the lemon juice and the salt.
2 Bring the fish stock slowly to the boil in a separate pan, over a low heat. Then pour the stock, a little at a time, onto the egg white mixture, stirring constantly with a whisk or a wooden spoon.
3 Bring slowly to the boil, stirring. When the mixture boils, stop stirring and reduce the heat. Allow the foam to rise, then simmer for 5 minutes, uncovered, without stirring. Remove the pan from the heat, cover and infuse for 10 minutes.
4 Line a large sieve or colander with

Trout in wine aspic

muslin and stand it over a bowl. Gently draw the scum away from one-quarter of the clarified stock. Lower a ladle into the gap and, disturbing the scum as little as possible, ladle the clarified stock into the muslin-lined sieve. (If you find that the resulting consommé is not absolutely clear, strain it and start again.) Measure 60 ml /4 tbls of the consommé into a small bowl and leave it to get cold.
5 Sprinkle the gelatine over the consommé in the small bowl. Leave it to soften, then stand the bowl in a pan of simmering water until the gelatine has dissolved.
6 Strain the dissolved gelatine mixture into the remaining warm consommé and stir thoroughly. Allow the mixture to cool until it is very syrupy (the consistency of unbeaten egg white) and on the point of setting. The aspic is now ready to use.

Basic chicken aspic

◖◖◖ making chicken stock, then
◖◖◖ about 3 hours, plus cooling

Makes about 1 L /2 pt
175 g /6 oz pie veal or chicken, minced
2 leeks, trimmed and fairly finely chopped
2 celery sticks, fairly finely chopped
2 carrots, fairly finely chopped
½ Spanish onion, fairly finely chopped
frothed whites and crushed shells of 2 eggs
1.7 L /3 pt cold home-made chicken stock, skimmed of all fat
45–60 ml /3–4 tbls powdered gelatine

1 In a large, heavy-bottomed saucepan, combine the minced pie veal or chicken, the chopped leeks, the celery sticks, the carrots, the onion and the frothed whites and crushed shells of the eggs.

2 Place the stock in a separate pan and bring it slowly to the boil. Pour the stock onto the egg white mixture, a little at a time, stirring constantly with a balloon whisk or a wooden spoon.

3 Bring the mixture slowly to the boil over a low heat, stirring all the time. When the mixture boils, stop stirring and reduce the heat. Allow the thick foam to rise to the surface, then simmer gently for 1 hour, uncovered, without stirring.

4 Line a large sieve or colander with muslin. Gently draw back the scum from one-quarter of the clarified stock. Lower a ladle into this gap and, disturbing the scum as little as possible, ladle the clarified stock into the muslin-lined sieve. Measure 60 ml / 4 tbls of the consommé into a small bowl and leave it to get cold.

5 Sprinkle the gelatine over the cold consommé in the small bowl. Let it soften for a few minutes, then stand the bowl in a pan of simmering water until the gelatine has completely dissolved.

6 Strain the dissolved gelatine mixture into the remaining consommé and stir thoroughly. Allow the mixture to cool until it is very syrupy (the consistency of unbeaten egg white) and on the point of setting. The aspic is then ready to use immediately, as desired.

● Basic chicken aspic can also be flavoured with fresh or dried tarragon leaves.

Trout in wine aspic

3½ hours, plus
cooling and chilling

Serves 6

6 trout complete with heads and tails, cleaned (each about 225 g /8 oz cleaned weight)
salt and freshly ground black pepper
1 Spanish onion, thinly sliced
1 sprig each of thyme and parsley
1 bay leaf
1 clove garlic, flattened with a knife
700 ml /25 fl oz bottle red wine
butter, for greasing

For the fish aspic

3 egg whites
100 g /4 oz minced white fish
½ Spanish onion, finely chopped
1 carrot, finely chopped
white part of 1 leek, finely chopped
3 parsley stalks
3-4 mushroom stalks, finely chopped
10 white peppercorns
1 bay leaf
a pinch of dried thyme
1.5 ml /¼ tsp tomato purée
juice of 1 lemon
1.5 ml /¼ tsp salt
45 ml /3 tbls powdered gelatine

For the decoration

12 thin slices of carrot
salt
the white of 1 hard-boiled egg
the peel of ½ cucumber, cut in wide strips
1 lemon
a small bunch of parsley
6 cooked prawns, in their shells

1 Season the trout inside and out with salt and freshly ground black pepper. Place the trout side by side in a roasting tin, cover with the sliced onion, then add the thyme, the parsley, the bay leaf and the flattened garlic clove. Pour in the red wine and enough cold water to just cover the fish. Then cover the fish with a sheet of buttered greaseproof paper, place over the heat and bring it to the boil. Turn the heat down and poach the fish very, very gently for 15 minutes. They should be cooked but still firm.

2 Use a fish slice to remove the trout from the roasting tin, taking care not to break them. Leave the fish to cool. Strain the stock from the roasting tin, then pour 1.1 L /2 pt into a saucepan, making up the quantity with warm water if needed. Use the stock to make the fish aspic, following the recipe for Basic fish aspic (see recipe).

3 Remove the skin of the trout decoratively. Do this by cutting through the skin at the neck and the tail end of the fish in a zig-zag pattern. Turn the trout over and cut in the same way on the other side, then peel off the skin.

4 Transfer the trout to a rack set over a baking tray and chill in the refrigerator while you prepare the decoration. Cook the thinly sliced carrots in boiling salted water for 5 minutes, or until soft. Drain and refresh under cold running water. Cut V-shapes from the edge of each carrot slice to make a flower shape. Thinly slice the hard-boiled egg white and cut tiny squares to use as the centre of the carrot flowers. Blanch the strips of cucumber peel in boiling water for 3-4 minutes so that they keep their colour. Drain and refresh under cold running water. Slice some of the strips of peel into leaf shapes by cutting the edges in a tiny zig-zag pattern. From the remaining cucumber peel, cut strips for the stalks.

5 When the aspic has cooled sufficiently to be syrupy, remove the trout from the refrigerator. Dip the little pieces of decoration, one at a time, into the syrupy aspic and lay them in position on the fish. Return to the refrigerator to chill for 15 minutes.

6 Set the rack with the trout over a baking tray. Spoon 45 ml /3 tbls syrupy aspic over each fish, covering it from head to tail. Chill until set. Pour the remaining aspic into a large shallow dish (the aspic should be 5-10 mm /¼-½ in deep). Chill until set.

7 Remove strips from the lemon with a sharp knife so that the lemon is striped. Slice it thinly and cut the slices in half.

8 To serve, lay the trout side by side on a long, flat serving dish (or use several smaller dishes). Turn out the layer of aspic and chop it roughly. Surround each trout with a little chopped aspic and decorate the plate with lemon slices, tiny sprigs of parsley and the unpeeled prawns.

● To cook the trout successfully, the liquid should barely simmer. If you find it difficult to control a low temperature on top of the stove, cook the trout in the oven instead. Heat the oven to 170C /325F /gas 3. When you are ready to cook the fish, bring them to the boil over the heat on top of the stove then transfer them to the oven and cook them for 15 minutes.

American vegetable aspic mould

This pretty vegetable aspic can be made in one large or six individual moulds.

⏱🍴 making the stock, then 1 hour, plus cooling and chilling

Serves 6
275 ml /10 fl oz cold home-made chicken
    stock, skimmed of all fat
30 ml /2 tbls powdered gelatine
275 ml /10 fl oz mixed vegetable or tomato
    juice
freshly ground black pepper
50 g /2 oz finely shredded raw cabbage
50 g /2 oz peeled carrot, coarsely grated
2 celery sticks, diced
½ green pepper or ½ canned pimento, diced
salt
lemon juice
To decorate a large mould
1 carrot
sprigs of parsley
8 black olives, stoned
6 tiny lettuce leaves
To decorate small moulds
6 small cucumber slices
60 ml /4 tbls mayonnaise

1 Measure 45 ml /3 tbls of the chicken stock into a small bowl and sprinkle the gelatine over it. Leave to stand for a few minutes, then stand the bowl in a pan of simmering water until the gelatine has completely dissolved.
2 Put the remaining chicken stock in a saucepan with the mixed vegetable or tomato juice and the freshly ground black pepper to taste. Gently warm the mixture. Strain the dissolved gelatine into the warm mixture and stir well. Leave it to cool until it is syrupy (the consistency of unbeaten egg white) and on the point of setting.
3 Sprinkle the prepared vegetables with salt and a squeeze of lemon juice and toss well, then fold them into the syrupy aspic. Pour the mixture either into a 1 L /1½ pt loaf tin or mould, or six 150 ml /5 fl oz dariole moulds or ramekins. If any vegetables stick out, push them gently under the aspic so they are well coated. Chill until set.
4 If you are using a large mould, make some carrot curls for decoration: peel the carrot, then, with a potato peeler, shave off thin strips down the length of the carrot. Choose 9 good strips about 15 mm /½ in wide and discard the rest. Put the 9 strips in a bowl of iced water and place in the refrigerator until the strips have curled.
5 To turn out the mould (or moulds), hold a hot, damp tea-towel around the mould for a few seconds to loosen the jelly. Invert a large flat serving plate (or an individual plate) over the mould, then reverse them. Give the mould a shake when halfway over, then invert it completely and give it a couple more shakes so the jelly slips out onto the plate.
6 To decorate the large mould, drain and dry the carrot curls on absorbent paper, then form each one into a tight curl. Arrange 5 of the carrot curls in a small circle in the centre of the mould, then put a ring of tiny parsley sprigs just inside the circle of carrot curls. Place 5 black olives around the carrot curls. Put a few tiny lettuce leaves at either end of the mould, and decorate them with 2 carrot curls and a black olive.
7 To decorate the small moulds, place a cucumber slice on top of each of them, then put 10 ml /2 tsp mayonnaise on each slice.

● Do not prepare this recipe more than 24 hours in advance as the vegetables will deteriorate.
● To serve the large mould, use a sharp knife first dipped in boiling water, and cut with a sawing motion to slice through the vegetables without pulling at the aspic.
● A quicker method is to substitute 600 ml / 1 pt aspic jelly from a packet mix for the liquids and gelatine. Flavour it with 15 ml / 1 tbls lemon juice and white pepper.

Boeuf à la mode

⏱🍴 marinating overnight, then 7 hours preparing and chilling

Seafood moulds

Serves 6
1 kg /2 lb lean boned shin or brisket of beef
3 Spanish onions
2 carrots, sliced
1 bouquet garni
425 ml /15 fl oz dry white wine
60 ml /4 tbls brandy
salt and freshly ground black pepper
90 ml /6 tbls olive oil or 75 g /3 oz lard
225 g /8 oz lean bacon, diced
1 calf's or pig's foot, split
4 garlic cloves, peeled
1 piece dried orange peel (see note)
275 ml /10 fl oz hot beef stock
For the aspic
175 g /6 oz lean minced beef
1 leek, trimmed and fairly finely chopped
1 celery stick, fairly finely chopped
1 carrot, fairly finely chopped
¼ Spanish onion, fairly finely chopped
1 soft, over-ripe tomato, coarsely chopped
frothed white and crushed shell of 1 egg
22.5 ml /1½ tbls powdered gelatine
For the decoration
4 carrots, cut into 5 mm /¼ in slices
50 g /2 oz frozen peas
lettuce leaves
3 tomatoes, cut in half
6 gherkin fans

66

1 Place the meat in a large bowl. Slice 1 Spanish onion and add it to the bowl with the sliced carrots, bouquet garni, dry white wine and brandy; season to taste with salt and pepper. Marinate for about 8 hours, or overnight, turning the meat once or twice.

2 Heat the oven to 150C /300F /gas 2. Quarter the remaining 2 Spanish onions. Heat the olive oil or lard in a large, heavy-based casserole and fry the diced bacon and quartered onions until they are brown. Remove from the pan with a slotted spoon.

3 Drain the meat, reserving the marinade; pat the meat dry with absorbent paper. Sauté the meat in the casserole until it is brown on all sides. Return the bacon and onion to the casserole and add the calf's or pig's foot, the garlic cloves and the dried orange peel, then pour over the marinade and the hot beef stock. Cover the casserole and cook it in the oven for 1–1½ hours, turning the meat from time to time. The liquid should barely simmer — so reduce the oven temperature if it appears to be cooking too quickly.

4 Remove the casserole from the oven and let it cool slightly. Take out the meat and keep it on one side, then skim any fat which may be on the surface of the casserole and strain the liquid into a clean saucepan. (If you have time, cool the meat in the liquid.)

5 Use the strained stock to make the aspic, following the instructions for Basic beef aspic (see recipe).

6 Cut 12–16 wafer-thin slices from the beef. (Use the left-over beef in another recipe.)

7 Prepare the decorations: boil the sliced carrots in salted water for 10 minutes, until cooked. Cook the peas in boiling salted water for 3 minutes. Cool and chill. Pour a layer of syrup aspic into a 1 L/2 pt mould or soufflé dish and chill until set.

8 Decorate the edge of the set layer of aspic with a circle of 9 carrot slices. Place a few peas in the centre. Spoon over enough syrupy aspic to just cover the vegetables, taking care that you do not move them. If they move, simply put them back into position with the point of a knife. Put the mould into the refrigerator, being careful not to disturb the decoration. Chill until set.

9 Arrange half the beef slices, overlapping over the layer of set aspic. Cover with syrupy aspic and chill until set.

10 Make another layer of vegetables, cover with aspic and chill, then make another layer of beef, cover with aspic and chill.

11 Arrange 24 carrot slices attractively over the set aspic, then cover the carrots with the remaining aspic. Chill until the aspic is set.

12 To turn out, hold a hot, damp tea-towel around the mould for a few seconds. Invert a serving plate over the mould and then reverse them; give a couple of firm shakes so that the jelly slips out onto the plate. Garnish with lettuce leaves, tomato halves and little gherkin fans.

● For dried orange peel, cut the peel from an orange into strips 5 cm×5 mm /2×¼ in. Dry out in a 140C /275F /gas 1 oven for 30 minutes.

Seafood moulds

making the stock, then several hours preparation and chilling

Serves 6
225 ml /8 fl oz boiling water
15 ml /1 tbls aspic granules or powder
6 thin slices of peeled cucumber
275 ml /10 fl oz cold home-made chicken stock, skimmed of all fat
30 ml /2 tbls powdered gelatine
275 ml /10 fl oz tomato or mixed vegetable juice
225 g /8 oz diced peeled shrimps or prawns, or shredded crabmeat or lobster
1 celery stick, diced
freshly ground black pepper
6 tiny sprigs of fresh parsley or chervil
1–2 tomatoes, sliced
1–2 hard-boiled eggs, sliced

1 Pour the boiling water over the aspic granules or powder and stir until dissolved. Strain if necessary, then spoon 10 ml /2 tsp of the aspic into each of six 150 ml /5 fl oz ramekins. Chill until set.

2 Carefully place a cucumber slice in the centre of the layer of set aspic in each mould. Spoon over enough cooled aspic to just cover, then chill until set. Pour the remaining aspic into a small, flat container (the aspic should be 5–10 mm /¼–½ in deep) and leave to set. (This aspic will be used for decoration.)

3 Measure 45 ml /3 tbls of the cold chicken stock into a small bowl and sprinkle the gelatine over it. Let it soften for a few minutes, then stand the bowl in a pan of simmering water until the gelatine has completely dissolved.

4 Put the remaining chicken stock into a saucepan with the tomato juice and warm through. Strain the dissolved gelatine into this mixture and stir well. Add the seafood and celery, and season to taste with freshly ground black pepper. Divide the mixture among the ramekins and chill until set.

5 Hold a hot, damp tea-towel around a mould for a few seconds, invert a plate over the mould then reverse it and give it a couple of firm shakes so that the jelly slips out onto the plate. Transfer to a large plate. Repeat with the remaining moulds.

6 Turn out the extra aspic and cut it into dice. Decorate each serving with a tiny sprig of fresh parsley or chervil. Place a spoonful of chopped aspic by the side of each mould and lay a slice of tomato and a slice of hard-boiled egg, overlapping, on top of each serving of chopped aspic.

GALANTINES & BALLOTINES

For a special occasion or cold buffet a galantine makes a memorable dish. A large bird is first boned out, then stuffed, re-shaped and poached. It is easy to carve and will look beautiful in individual slices.

A galantine will certainly give you a reputation as a cook among your friends. The preparations require patience, but none of the processes involved is difficult and your careful work will be rewarded on the day with a dish which looks and tastes splendid.

A galantine is made by stuffing a boned-out bird (or some other meat), re-shaping it carefully and then cooking it, to serve cold. The preparations are time-consuming, but a buffet party will always need a couple of days' work beforehand and a galantine has several advantages in addition to its stylishness. For one it is quite economical as the stuffed bird will feed twice the usual number of people. Advance preparation actually improves a galantine as a little maturing helps the flavour to develop fully. But most important, with galantines there are no carving problems. They slice like a loaf so you are entirely free from intricate carving at the time of serving.

Galantines were originally invented as a way of serving chickens. Now game birds, fish and meat such as veal, are all used in the same way — boned, stuffed and then poached.

Ballotine means 'little ball' and the word is sometimes still used for small stuffed parcels, for example a stuffed turkey leg, which can be served hot or cold. Generally, the names galantine and ballotine are used interchangeably when the dish is cold.

Boning out birds

Your butcher may bone the bird for you but scraping away the flesh from the bones of birds is really very straightforward to do yourself — although it does need a little practice. After the first attempt, you should be able to do it in about 25 minutes.

The main point to remember is not to puncture the skin because it is the skin which holds the whole thing together during cooking. The secret is to feel your way with your fingers, locating the bones and joints. Use a small, sharp knife and always keep it pressed flat against the bone as you scrape the flesh free from it. Work parallel to the skin rather than cutting towards it.

Removing the carcass

Cut off the wing tip and the middle section, leaving the largest bone intact. Place the bird, breast side down, on a flat surface. Slit the skin down the length of the backbone. Lift the cut skin and scrape the flesh away from one side of the rib cage. As you cut, sever the white, stringy sinews.

Now grasp the wing — on the side you are working — and bend it outwards so that its ball joint pops out of its socket. Cut all the sinews around the joint, pushing the bone inwards towards the centre, to expose them. Repeat with the leg. Freeing the joints will help create a flatter shape which makes the rest of the work easier. Returning to the slit

skin by the backbone, repeat the process on the other side.

Now free the flesh from over the breast bone — work carefully because it has a tricky shape with a pointed ridge. As this ridge is separated from the skin by only a very thin covering of flesh, this is the most difficult part.

At the neck opening, find the wishbone. Feel for the little knob of bone at the top of the upside down 'V' shape, then snap it free and lift out the carcass. You will be left with the flattened chicken. Scrape the wishbone and collar bones free.

Boning the legs and wings: to remove the leg and wing bones, leaving the flesh in place, hold one leg by the drumstick and push the thigh towards the middle of the chicken. Scrape the flesh from the thigh

bone, pushing inwards to expose it. When you reach the knee joint stop and cut the thigh bone free. Turn the flesh the right way out again by pulling the drumstick outwards. Lay the drumstick flat on the board and cut it off. Don't worry about the cut that you make across the skin, it will be stitched later.

Bone the upper joint of the wing in the same way, then repeat on the other side. This will give you a neat, almost rectangular shape. Remove the skin and bones from the drumstick and reserve the meat.

Finishing off: once the bird is boned and lying flat, skin-side down, slice horizontally across some of the thicker parts of the breast flesh and lay these slivers of flesh with the reserved drumstick meat over the parts of the bird where the flesh is sparse. This helps to create an even, flat shape. Cover the whole thing with cling film and bat it out carefully with a meat bat or rolling pin until the flesh

Galantine of veal garnished with chicory, radish and cucumber

Preparing a galantine

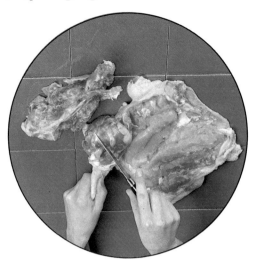

Cut the flesh from the carcass; remove the carcass whole. To remove leg and wing bones, push the bone towards the middle. Use a sharp knife to scrape off the flesh.

Bring the two long 'slit' edges together. Use a skewer to make a stitch and hold the skin. Pat the bird into shape and oversew it, working from vent to neck along the back.

Wrap in a double-thickness of muslin and twist the ends like a Christmas cracker. Tie the twists and then tie round the parcel at intervals and finally from end to end.

is an even thickness all over. This will make an even layer of meat so the finished dish will look neat when sliced.

The stuffing

Stuffing is used to fill the centre of a boned bird and to give it back its shape. Clearly the stuffing must complement the casing.

A savoury stuffing is usually used: a mixture of minced meats which can include veal, pork belly or sausage-meat. Pork or bacon is often included because these are fatty meats and therefore help prevent the galantine from drying out when cooked.

If there are trimmings left over when the outside casing is shaped, these can be added to the stuffing. Season the minced meats generously and add other ingredients, such as finely chopped onion, that will enhance the flavour. Bindings such as eggs and cream are incorporated to hold the mixture together.

Testing the basic mixture: season the un-cooked mixture well because you can't adjust seasonings once the galantine is cooked! Cooking changes flavours so to check what its taste will be once it is cooked, roll a little stuffing into a ball and fry it in butter, then taste and adjust the seasoning if necessary.

Layered stuffings: to vary the texture of the stuffing and to make the appearance more decorative when sliced, chunky solid ingredients are included: strips of chicken, cubes of tongue, sautéed bacon, ham and chopped nuts and herbs are popular. Use them to create pretty contrasts of colour and exciting combinations of texture.

Enclosing the stuffing

The idea is to make an even-shaped cylindrical parcel so the sewing up of the galantine is important. A good trussing needle makes the job easier.

Reshaping the bird: bring the two long edges (the slit back of the bird) together. With a thin skewer, take a 'stitch' through both skins down the length of the bird to

make a roll. Pat the bird into shape around the stuffing, drawing up any slack skin. The aim is to fill the shape comfortably — not too tightly, but without air pockets inside. Push the open ends of skin and flesh, where the legs and wings were cut, into the bird. At the leg end of the chicken pull the vent skin neatly together and over-sew it, then work up and along to the end of the bird's back, removing the skewer as you go. Where the skin feels a bit thin — and likely to split — make a stronger, wider seam that incorporates some flesh as well.

Pull the bird's neck skin to make sure that the end of the cylinder is flat, and pat the stuffing finally into shape. Trim away the excess skin to make a neat seam and stitch it up. Now 'darn' the slits where the legs and wings were pushed in.

Wrapping in muslin: double-thickness muslin or single thickness cheesecloth is wrapped around the parcel to help preserve the shape while it is cooked. The rectangle must be large enough to go right around your parcel twice, with spare material at either end, and these end pieces should be long enough to twist like a Christmas cracker. Either trim away excess cloth from these twists, or spread it out a bit so that it isn't lumpy.

Tying the parcel: string is the easiest way to tie the parcel, or you can use bandage or strips of muslin — about 25 mm /1 in wide. The latter gives a really super finish to the galantine because it leaves no dents across the surface of the galantine as string does. String works well too — but don't tie it up tightly. Tie the end twists, and tie at intervals down the whole length of the roll, then make one tie from end to end (see instructions above).

Cooking the galantine

The most common way to cook a galantine is to poach it in chicken stock. This moist, gentle treatment helps to keep a bird's lean, delicate flesh from drying out, and poached birds have an almost white skin. This pale finish gives you the option of coating the bird with aspic or a white chaudfroid if you wish. You can make a stock from the bones of the bird that will be ready in time for poaching the galantine, if you start making the stock as soon as you remove the bird's bones. However, for maximum flavour, I like to poach the bird in a rich pre-made stock, or a good quality bought stock cube, and I then intensify the flavour further by adding the bones to the poaching pan.

The other way to cook a galantine is to roast it (without the muslin wrapper) which colours and crisps the skin. Roasting suits duck especially (see recipe), which is fatty.

Serving the galantine

I like simple presentation best, relying on the decorative effect of the slices, layered meats and stuffings for eye-appeal. For a buffet, arrange the slices on a platter or slice three-quarters of the galantine and arrange it with the unsliced section. Garnish the plate discretely with something green, such as a little shredded lettuce, or little bouquets of parsley or watercress. If you are serving the galantine as a starter, you can dress each slice on an individual plate.

Galantines are easy to carve in front of the guests. If you want to display your masterpiece whole, you can coat it with chaudfroid, and/or aspic (see Galantine of turkey). A chaudfroid is a gelatinous white sauce using a bechamel sauce as the base. Stand the galantine on a wire rack over a tray and spoon the sauce over the top, then transfer it to the refrigerator for the sauce to set. If you wish, you can then garnish the coated galantine with herbs and finely sliced salad vegetables and top it with a coat of glistening aspic.

Galantine of veal

⏱️🍴 3 hours,
plus overnight chilling

Serves 12
1.4 kg /3 lb boned out brisket end of breast of veal (about 2.7 kg /6 lbs, unboned)
salt and freshly ground black pepper
2 thick slices of cooked ham, 175 g /6 oz together
2.3 L /4 pt chicken stock, home-made or from a cube
1 knuckle bone of veal
bouquet garni
For the stuffing
15 g /½ oz shelled pistachio nuts
225 g /8 oz cooked ham
225 g /8 oz boneless veal
125 g /4 oz unsmoked lean bacon, rind removed
½ Spanish onion, finely chopped
25 g /1 oz fresh white breadcrumbs
2.5 ml /½ tsp dried rosemary
30 ml /2 tbls brandy
salt and freshly ground black pepper
For the garnish
1 head chicory
½ cucumber, sliced
4 radishes, sliced
sprigs of flat-leaved parsley

1 Start at least one day before you intend to serve the galantine. Lay the breast out flat on a board with the side from which the rib bones have been removed downwards. Cut away — and discard — excess fat from the top layer and any scrappy bits of flesh and skin.
2 Turn over the breast. Remove and discard any fat from the outside edge. You will have a slightly triangular shape; to make a rectangle, trim away — and reserve — the bits of flesh from the pointed end. Next, feel across the uppermost layer of flesh to find a triangular-shaped flap with a pocket beneath. Extend the pocket by peeling it back with your fingers, then cut through the connective tissue until the whole flap is free. Reserve this with the trimmings. You will now be left with an almost rectangular piece of meat — about 30–36 cm /12–14 in long — with a smooth surface.
3 Lay the breast between two sheets of cling film and bat it out as flat as possible with a meat bat or rolling pin.
4 Cut away, and discard, all the sinews from the trimmings, then bat the trimmings flat. Cover and reserve.
5 For the stuffing, pour boiling water over the pistachio nuts. Leave for 30 seconds, drain and then rub in a tea-towel to remove the skins. Coarsely chop the nuts.
6 Coarsely chop the ham, the veal and the bacon, then pass them through the finest blade of your mincer twice to make a smooth paste.
7 Put the paste into a large mixing bowl. Stir in the nuts, the finely chopped onion, the breadcrumbs and the dried rosemary. Mix well. Stir in the brandy and mix again. Season to taste with salt and pepper.
8 Heat the oven to 180C /350F /gas 4.
9 Lay a rectangle of about 60 × 45 cm / 2 × 1½ ft of double thickness muslin on a work surface. Put the breast, fleshy side up, in the centre. Season with salt and pepper.
10 Arrange the thick slices of ham, side by side, on top. Spread out the stuffing in an even layer, leaving a 25 mm /1 in border all round. Arrange the trimmings in a row down the centre of the stuffing.
11 Lift one long edge of the muslin and use it to help you to roll one long side of the breast over the stuffing. Pulling upwards with the muslin, roll the veal as tightly as you can — like a Swiss roll.
12 Roll the meat to the edge of the muslin, then roll the muslin tightly around the veal. Make a series of ties around the parcel and then one from end to end.
13 In a roasting tin, bring the stock to a boil on top of the stove. Add the galantine, the knuckle of veal and the bouquet garni. Cook in the oven for 20 minutes.
14 Because the roasting tin and the stock is shallow, the galantine will be only partially submerged and will need to be turned in the hot liquid every 20 minutes throughout the cooking. Cook for about 2 hours.
15 Remove the roasting tin from the oven and leave the galantine to cool in its stock for 1 hour, turning it once.
16 Set a wire rack on a tray. Transfer the lukewarm galantine to the rack. (Discard the knuckle and the bouquet garni but save the stock for another dish.) Carefully remove

the strings and muslin and leave the galantine on the rack to get cold.
17 Dip absorbent paper in hot water and wipe off all fat from the surface of the meat. Tightly cover with cling film and refrigerate until 1 hour before serving.
18 To serve, cut into thick slices and garnish with salad vegetables.

● Make a green mayonnaise to serve with this galantine. To 150 ml /5 fl oz of mayonnaise add the same quantity of thick cream, a bunch of chopped watercress and 45 ml /3 tbls parsley juice. Season to taste.

Chicken ballotine with hazelnuts

⏱️🍴 5½ hours, including marinating, then chilling

Serves 8
1.4 kg–1.5 kg /3–3½ lb chicken
½ chicken, about 700 g /1½ lb
60 ml /4 tbls brandy
50 g /2 oz shelled hazelnuts
15 g /½ oz butter
½ Spanish onion, very finely chopped
4 slices lean bacon, rind removed
225 g /8 oz sausage-meat
1 large egg
30 ml /2 tbls thick cream
50 g /2 oz ground almonds
salt and freshly ground black pepper
¼ tsp ground allspice
chicken stock to cover, home-made or from a cube

1 At least one day before you intend to serve the galantine, bone the whole chicken carefully, without splitting the skin (see text); reserve the carcass. Bone and skin the half chicken, reserving the bones. Chop the leg meat coarsely and cut the breast lengthways into six strips.
2 Lay the boned whole bird on a board, skin-side down. Cover it with cling film and flatten it with a meat bat or rolling pin to an even thickness all over. Lay it skin-side down in a wide, shallow dish and sprinkle it with 15 ml /1 tbls of the brandy.
3 Add the chopped chicken leg meat and the strips of breast meat, and moisten with another 15 ml /1 tbls brandy. Cover and leave to marinate for 2–3 hours.
4 Meanwhile, heat the grill to high. Spread the hazelnuts in the grill pan and grill them for 3–4 minutes, shaking the pan to turn them, until browned all over. Let them cool a little, then rub off the skins in a dry tea-towel. Pick off any remaining skins carefully by hand and cut the nuts in half.
5 Melt the butter in a small frying-pan, add the very finely chopped onion and sauté for 2–3 minutes until transparent. Remove with a slotted spoon.
6 Add the slices of bacon to the fat remaining in the frying-pan and sauté until it is lightly cooked. Remove from the pan and chop coarsely.
7 Using a slotted spoon, lift the chopped leg meat out of the marinade, letting the juices drain back into the dish. Mince the leg

Ballotine of duck

meat to the same consistency as the sausage-meat, then thoroughly blend the two together in a large bowl.

8 In another bowl, mix the egg with the thick cream and the remaining brandy. Carefully drain off all the marinade juices and add them to the bowl. Beat until just blended. Add the sautéed onion and the ground almonds, and mix well.

9 Blend the cream and almond mixture thoroughly into the minced chicken and sausage-meat mixture. Season liberally with salt, freshly ground black pepper and a pinch of ground allspice. Gradually add the halved hazelnuts, mixing until they are evenly distributed throughout the stuffing.

10 Lay the whole chicken out on a board again, skin-side down, and season the surface with salt and pepper. Spread half the meat mixture down the centre of the chicken. Cover with half the strips of chicken breast and all the sautéed bacon. Spread the remaining minced meat mixture on top and lay the remaining strips of chicken breast down the centre.

11 Pull up the skin to enclose the stuffing and sew up the ballotine from the vent end. Wrap it securely in muslin and tie up the parcel several times along the length and once from end to end.

12 Put the parcel in a large saucepan, cover with chicken stock and add the bones. Bring to the boil on top of the stove, then reduce the heat, cover, and simmer gently for about 1½ hours. Make sure that the stock never actually boils since the meat will stay succulent if it cooks gently.

13 Remove the pan from the heat and leave the ballotine to cool in its stock for about 30 minutes. Set a wire rack on a tray. Transfer the ballotine to the rack; discard the bones

and reserve the stock for soup. Leave the ballotine to drain and cool, which will take about 1½ hours. Then carefully remove all the strings and the muslin and leave until it is completely cold.

14 Dip absorbent paper in hot water and wipe off all fat from the surface of the skin. Remove the stitching and cover the ballotine tightly with cling film. Refrigerate overnight and until 1 hour before serving.

15 Cut into thick slices to serve.

Ballotine of duck

3½ hours, then overnight chilling

Serves 12–15

1.8 kg–2.3 kg /4–5 lb duck
30 ml /2 tbls shelled pistachio nuts
500 g /1 lb lean pork
500 g /1 lb pie veal
125 g /4 oz boneless chicken leg meat
50 g /2 oz cooked tongue
50 g /2 oz cooked ham
2 eggs
60 ml /4 tbls brandy
a generous pinch each of cayenne pepper,
  ground ginger, cloves, cinnamon, coriander
  and cumin
salt
freshly ground black pepper
30 ml /2 tbls olive oil
To garnish
orange slices
white grapes, seeded

1 Bone the duck carefully without splitting the skin.

2 Put the pistachio nuts in a small bowl and pour boiling water over them. Leave for 30 seconds, drain, and rub in a tea-towel to

remove the skins. Chop the skinned nuts coarsely, then set them aside.

3 Remove any skin, fat and sinews from the pork, veal and chicken meat. Dice and pass through the finest blade of your mincer three times, or until the meats are reduced to a very fine paste. Cut the tongue and ham into dice.

4 Put the minced meats in a bowl, add the eggs, chopped pistachios, brandy and the diced tongue and ham and blend thoroughly. Season to taste with the spices, salt and pepper. The mixture should be highly seasoned as the flavours tend to weaken when the ballotine has been cooked.

5 Heat the oven to 190C /375F /gas 5.

6 Lay the boned duck, skin-side down, on a board. Cover with cling film and flatten with a meat bat or rolling pin to an even thickness. Spread the meat stuffing over the duck, leaving a 25 mm /1 in border all round.

7 Pull up the skin to enclose the stuffing and sew up the ballotine from the vent end. Tie up the parcel several times along the length and once from end to end.

8 Put the ballotine in a roasting tin and pour the olive oil over it. Roast for 1½ hours, basting frequently with the pan juices to make the skin crisp and amber. (If the duck browns too quickly before it is cooked through, cover it with a piece of crumpled foil.)

9 Stand the ballotine on a wire rack and leave it to cool. When cold, remove the string and stitching, then wrap in cling film and chill until 1 hour before serving.

10 To serve, cut into thick slices and garnish with slices of orange and some seeded white grapes.

● This ballotine of duck can be served as a main course with salad, or try it sliced thinly and eaten with toast as a starter.

Galantine of turkey

To prepare a turkey galantine, you need a really large pot, such as a preserving pan, in which to cook it.

5½ hours, plus overnight chilling

Serves about 30

5.4 kg /12 lb turkey
salt and freshly ground black pepper
15 ml /1 tbls mixed dried thyme, marjoram and rosemary
225 g /8 oz fresh breadcrumbs
milk
60 ml /4 tbls pistachio nuts
500 g /1 lb boneless veal
500 g /1 lb boneless pork
225 g /8 oz unsmoked fat bacon, rind removed
grated zest of 1 lemon
90 ml /6 tbls finely chopped fresh parsley
30 ml /2 tbls brandy
60–90 ml /4–6 tbls dry sherry
225 g /8 oz cooked ham, cut in strips
3 hard-boiled eggs, quartered
1.5 ml /¼ tsp ground mixed spice
chicken stock to cover, home-made or from a cube

1 At least one day before you intend to serve the galantine, bone the turkey carefully, without splitting the skin; reserve the carcass to be used later.

2 Lay the boned turkey, skin-side down, on a flat board. To distribute the flesh more evenly over the skin, slice away some of the thick breast meat and lay it over the thin-fleshed parts. Cover with cling film and flatten it by banging with a meat bat or rolling pin to an even thickness all over. Season generously with salt and freshly ground black pepper and sprinkle with the dried mixed herbs.

3 Put the breadcrumbs in a small bowl, cover them with milk and leave them to soak. Meanwhile, put the pistachio nuts into a separate bowl and pour boiling water over. Leave for 30 seconds, drain and then rub in a tea-towel to remove the skins. Coarsely chop the skinned nuts.

4 Coarsely chop the veal, pork and fat bacon and pass them through the finest blade of your mincer twice to make a smooth paste. Squeeze excess moisture from the bread-crumbs and blend them into the minced meats. Add the grated lemon zest, 60 ml / 4 tbls of finely chopped parsley and the brandy; add sherry to taste. Mix well.

5 Spread the stuffing evenly over the boned turkey, leaving a 25 mm /1 in border all round. Arrange the ham strips and quartered hard-boiled eggs on top of the stuffing, alternating them. Sprinkle with the remaining finely chopped parsley, the ground mixed spice and the pistachio nuts.

6 Pull up the skin to enclose the stuffing and sew up the galantine from the vent end. Wrap it in muslin and tie the parcel several times along the length and then end to end.

Galantine of turkey garnished and coated with elegant chaudfroid

7 Put the parcel in a large saucepan or a preserving pan and cover it with chicken stock. Break up the carcass and add the bones if there is room. Bring to the boil on top of the stove, then reduce the heat, cover and simmer gently for 3–4 hours.

8 Allow the galantine to partially cool in the liquid because it will then absorb more flavour from the stock.

9 Remove the bird from the stock and drain; press the galantine between 2 boards with a weight on top, so that the roll is flattened and the filling compacted. Discard the bones from the stock and reserve the stock for soup or for aspic — see note below. When the galantine is cold, carefully remove the strings and muslin.

10 Dip absorbent paper in hot water and wipe off all fat from the surface of the skin. Remove the stitches and lightly cover the galantine with cling film. Refrigerate it until 1 hour before serving.

11 To serve, cut into thick slices.

● If wished, the turkey may be coated with a white chaudfroid for a centrepiece. Use Bechamel sauce (*page 9*) and stir in 10 ml / 2 tsp gelatine dissolved in 60 ml /4 tbls water. Decorate with a selection of fresh herbs and thinly sliced radishes, mushrooms, carrots and cucumber. Then use 600 ml /1 pt Basic chicken aspic (*page 64*) to coat the galantine and secure the garnish.

CARVING A PARTY HAM

A whole gammon on the bone makes the ideal centrepiece for a large buffet party and will feed a crowd. Learn how to carve the ham expertly and professionally to ensure a beautiful presentation with no wastage.

The average weight of a whole raw gammon is about 7.3 kg /16 lb. This will reduce to 5.9 kg /13 lb after cooking and it will feed 30–35 people. A half ham will give you 12–18 portions.

Remember your ham may differ from that in the pictures, depending on whether it is from the left or right side of the pig.

Ham or gammon?

A gammon (the hind leg of the pig, cured with the side and then cut free) and a ham (cut off the pig before curing) are cooked and served in an identical way. The leg bones of the pig are obviously the same in both cases but the shape of the meat around the top of a whole 'ham' and the amount of pelvic bone present may vary according to which ever way the leg was cut.

Inspect your ham after cooking and cooling. If a large amount of the pelvic bone is exposed on the surface, running down to a round ball joint near the hip bone, take a small sharp knife and cut all around this exposed bone neatly. Then free it with your fingers and pull it out in two pieces. The ham may now be carved as shown in the diagrams below, omitting the step shown in the first photograph.

Tackling the carving

A very sharp, thin, long-bladed knife, often known as a ham knife, is absolutely essential when you come to carve the ham. It ensures that the meat slices smoothly and tidily, without jagged chunks.

The ham is carved more easily if it is on a flat board or plate. The initial position will vary according to whether your ham is whole or halved. A half ham will stand solidly on its cut end. A whole ham will lie on the board and the main portions will be carved while it is bone side down. A napkin, foil or a ham frill is used to cover the bone and give the carver something to hold on to.

Carve the gammon as close to the serving time as possible and arrange the meat slices on a large platter. Keep the slices from different parts of the ham separate so that you can give each person some of each part of the leg. Cover the platter and meat with cling film until it is needed.

If you want to serve a whole ham at your buffet, tackle the end bone in the kitchen first and take off some of the end slices and some of the slipper underneath so that the ham sits securely (see the first and second photographs). Then you can carve the main slices from the ham without too much difficulty in front of your guests.

Carving a whole gammon

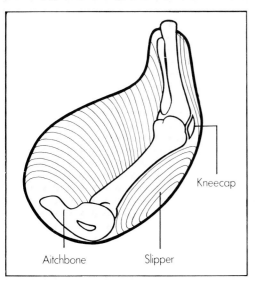

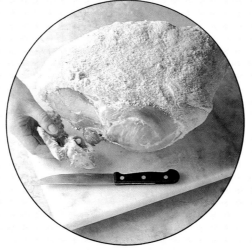

Place the gammon meaty side up and carve away the smaller corner of the meat at the rounded end. Remove the aitch bone.

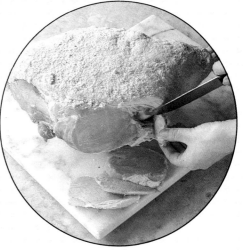

Carve slices from the slipper, with the grain, towards the knuckle end, until the bone is reached. Remove the hard kneecap.

Turn the joint onto a flat area. Cut a 'V' below the knuckle and remove the small bone. Carve towards the bone; release the slices by cutting parallel to it.

Continue carving the main meat of the whole gammon in thin slices, towards the bone, away from the knuckle end. Hold the knuckle end with a napkin while you carve.

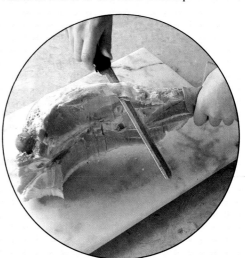

Turn the gammon over and slice the remaining meat from the bone, working parallel to the bone. Make sure that the slices you cut from this are as neat as possible.

PREPARING GAME BIRDS

Plucking and drawing game birds are simple tasks which need only take a short while. If you know how to do them yourself, you need never miss out on these delicious birds because you cannot cope with the initial stages.

Game birds, because of the controlled season and the expense of shooting, are considered a great luxury. Each type of bird needs to be hung for a specified number of days, complete with feathers and undrawn, that is, with its innards still in place. If you buy game from your local butcher or poulterer he will hang the bird for the specified time and supply it, plucked and drawn, ready for the oven, on the day for which you ordered it.

You may be able to buy them feathered and undrawn in a market or be given them by a shooting friend but rather than forego the chance of enjoying game birds at their best, pluck them and prepare them yourself; you have secured a luxury and have saved quite a bit of money by avoiding

preparation charges. If you are lucky enough to be given a bird by a friend and know how to prepare it, your luxury will cost you nothing!

Hanging improves the flavour of almost all game. Grouse, partridge, pheasant, snipe and woodcock are all hung by the beak, complete with feathers and undrawn, for approximately 3–4 days, the shorter period in warm weather, the longer period in cold weather. Wild duck — mallard, teal and widgeon — should be hung for 2–3 days. Wood pigeon are drawn immediately after shooting and need not necessarily be hung. However, they can be hung for one day in mild weather and up to seven in cold weather if it suits you, and the flavour will be improved.

Some people like their game very high —

to give a much richer, fuller flavour — and will hang it 1–2 days longer than these times. Others prefer a more delicate flavour; for this, hang birds for only 1–2 days.

Skinning feathered birds

If you are going to roast the birds, then plucking is essential, because the skin is needed to hold the bird in shape. However, there is an alternative if you are planning to casserole the birds or joint them for a dish.

The old country method is to skin the bird without plucking it first. To do this, plunge the bird in boiling water, head first, to loosen the skin. Next, cut off the bird's head with a cleaver or sharp knife. Make a slit down the bird's breast from neck to tail. Catch hold of the skin round the neck and tug it over the bird's back and down towards the tail. Pull it down over the wings until the second joint is exposed, then cut through the joint on each wing. Now pull the skin over the tail and down the legs. Cut off the legs at the knees, releasing the skin with all the feathers still

Freshly-killed game birds

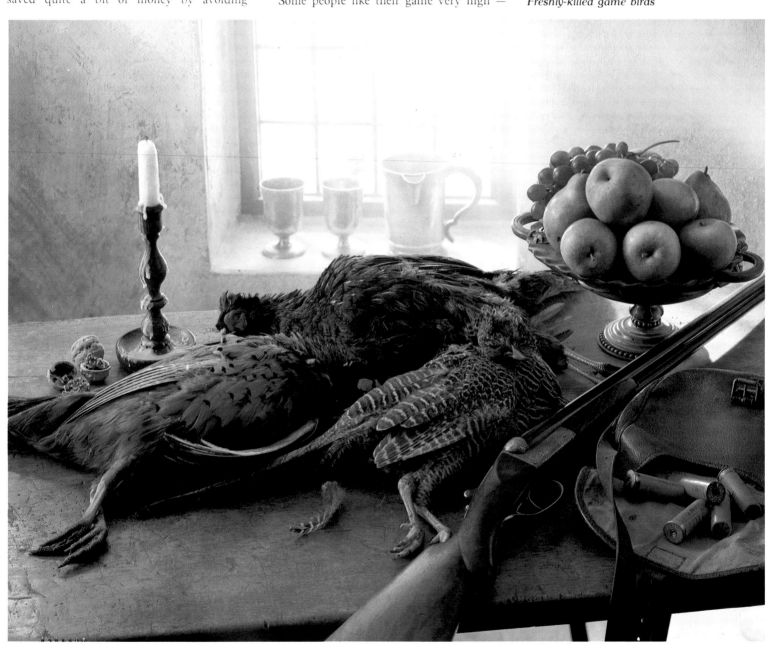

attached. This method is ideal for wood pigeons since the breasts contain 90% of their meat. Cut the wings off at the first joint — they have little meat, and there is really no point at all in plucking what you cannot eat.

Plucking birds

For roasting, a bird must be plucked. This is less daunting than it sounds (and it is almost impossible to spoil the bird). It takes about 4–5 minutes for a pigeon, 5–10 minutes for a pheasant. Give yourself plenty of working space, preferably next to the sink or a source of cold running water. Have a bin nearby to throw the feathers into, and keep the vacuum cleaner handy.

With the exception of duck, all game birds, including guinea fowl, are plucked and drawn following the step-by-step instructions and pictures opposite. Duck are plucked from the tail to the neck. Do not pull too many feathers at a time, two (with the downy feathers underneath them) is about right. Take care not to break the skin over the breast and work carefully around any gunshot wounds. Keep the tail feathers of a pheasant to garnish the finished dish.

Geese, chickens and turkeys are plucked in much the same way as game birds. However, there may be the problem of quills left in the bird's skin: nasty tenacious ends of the feathers. These can be pulled out individually with pliers or tweezers. If quills are present in game birds, it is a sign of age and the bird should be casseroled not roasted! Ducks and downy birds will probably need to be singed to remove all the quills. Hold the bird by its legs and neck and pass the body over a flame or pass a lighted taper over the bird until the skin appears quite smooth.

Drawing birds

Clean the work surface of all feathers and wear a pair of rubber gloves if you like. With a sharp knife slit the skin of the neck. Push your fingers into the neck, move your fingers around to loosen the windpipe and gullet. You can omit this if you want but it does make the eventual drawing easier.

Turn the bird around and, using a pair of sharp scissors, cut through the skin of the vent and make a slit about 4 cm /1½ in long. Put your forefinger inside this and feel for the top of the body cavity. Next, hook your finger around the innards at the top of the cavity and pull out the entire contents. Generally it is 'hook, pull and don't look'!

Reserve the giblets — heart, liver and gizzard — for stock. Slit the big gizzard down one side, empty out any grit that may be in it and wash it out well. Discard the other entrails. Alternatively keep the liver separate, sauté it in a little butter and mash it to a paste to enrich the gravy.

There are two game birds that are sometimes cooked without being drawn — snipe and woodcock. When they are roasted they are traditionally cooked with their heads left on and undrawn; the long bill which is characteristic of both birds can be used as a skewer and pushed through the legs and body of the bird to truss it. However, if the birds are to be casseroled, then they too are plucked and drawn.

Plucking a pheasant

Pull the feathers from the breast, 2–3 at a time, flipping them upwards, against the natural lie of the feathers. Remove all the breast feathers, working down to the tail.

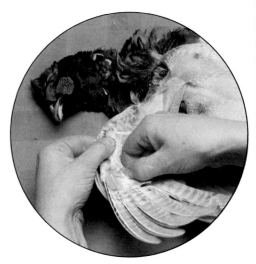

With the bird on its back, first pluck the smaller feathers, then the larger feathers on the wings. Work from underneath the wings first, then pluck the tops of each wing.

Turn the bird on its back and remove all the downy feathers from the wings, breast and legs. Turn the bird on its breast and pluck the feathers from the back.

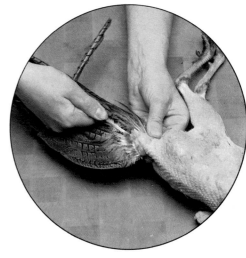

Hold the bird firmly; tug to remove the tail feathers. Reserve these for decorating the bird when cooked. Cut off the feet, head and neck and discard.

With scissors, cut through skin from the vent. Insert your forefinger into the cavity, hook the innards at the top and pull everything out.

Reserve neck and giblets for stock. Wash the inside of the bird, dry with a cloth, then absorbent paper. Truss it for roasting or joint it.

ICING

A delicately iced cake or an exquisite collection of sugar flowers on a birthday cake are guaranteed to bring compliments. In this chapter I show you some ways of making your cakes look as good as they taste.

The next few pages concentrate on the more complicated methods of cake decoration: clever ideas for moulding flowers, piping flowers, crystallizing flowers and making beautiful chocolate decorations. It requires patient practice to perfect each of these techniques; there are no short-cuts to success. But once you have acquired the art, you will be able to produce beautiful, professional-looking cakes.

The decoration of your cake will depend very much on the occasion for which it is being made. Christmas and wedding cakes are usually white, but you can produce interesting results by using two colours for cake icing. Pastel shades usually look best, particularly for wedding cakes.

Match the icing carefully to your chosen cake. You must then decide on the type of decoration you want to use and, most important, the design. A light sponge cake is complemented by flowers piped in soft icing. A rich fruit cake is best decorated with piped Royal icing shapes and borders, with flowers which may be piped in Royal icing or moulded from fondant icing or almond paste. Chocolate shapes and leaves are always an ideal decoration for chocolate cakes, and delicate crystallized flowers make a delightful decoration for sugar-iced cakes.

Remember, icing sessions need to be carefully planned. If made in an electric mixer, the icing has to stand for 24 hours before use, so allow time for this. Choose your colour scheme carefully and work out the design in advance.

Decorating rich fruit cakes

If you are making a rich fruit cake, plan well ahead. You need to allow a minimum of 8 days for cooking and icing the cake. A rich fruit cake is usually covered with almond paste (which you may find easiest to buy) before it is iced and decorated. You must leave the almond paste to dry, at room temperature, for 5–7 days, because otherwise the Royal icing will absorb colour from the moist almond paste.

When the almond paste has dried completely, cover the cake with Royal icing, tinted if you wish. It is easiest to do this by first sticking the cake to a cake-board with a dab of icing. Now put a mound of icing on top of the cake and draw an icing ruler towards you, over the cake, to smooth the top. Work the icing round the sides of the cake using a palette knife to smooth the sides.

My recipe for Royal icing is enough for a 20 cm /8 in round or 18 cm /7 in square cake and will cover it completely and still allow enough for piping. To prevent unused icing from drying out while the cake dries, cover the bowl with a clean damp cloth and leave it in a cool place. The cake must be left until the layer of flat icing has dried out completely before it can be decorated.

Pricking out guide marks

For simple repeat patterns such as borders you need no guide marks, but for a more formal design you will need to mark the cake with guide points to help you when piping. Cut a sheet of greaseproof paper to the size of the top of the cake. For a symmetrical design, fold the paper into quarters, then eighths. Open it out on top of the cake and use the creases as guide lines to divide it up, pricking through the creases with a pin. For an all-over design, draw the whole pattern on the paper and prick it out onto the icing.

If you want to pipe a name on top of the cake, draw it on the greaseproof paper until you are satisfied with its appearance, then position it and prick it through onto the cake to guide you when piping.

Equipment

Assemble all the equipment before you start.
Turntable: if you are an icing addict, a cake decorating turntable is a most useful piece of kitchen equipment. It is perfectly possible to

Royal-iced wedding cake

ice a cake without one, but a turntable makes the job easier and helps give the cake that smooth professional-looking finish.

A good turntable has a perfectly flat surface that spins around smoothly when you turn it. Place your cake on an appropriately sized serving plate or cakeboard on the turntable. Revolve the cake away from you instead of moving your hand — this way you can hold an icing ruler against the side of the cake to smooth it.

Icing ruler: this is a thin, flat piece of metal or plastic used to create a smooth, even surface.

Making a greaseproof paper bag: even if you bought an icing bag with your icing nozzles, it is extremely useful to know how to make a greaseproof paper bag. Most professional icers find that greaseproof paper bags used with nozzles give the best results. They are also convenient if you are icing in more than one colour — simply make several bags instead of having to wash out a bought icing bag each time. A greaseproof bag can also be used without a nozzle.

Cut a 25 cm /10 in square of greaseproof or silicone paper. Lay the sheet on a work surface and cut it in half from corner to corner. Continue to fold it to make a cone. This makes a small, neat bag which is easier to use when full of icing than a larger one.

Snip off the tip of the bag and drop in a decorating nozzle. Aim to have 10 mm /½ in protruding. Like this the nozzle will fit tightly and icing cannot leak out. You can also snip off a small point and use the bag without a nozzle.

Put in the icing to fill the bag until it is three-quarters full. Fold the top flap down, thus enclosing the front edge and sealing the bag.

Nozzles

To pipe, you will need a piping bag and a selection of small nozzles, preferably made of metal. There are a great number of nozzles to choose from and the numbering system varies from manufacturer to manufacturer and from country to country.

Plain or writing nozzles have a round hole at the top and come in a number of sizes, from a pin hole to 5 mm /¼ in. They will pipe lines, words, dots and strings of 'pearls'. This is the nozzle to use for dividing a cake into areas for separate decoration or for creating running lines and loops for lace-like effects.

Star nozzles have a series of little teeth at the top which are bent inwards. There are a number of different sizes and the number of points to the star may vary from 5 up to 12. Held at right angles to the cake, they produce a star or rosette. Held at a smaller angle and moved with varied pressure, they produce ropes and zigzag scrolls.

Shell nozzles are similar to star nozzles but the teeth at the top of the nozzle are straight. Held at an angle and moved with varied pressure, they give you shell shapes and scrolls. Half shell nozzles have teeth on one side only.

Fluted ribbon nozzles have a rectangular aperture at the top with little teeth at either side. They produce a continuous ribbon with markings along its length.

Making a greaseproof paper piping bag

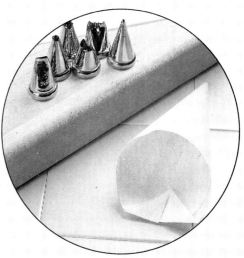

Cut a 25 cm /10 in square of greaseproof paper in half diagonally. Roll one of the matching corners over and lay it on top of the right-angled corner in the centre.

Roll the other corner around the cone. Fold down the protruding angle at the top. Cut off the bottom to hold the nozzle, so it projects 10 mm /½ in. Fill three-quarters full.

Petal nozzles: there are various nozzles for different flowers, and they come in several sizes. They have a long, narrow slit at the top, eyebrow-shaped for roses, straight for some other petals.

Leaf nozzles have a flattened triangular point with a semi-circle cut into the tip. They make wavy leaf-like lines which can be used as a decoration with flowers.

Using a piping bag

Make sure the icing is the right consistency before you start. You should be able to squeeze it out of the nozzle without any difficulty, but the piped decoration should hold its shape.

Filling the bag: drop the nozzle you have chosen into the icing bag, then stand the bag in a tall tumbler. If you are using a fabric bag, fold down the top half around the outside of the tumbler like a cuff. Now spoon icing into the bag until it is no more than three-quarters full. Pull the top of the bag together and rotate it into a tight screw. If you are using a greaseproof paper bag, support it in a tumbler but do not turn down the top. Fill it in the same way as the fabric bag, then fold the top down.

Piping: hold the bag with your thumb on the top. If it is a fabric bag, hold the twist firmly with your thumb. If the bag is paper, your thumb will naturally hold the bag shut. Your forefinger down the side of the bag should direct it. The rest of your fingers, curved underneath, supply the pressure to squeeze out the icing. Hold the bag at the correct angle for the decoration you have chosen and squeeze firmly.

When making shells, rosettes and other individual shapes, gradually decrease the pressure to give a tapered finish. Press continuously for a design such as a ribbon. For a running border, always work the design by drawing the bag towards you, never away from you. Vary the pressure on the bag according to the design and always release

the pressure just before removing the nozzle from the piped design.

Practise your patterns before you start on the cake itself. It is a good idea to cover a cake-board or chopping board with cling film. The icing can be scraped off this easily and returned to the bowl for use.

Piping borders

The first four borders described here may be piped in whipped cream or Royal icing, but only Royal icing is suitable for the ribbon loops.

Rosette border: use a star nozzle. Hold the bag so that the nozzle touches the cake at a right angle. Apply pressure, lifting the nozzle about 5 mm /¼ in from the cake, then ease off the pressure so that the rosette finishes with a point.

Shell border: shells are made by varying the pressure on the bag so that the icing emerges in an uneven thickness — thick for the body and thin for the tail end of the shell. Use a star or shell nozzle. Hold the bag so that the nozzle touches the cake at a 60° angle. Apply pressure to the bag, lifting the nozzle about 5 mm /¼ in from the cake to arch the shell. Gradually ease off the pressure, bringing the shell down to a point. Make a line of shells, overlapping.

Reverse shell border: make the border as described above, guiding the nozzle so that the shell arches alternately to the left and to the right.

Zigzag border: use a star nozzle or, for a flatter pattern, a fluted ribbon nozzle which provides a wide, crimped band. Hold the piping bag so that the nozzle is at a 45° angle to the cake. Guide the nozzle in a zigzag line, applying even pressure to the bag.

Ribbon loops are used on the sides of cakes. Use a very fine plain nozzle and slightly thinned Royal icing. The icing should be thin enough to flow smoothly, but not so thin that it does not hold together. Touch the top edge of the cake with the nozzle, then apply pressure to the bag so that a string of icing emerges from the nozzle. Squeeze out a string that is long enough to make a loop that will hang down 25 mm /1 in when the other end of the loop is attached to the cake about 4 cm /1½ in from the first. Make a second loop, starting and finishing it in the same places as the first loop, allowing it to hang down only 20 mm /¾ in. Continue to make loops all the way round the cake.

Always keep the nozzle level with the top of the cake so that the loops hang down into place. Do not try to stretch the icing or it will break. To make 'bows' where the loops join, pipe a horizontal figure 8 at the top of each join, then pipe two short strings, attaching them at the centre.

Piping flowers and leaves

Flowers and leaves are piped individually onto squares of waxed paper. When dry, they are removed from the paper and arranged on the cake in sprays, circles or horseshoes. They can be used both on the top and sides of the cake; they should be attached with a dab of icing.

You can use either Royal icing or Creamy decorative icing (see recipes) to make your flowers and leaves. If they are made of Royal icing, they will set hard and can be attached to the cake several days before you want to use it. Flowers and leaves made from Creamy decorative icing will become firm but never hard and are therefore more suitable for sponge cakes. They should be attached to the cake no more than 1 hour before serving.

A special flower nail, made of metal or plastic, which looks like a large nail with a flat top, is sold with icing sets. Its thin 'stem' is easily rolled between the fingers, enabling you to turn the flower as you are piping it, keeping the piping bag still. However, I find that squares of paper on top of a jam jar serve just as well — and mean you can stop and rest in the middle too!

If you are using two shades of icing for each flower, you will need two greaseproof paper piping bags, each fitted with the appropriate nozzle. Alternatively, you can pipe all the centres first and outer petals afterwards. Leave the flowers and leaves to dry for a minimum of 1 hour.

Modelled roses

Roses can be modelled. Use either fondant icing or almond paste, both of which can be bought. Flowers made from fondant icing will fit better into a pastel scheme. Almond paste flowers will give you brightly coloured blooms. Once they have been made, almond paste flowers may be frozen and kept for up to 3 months.

Crystallized flowers

A number of real flowers can be candied in all their beauty to make decorations for your cake. Alternatively, only the petals may be used. Do not crystallize flowers grown from bulbs as these are poisonous. Suitable whole flowers are apple blossom, flowering cherry, primroses and wild violets. Violet and rose petals are also useful cake decorations (and expensive to buy ready-prepared). Choose rose varieties that have a good scent.

For a flower decoration for a very special occasion, you need only egg white and sugar (see recipe). To crystallize flowers so that they may be stored for up to a year you will need gum arabic, which is rather difficult to use. Once they are made, store them in an air-tight container in the dark.

Chocolate decorations

Chocolate shapes and leaves can be used to decorate mousses and pastries, as well as cakes and gateaux. Do not handle chocolate decorations or they will lose their gloss. Keep them in the refrigerator until they are required.

Cut-out chocolate shapes: melt chocolate in a bowl set over a pan of hot but not boiling water. Spread a thin layer of melted chocolate on a sheet of waxed paper and leave it to set until it is just firm. Cut out shapes

using petits fours cutters — or cut squares or triangles with a sharp knife.

Caraque is elegant chocolate curls. Melt the chocolate as above, spread it on an oiled surface and leave it until cold. Shave it into long curls with a small, sharp knife.

Chocolate leaves (see recipe) can be made by coating the underside of rose leaves. This gives them all the genuine leaf markings, including tiny veins.

Creamy decorative icing

This icing is easy to work with and is ideal for making flowers and leaves for a sponge cake. It sets, so the flowers can be arranged on the cake, but it never becomes hard. It keeps in the freezer for 1 year so you can make up a batch and use it as needed for flower and leaf decorations. Do not use it for covering the cake as the taste is not particularly exciting. Use a fondant icing or butter-cream for the basic cake icing and for sticking on the decorations.

⏱ 5–10 minutes,
plus 1 hour chilling

Makes 800 ml /1½ pt
225 g /8 oz hard white vegetable fat
150 g /5 oz butter
550 g /1¼ lb icing sugar
5 ml /1 tsp almond essence
a few drops of food colouring

1 Place the vegetable shortening in a bowl with the butter and cream them together until they are smooth.
2 Sift in the icing sugar a little at a time, mixing well after each addition.
3 Add the almond essence and beat the mixture until it is light and fluffy. Add a few drops of food colouring and mix well. Chill for 1 hour before piping.

Piping many-petalled roses

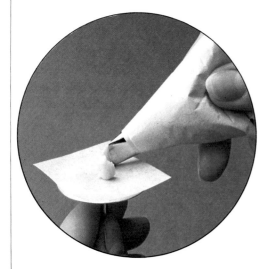

Make a tall blob for the centre. Hold the nozzle thin edge uppermost. Start halfway up the base and wrap an icing petal round.

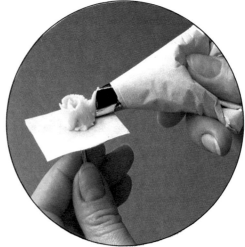

For an inner petal, slant the nozzle outwards. Squeeze out the icing, revolving the paper away from the nozzle. Release the pressure.

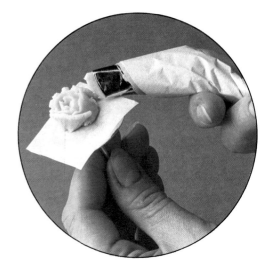

Use a paler icing for the outer petals; use the nozzle with the thin edge at the petal tip and slant the top well out.

Modelling roses from fondant or almond paste

Roll paste into 10 mm /½ in balls and insert into dusted cling film. Flatten to a petal shape making the petal tip extra thin.

Roll first petal for bud centre. (Dry fondant petals for 10 minutes before assembly.) Wrap petals round the bud thick edge downwards.

Stick roses and sugar leaves to the cake with dabs of icing. (Leave fondant roses to set for 1 hour before attaching them.)

Many-petalled piped roses

These roses look like hybrid tea roses, and you can vary the design of them by using either one or two shades of pink for each little flower.

making and chilling the icing,
plus 1 hour, then chilling

Makes 15–20 roses
⅓ Creamy decorative icing (see recipe)
red food colouring

1 Divide the icing in half and colour one half pale pink and the other half a darker shade of pink. Place the pale pink icing in a bowl and cover it with a clean damp cloth. Put a large petal nozzle into a piping bag, stand the bag in a tumbler and, if you are using a fabric bag, turn down the top. Fill the bag three-quarters full with the darker icing and hold the top with your thumb.
2 Cut 15 pieces of greaseproof or silicone paper, each 5 cm /2 in square. Stick the first one to an upturned jam jar bottom or icing nail with a dab of icing.
3 Guiding the bag with your forefinger and with the rest of your fingers curved around the bag, squeeze a small mound of the darker colour in the centre of the square to make a base for the rose.
4 To form the centre of the bud, hold the nozzle so that the thin edge is uppermost. Squeeze out the icing, wrapping it tightly around the base. As you squeeze, hold the bag still and rotate the jar or icing nail with your other hand, making a single petal.
5 To make the first row of petals, slant the nozzle slightly outwards so that the flower will begin to open. Make a row of 2–4 overlapping petals around the bud, each about 20 mm /¾ in wide, squeezing out the icing with a circular movement.

6 Fit a second piping bag with a rose nozzle and fill it with the paler icing, as in step 1. To finish the roses, make a further row of outer petals, still with the thick edge against the base of the rose. Slant the top decidedly outwards.
7 Chill for at least 2 hours to allow the roses to firm up before handling.
8 About 1 hour before serving, attach the roses to the cake with dabs of icing.

● If you want to make shaded roses but do not have two icing bags, it is easier to make all the dark centres first. As you finish, move the piped petals to the refrigerator to set, then pipe all the paler petals in one go.
● The icing flowers may be made ahead and refrigerated for 1 week.
● The roses may be frozen in a rigid container until needed.

Sugar leaves

30 minutes,
plus a minimum 2 hours setting

Makes about 20 leaves
⅙ Creamy decorative icing (see recipe)
a drop of green food colouring

1 Tint the icing with the green food colouring. Now fit an icing bag with a leaf nozzle.
2 Cut 20 pieces of greaseproof or silicone paper, each 5 cm /2 in square. Stand the piping bag in a tumbler and, if you are using a fabric bag, turn down the top. Fill the bag three-quarters full with icing and then close the top.
3 Guide the bag with your forefinger and curve the rest of your fingers around the bag. Hold the tip at 45° to the paper and pipe the icing with a slight up and down motion to make a crinkled edge. Pipe the leaves in varying sizes from 25 mm–4 cm /1–1½ in long. Release the pressure and lift the nozzle to complete each leaf. Place the leaves on a

baking sheet in the refrigerator and leave them for a minimum of 2 hours to set.
4 About 1 hour before serving, attach the leaves to the cake with dabs of icing.

Royal icing

Royal icing is the grandest of the plain white icings and the one used for wedding cakes. It sets very hard and is therefore ideal for a perfect smooth surface and for piping.

30 minutes, plus 24 hours standing
for flat icing or piping

Covers a deep 20 cm /8 in round cake
4 egg whites
900 g /2 lb icing sugar
colouring (optional)
10 ml /2 tsp lemon juice
a few drops of glycerine

1 In a large bowl, whisk the egg whites until they are just frothy. Sift the icing sugar into the bowl a little at a time, whisking well between each addition. Add a few drops of colouring if you wish.
2 Add 10 ml /2 tsp lemon juice and a few drops of glycerine. Continue to whisk until peaks form.
3 If you are making rough icing, you can use the icing straight away. If you are flat icing or piping, however, it is best to let the icing stand for 24 hours so that the bubbles made by the mixer can subside. When not using the icing cover it with a damp tea-towel to prevent a crust forming.
4 If, when you start to use the icing, you find that it is too stiff to work, particularly for piping, soften it with a few extra drops of lemon juice. Remember to keep the surface of the bowl covered while you are working.

● If this icing is to be used for a 3-tier wedding cake, omit the glycerine because the surface needs to be hard to support the pillars.

Crystallized flowers

Candy tiny flowers from your garden to make beautiful cake decorations, or crystallize sweet-smelling petals. If you want a decoration to eat immediately, the flowers may be treated with just egg white. For long-term storage, fresh flowers should be treated with gum arabic.

⏲ 30 minutes,
plus drying time

Candies 6 or more flowers
1 egg white
fresh flowers, such as apple blossoms, cherry blossoms, primroses or petals from sweet-smelling roses or violets (avoid flowers from bulbs, which are poisonous)
caster sugar

1 Lightly beat the egg white.
2 Make sure the flowers or petals are dry. Carefully brush them all over with the lightly beaten egg white using an artist's paint brush. Be sure to coat the flowers or petals thoroughly as any exposed parts will darken and wilt. Do not coat too thickly or the caster sugar will adhere in lumps.
3 Sprinkle the flowers or petals with caster sugar, completely covering the surfaces. Leave them to dry, then dust again with caster sugar. Leave them to dry completely. Shake off any excess sugar.

● Flowers treated with egg white will keep for up to 2 days. For longer term storage, use gum arabic dissolved in rose-water or orange-flower water. Gum arabic is quite difficult to use, so follow the manufacturer's instructions carefully and dissolve the crystals completely before use. Flowers treated with gum arabic will keep for up to a year.

Yellow wild roses

⏲⏲ 1 hour,
plus a minimum 2 hours setting

Makes about 5 large and 15 small roses
⅓ Creamy decorative icing (see recipe)
a few drops of yellow food colouring
a few drops of red food colouring
a few drops of green food colouring

1 Cut 20 pieces of greaseproof or silicone paper, each 5 cm /2 in square. Stick the first one to the bottom of an upturned jam jar with a dab of icing.
2 Divide the icing in half and set one half aside in a bowl covered with a clean damp cloth. To make large yellow roses, tint the other half with 3–4 drops of yellow colouring. Reserve 15 ml /1 tbls of icing for the rose centres. Put a large rose petal nozzle into a piping bag, stand the bag in a tumbler and, if you are using a fabric bag, turn down the top. Fill the bag three-quarters full with icing and close the top.
3 Guide the bag with your forefinger and curve the rest of your fingers around the bag. Holding the wide end of the nozzle at a 45° angle and turning the jam jar with the other hand, press out the icing to make a round petal on the paper. It should be about 20 mm /¾ in across. Make 5 petals in all, meeting in the centre to make a round flower about 4 cm /1½ in diameter. As the roses are completed, remove them from the top of the jam jar, still attached to the greaseproof silicone paper. Put them on a baking sheet in the refrigerator and leave them to set.
4 To make small wild roses, colour the

Iced fancies with Yellow wild roses and Sugar leaves, and Chocolate leaves

second quantity of icing orange with 2–3 drops each of yellow and red food colouring. Reserve 15 ml /1 tbls icing for the centres.
5 Use the same size nozzle and pipe the small rose petals in the same way as the larger ones, but keep the size of the roses to 20 mm /¾ in diameter. Place the roses in the refrigerator to set.
6 To make the centres of the large roses, add red colouring to the reserved icing. Fit the piping bag with a plain nozzle and carefully pipe 5 dots in the centre of each rose.
7 To make the centres of the small roses, add a drop of green food colouring to the reserved icing. Using the same nozzle, pipe 5 dots in the centre of each small rose. Chill the roses in the refrigerator for a minimum of 2 hours until set.
8 About 1 hour before serving, attach the roses to the cake with dabs of icing.

Chocolate leaves

These beautifully marked leaves of chocolate can be arranged in sprays with flowers or silver balls and then used to embellish a sophisticated chocolate cake or an elegant dessert.

⏲⏲ 45 minutes,
plus setting and arranging

Makes 12–15 leaves
50 g /2 oz plain chocolate
12–15 small fresh rose leaves

1 Break up the chocolate and melt it in a medium-sized bowl over a pan of hot but not boiling water. Meanwhile wash and dry the rose leaves.
2 Coat the underside of each leaf with melted chocolate, using an artist's paint brush. Place the coated leaves in the refrigerator to harden.
3 Just before you wish to use them, peel away the rose leaves.

Chocolate leaves

Using a clean artist's paint brush, coat the underside of clean rose leaves with melted chocolate. Chill until firm. Peel away the leaf.

With a Foreign Flavour

STIR-FRYING

The quick stir-fried dishes of China are derived from one of the most ancient cuisines in the world. They represent the successful blending of thousands of years of careful experiment, and yet are simple, quick and easily learned.

If you are like many of my friends who admit they love Chinese food but are afraid to cook it themselves because it is too different and exotic, let me try to persuade you otherwise. Chinese food *is* different, but the stir-fry method — once you learn the knack — is quick and easy to do.

Although most dishes may be served individually, they are generally meant to be eaten three or four together. Serve them in individual dishes and keep them warm, if possible, in the centre of the table on table-top warmers. Guests take a little from the dish of their choice with chopsticks. I find that food eaten in this manner actually tastes better than when it is eaten Western-style, all on one plate and using a knife and fork.

In a Chinese meal, individual rice bowls are always used. I like to use mine as a 'dripping bowl', taking each morsel of tender meat or crispy vegetable by the chopstickful and carrying it over my bowl to allow some of the juices to drip into it, and add flavour to the rice.

Equipment
When most people think about stir-frying they think of using a *wok*. A wok is a large semi-circular pan which is put directly over the heat on the top of the stove. The heat always remains greatest in the base of the wok, and food can be pushed up the sides — out of the direct heat — whenever necessary, so it is easy to avoid over-cooking.

If you are a beginner at stir-frying you may prefer to use a large frying-pan instead of a wok. Heat the pan over a small, central flame as it is important to concentrate the heat only in the middle of the pan.

As all the ingredients need to be chopped up before you start cooking, a good-sized chopping board is a must. You will also need a sharp knife or a flat cleaver. Stir-fried food can be stirred with wooden chopsticks, a pair of forks or, if you prefer, the shovel-like wok scoop.

What to stir-fry
The most commonly stir-fried foods are savoury vegetables, fish and meats. Cut into small even-sized pieces, they are cooked quickly before the flavour has time to escape or the food becomes tough.

Vegetables are especially suitable for stir-frying. They should first be blanched in boiling, salted water so that they keep their bright, fresh colour. Then they are cooked briefly to retain their crispness, and the bite-sized pieces are eaten whole. As the appearance of food is almost as important as the flavour, choose vegetables of contrasting colours and textures — carrots, broccoli and red peppers — for an attractive dish.

Fish, particularly prawns, are very often served stir-fried. They should be shelled and then sprinkled with salt about 15 minutes before cooking. This makes them slightly firmer. As they are already quite small, there is no need to chop them up; they will cook quickly and still remain tender.

Meat is usually cut into strips about 4 cm / 1½ in long and so cooks in the hot oil in a few minutes. To add extra flavour to the meat, marinate it for at least 20 minutes in a mixture containing soy sauce and Chinese wine, or sherry. Beef, pork, lamb, chicken and duck can all be stir-fried Chinese-style.

How to prepare the ingredients
Everything should be prepared before you start cooking — once you've begun you won't have time to chop or cut any extra ingredients. Cut the vegetables or meat to size and place them near the stove on individual plates, or prepare them in advance and keep them in covered containers in the refrigerator. Stored like this they will keep in perfect condition for up to 8 hours.

The cutting of ingredients is all-important; it determines the length of time the food has to be cooked (the smaller the pieces, the shorter the cooking time) as well as the final appearance of the dish.

Cubing and dicing: cut the food to be cooked into thick slices, cut the slices into strips, then cut the strips across to make cubes. Use the same method to cut dice, making all the cuts at shorter intervals.

Slicing: place the point of the knife or the tip of the cleaver down on the chopping board, push the vegetable to be cut under it and bring down the cutting edge to the chopping board. Repeat this action rapidly and gently along the vegetable. Meat, fish and poultry can be sliced in the same fashion — you'll get neater slices if they are slightly frozen. Tender vegetables such as spring onions and young leeks are cut across into rounds. Firmer vegetables such as carrots, celery and asparagus can be cut diagonally to produce larger slices.

Cutting into strips: slice the food lengthways, then make a pile of slices and cut the pile into strips. Carrots, bamboo shoots and turnips are suitable for this method.

Quick stir-fried vegetables

20 minutes

Serves 4
450 g /1 lb vegetables of your choice
30 ml /2 tbls oil
1.5 ml /¼ tsp salt
15 ml /1 tbls soy sauce
15 ml /1 tbls sake or dry sherry

1 Put a large pan of salted water on to boil. Wash the vegetables and cut them as desired (see introduction).
2 Blanch the cut vegetables in the boiling salted water, adding those that require the longest blanching time first and gradually adding those that require less time, for example 5–6 minutes for carrots, 3 minutes for courgettes, 2 minutes for celery. Drain them well.
3 Heat the oil in a wok or a large, heavy frying-pan, add the blanched vegetables and stir-fry for 1–2 minutes. Add the salt and 150 ml /5 fl oz water and stir-fry for a further 2–3 minutes. Add the soy sauce and sake or dry sherry and stir-fry for 1 minute. Serve the vegetables immediately.

Stir-fried beef with broccoli

Stir-fried beef with broccoli

20 minutes, plus 30 minutes marinating, then about 30 minutes

Serves 4 with 2 other dishes
450 g /1 lb rump or skirt steak
225 g /8 oz broccoli
90 ml /6 tbls peanut or vegetable oil
5 ml /1 tsp salt
4 garlic cloves, finely chopped
3 spring onions, cut into 25 mm /1 in
  sections, white and green parts reserved
  separately
15 ml /1 tbls Shaohsing wine or medium-dry
  sherry
onion tassels, to garnish (optional)
For the marinade
1.5 ml /¼ tsp sugar
1.5 ml /¼ tsp salt
7.5 ml /1½ tsp thin soy sauce
7.5 ml /1½ tsp thick soy sauce
about 1.5 ml /¼ tsp freshly ground black
  pepper
10 ml /2 tsp Shaohsing wine or medium-dry
  sherry
7.5 ml /1½ tsp potato or tapioca flour
For the sauce
10 ml /2 tsp thick soy sauce
15–25 ml /1–1½ tbls oyster sauce
5 ml /1 tsp potato or tapicoa flour

1 Cut the beef across the grain into rectangular slices about 4 cm×25 mm / 1½×1 in and 5 mm /¼ in thick. Put them into a large, deep bowl.
2 Add all the marinade ingredients. Add 15 ml /1 tbls of water and with chopsticks or a fork stir vigorously in the same direction to coat the beef thoroughly.
3 Repeat the stirring once. This process is essential if the beef is to end up velvety and tender. Refrigerate for 20–30 minutes.
4 Peel and discard the hard outer layer of the broccoli stems. Cut the rest into bite-sized pieces. Mix the sauce ingredients with 90 ml /6 tbls water and reserve.
5 In a saucepan, bring plenty of water to the boil. Add 15 ml /1 tbls of the oil and the salt, add the broccoli, return to the boil, then continue to boil for about 3 minutes. Drain, then cool under cold water and drain again.
6 Heat a wok over a high heat until a wisp of smoke rises. Add the remaining oil and swirl it around. Add the garlic and the white parts of the spring onions, stir with a wok scoop or metal spatula several times. Add the beef and flip and toss it for 1–1½ minutes.
7 Splash the wine or sherry along the rim of the wok just above the beef and, while it sizzles, continue to stir. When the sizzling subsides and the beef is still underdone, transfer it to a warm plate, draining well.
8 Add the green part of the spring onion and the broccoli and stir until they are hot. Push the broccoli around the sides and pour the sauce into the centre, stirring well once. As soon as the sauce bubbles, return the beef to the wok and stir everything together until the broccoli is piping hot. Transfer it to a warm serving plate and garnish with onion tassels, if wished.

Stir-fried prawns in tomato sauce

 5 minutes, then 15 minutes resting, plus about 25 minutes

Serves 2 with 1 other dish
225 g /8 oz medium-sized raw prawns in
  their shells, defrosted if frozen
2.5 ml /½ tsp salt
225 g /8 oz ripe tomatoes
75 ml /5 tbls peanut or vegetable oil
4–5 garlic cloves, finely chopped
4 spring onions, cut into 25 mm /1 in
  sections, white and green parts reserved
  separately
10 ml /2 tsp thin soy sauce
2.5 ml /½ tsp sugar
2.5 ml /½ tsp potato or tapioca flour

1 Shell, devein and wash the prawns. Pat them dry with absorbent paper and then sprinkle them with half of the salt; this will firm them up. Leave them for about 15 minutes.
2 Put the tomatoes in very hot water for

Stir-fried prawns in tomato sauce

5–10 seconds. Peel off the skins and cut them into slices.
3 Heat a wok until a wisp of smoke rises. Add the oil and swirl it around until it is very hot. Add the garlic and half of the white part of the spring onions, stirring.
4 Add the prawns. Flip and turn them rapidly from the bottom of the wok with a wok scoop or metal spatula for 1 minute or until the prawns have curled up and turned pink. Scoop them onto a warm plate, leaving behind as much oil as possible.
5 Add the remaining white of the spring onions to the wok. Add the tomato slices and stir to incorporate the oil. Season with the salt, the soy sauce and the sugar. Cover and cook over a medium heat for 7–8 minutes.
6 Mix the potato or tapioca flour with 15 ml /1 tbls water. Remove the cover and add the flour mixture, stirring well.
7 Return the prawns to the wok and add the green of the spring onions. Turn up the heat, stir and turn until the prawns are very hot. Scoop everything onto a warm serving plate. Serve immediately while the fragrance is at its best.

MAKING PASTA

Learn from the Italians how to transform the simple ingredients of flour, eggs, oil and a drop or two of water into golden home-made pasta. Freshly made, it has a delicious flavour, and makes tasty, economical meals.

Only a very gifted people could transform very simple ingredients into such a bewitching variety of pasta shapes and sizes: tubes and strings, ribbons and bows, frills, stars, spirals and sea shells. Certainly the Chinese have eaten noodles for centuries, but pasta as we know it is the result of Italian inventiveness, a glorious monument to that nation's joyous spirit and hearty love of good food.

Not content with inventing well over a hundred different shapes, the Italians then married each one to the right dressing — rich thick sauces that cling to ropes and ribbons, rather thinner sauces to flow through and around tubed noodles, from neat little macaroni to great ribbed tunnels of *rigatoni*.

Sometimes a plate of perfectly cooked steaming noodles is served with just a dollop of butter and a bowl of freshly grated Parmesan cheese. Or try a light dressing of warmed, fruity olive oil, barely coloured with garlic and parsley. I like, too, a sauce made of pounded anchovies and finely chopped onion and garlic.

The strange thing is that no two pasta dishes taste alike, even if made with the same home-made dough and dressed with the same sauce. This is perhaps because the variations in size and shape of pasta give a different proportion of noodle to sauce, depending on the pasta used.

Buying pasta

Delicatessens and supermarkets stock a fairly wide range of dry pasta, most of it imported (although very acceptable pastas are also produced outside Italy). These pastas are dried and packaged and can safely be stored for a year or more. Commercially available pasta can roughly be divided into the following categories:

Ropes and strings: these include spaghetti, *spaghettini* (a thinner version of spaghetti) and *vermicelli*, the finest of all.

Ribbons: the most common names for ribbon noodles are *fettucine*, *tagliatelle* and *tagliolini*. *Lasagne*, however, are large flat strips of the same dough, much wider than the ribbons above, and are served in a different way.

Tubular pastas: the famous macaroni (*maccheroni*), *maccheroncini*, which are thinner tubes, and *rigatoni*, the ribbed noodles, which are much larger.

Pasta shapes: finally we are left with the whole range of *stricchetti* and *farfalletti* (bows and butterflies), *conchiglie* or 'little shells', little cupids' bows and kisses, stars and even letters of the alphabet.

Fresh egg pasta: housewives and cooks in Italy can buy fresh pasta the day it is made. This is also available from many Italian delicatessens outside Italy and increasingly from larger supermarkets, where it is sold vacuum packed. But if you do not have one of those shops near you, make it yourself.

Serving pasta

Choose the type of pasta that best suits the dish you are planning. Large shapes and tubes are served as a dish by themselves, with butter or a sauce. Smaller shapes or broken pieces are the best choice for adding to a soup; *pasta in brodo* may be anything from an elegant garnish of pasta shapes in a consommé to a hearty *minestre*.

Outside Italy most people think of pasta as an informal, quick and easy main dish for lunch or supper time. And very good it is, too, preceded by an *antipasto* platter in the Italian manner — a selection of cold meats — washed down with a bottle of Chianti and followed by a green salad and something very light for the sweet.

To make more of it, try slotting a pasta course between the appetizer or *antipasto*, which, literally translated, means 'before the pasta', and the main course. This is the way Italians serve pasta, and also rice. If you follow their example and serve the meat course on its own, or with a simple green vegetable or salad, you need have no fear of overwhelming your guests.

Home-made pasta

Although dried pasta is a convenience that few of us, if we were honest, would like to be without, there is a flavour in fresh pasta that cannot be matched, as well as the fun involved in making your own. The main ingredients of a pasta dough are flour and eggs in the proportion of 4 eggs to 500 g /1 lb flour. A perfectly acceptable pasta dough can be made with ordinary plain flour, but strong flour — the high gluten flour used to make bread — is nearer to the durum flour used in Italy and so will give a better result. The basic pasta dough, *pasta gialla*, is best made with fresh egg yolks. Dark yolks give the noodles an appetizing golden colour but unless you can get really fresh, dark-yolked eggs, I am afraid you are going to have to cheat a little by adding a drop or two of yellow food colouring.

By the time you have made your dough, rolled it out, cut the noodles into the chosen shape and left them to dry, you will probably have had enough for one day. I prefer to break off at this stage anyway, leaving the noodles to dry overnight, then I can set about cooking them with renewed enthusiasm the following day.

Coloured pasta: a border of pink or green noodles around a dish can look more stylish than plain ones. Or try a simple dish of buttered noodles, using three colours.

The recipe for green pasta, *pasta verde*, breaks the proportion rule of 4 eggs to 500 g /1 lb flour. Half the eggs are replaced by spinach, which changes the pasta from yellow to green. There is no need to add extra water to the dough as the spinach will add sufficient moisture. Start by adding 75 ml /5 tbls

Fresh coloured noodles served with butter and grated Parmesan cheese

spinach to the flour — if you find it is too dry add more spinach, 15 ml /1 tbls at a time.

There are different ideas about how to tint pasta pink for *pasta rosa*. Some people like to incorporate beetroot to give the pasta its colour, but I find that the colour tends to come out during cooking so I use tomato purée, which produces a good colour.

Making fresh egg pasta

Make a stiff dough. To knead, push the ball down and away with the heel of your hand.

Handling the pasta dough

The first thing that will probably strike you when you start mixing the ingredients is that there is far too little liquid to hold the dough together. Keep mixing a bit longer before you give up and decide to add more water. Of course, flours vary and some absorb more liquid than others, but you will probably find that with a little extra effort you will be able to force in all the flour.

Now start kneading in real earnest, pushing the ball of dough down and away from you with the heel of your hand, then pulling it towards you with your fingers as you draw your hand back. Each time you do this, turn the pad of dough round slightly so that every part of it is kneaded. If you can develop a smooth, relaxed, regular kneading rhythm, you will find it much less tiring.

After about 15 minutes steady kneading, the dough will have become smooth and elastic, though still very firm. Little air blisters just under the surface are a sure sign that it has had enough kneading.

Resting the dough: rolling the dough at this stage is very difficult indeed. The answer is to wrap the ball loosely in a polythene bag (to prevent the surface drying out) and leave it to rest for a minimum of 1 hour at room temperature — the longer the better. This gives the gluten in the flour a chance to relax and makes it yield more readily to the rolling pin. You can even leave it overnight at the bottom of the refrigerator, but make sure the bag is not sealed, otherwise the dough will tend to sweat.

Rolling the dough by hand

When dealing with a large amount of dough, you will find it easier to roll it out a piece at a time. Cut off a quarter and return the remainder to its polythene bag to keep moist.

Flour your working surface lightly and flatten the piece of dough with the palm of a lightly floured hand. Don't knead the dough at this stage: you will only revive its elasticity and make it more difficult to roll.

Dust your rolling pin with flour and start rolling the dough, using short light strokes, in one direction only, and always working outwards from the centre to make a circle. Check occasionally that the sheet of dough has not stuck to the working surface, flouring a corner of the surface from time to time and swishing the sheet of dough over it to ensure that the underside keeps dry. The sheet of dough will resist all the way but with perseverance you will finally roll it paper-thin. Press it firmly with a finger — it should leave only the faintest indentation.

Using a pasta machine

A machine which rolls and cuts the dough is useful if you make a lot of pasta. Dust the rollers lightly and cut off a quarter of the dough, keeping the rest covered. Set the rollers at their widest setting and turn the handle to roll the pasta through. Reduce the width between the rollers by one notch and re-roll. Repeat this until only one notch remains. If you are making stuffed shapes, lasagne or cannelloni, pass the pasta through the narrowest setting. Now cut it immediately, unless making ribbons.

If you are making ribbons, at this point it is best to hang up the strips for 30–60 minutes to dry. A well-scrubbed broomstick supported by two chairs will serve as a bar.

Your machine will have a second set of rollers which will cut the pasta into ribbon noodles, usually tagliatelli. Move the handle and roll the dough through. Some machines also have a third set which will give you a narrow linguini.

Cutting pasta by hand

When making stuffed ravioli-type pasta, the dough should be used as soon as it is rolled, while it is still moist enough to stick to itself under the pressure of your fingers and seal in the filling.

For ribbon noodles or large leaves of lasagne or cannelloni, it is safer to leave the sheet of dough for 10–15 minutes to dry slightly before proceeding.

When it is ready for cutting, flour your hands lightly and sweep them over the surface of the dough. If you are making cannelloni, there is no need to fold the dough, just cut it neatly into 10 cm /4 in squares. Otherwise, fold the sheet up loosely into a long strip about 7.5 cm /3 in deep. Using a very sharp knife which will slice through the dough with minimum pressure, trim off the uneven ends, then cut into noodles as follows:

Tagliarini or linguini: narrow ribbons 3 mm /⅛ in wide.
Fettuccelle or taglioni: narrow ribbons 3–5 mm /⅛–¼ in wide.

Lift the end as you draw back your fingers and slap the dough back into a ball.

Give the dough a quarter turn, then push it out again. Develop a rocking rhythm.

For ribbon noodles, roll the dough up like a Swiss roll, then slice it with a sharp knife.

Tagliatelle or fettucine: slightly wider version of fettuccelle, 5 mm /¼ in wide.
Fettucce or tagliolette: 10 mm /½ in wide ribbons.
Lasagne: to make, cut long strips 5 cm /2 in wide. Unravel each strip and divide into 10–15 cm /4–6 in lengths.
Cannelloni: to make, cut 10 cm /4 in squares to roll around a filling.

Drying and storing pasta

Fresh home-made noodles must be left to dry out for at least an hour before cooking (or preferably overnight) until they feel hard, if not exactly brittle like bought pasta. If they are not dry enough, they will absorb too much of the cooking water and turn slimy. You can use one of two methods:
On a tray: dust a clean cloth with flour and, as you slice the noodles, shake them out onto the cloth. If you intend to leave them overnight, lay another cloth over the top to cover them completely. Flat leaves should be laid out side by side, not overlapping.
Hanging up: another way of drying home-made noodles is to place two kitchen chairs, back to back, with a scrubbed broomstick between them and hang the noodles over this stick to dry in the warm air of the kitchen. The pasta loses weight as it dries.
Storing pasta: fresh pasta will keep for up to 1 week if stored, wrapped in a polythene bag, in the refrigerator.
● Both the unrolled dough and cut strips can be frozen for 6 months or more. Eventually, however, they dry out and lose the characteristics that distinguish them from dried pasta.

Cooking pasta

Always boil pasta in plenty of salted water — 3.5 L /6 pt per 500 g /1 lb of pasta is a reasonable amount — otherwise the noodles may stick together. When cooking dried pasta, it helps to add 15 ml /1 tbls olive oil to the cooking water.

Long noodles, such as spaghetti, should never be broken. To get them in the pan, hold a stiff, dry sheaf upright in the boiling water, pressing gently against the base of the pan. As you feel it soften, gradually curl it around in the pan until it is completely submerged. With smaller shapes, add the pasta gradually to the pan so that the water remains at a rolling boil.

Once the strands or shapes are all in the water, give them a good stir with a fork to separate them and dislodge any that may have stuck to the bottom of the pan. Never cover pasta while it is cooking, the water is sure to boil over and you will have a terrible job cleaning up the sticky mess.

Specifying a cooking time for pasta is always tricky, whether you are dealing with freshly made or dried. Roughly speaking, the former will take about 6–8 minutes and the latter anything up to 11 minutes and beyond, depending on size, shape and how long it has been on the shelf. Take care not to overcook it as it quickly turns slimy and unpleasant. The only reliable test is to lift out a strand or ribbon on a fork and bite it.

Al dente is a phrase which has found its way into international cookery terminology. We use it when speaking about pasta and rice

but, to the Italian cook, vegetables can also be cooked *al dente*. Literally meaning 'to the tooth', this phrase pinpoints a precise stage at which an ingredient is just cooked through and no more — no longer raw but still firm enough to offer a slight resistance when you bite through it.

I always boil pasta like lasagne or cannelloni until quite tender before layering it with sauce or rolling it with stuffing for baking in the oven. In my experience, no amount of subsequent cooking will soften it further once it has been boiled and allowed to cool. However, there are a number of 'quick' lasagnes sold now which the manufacturers say need no pre-boiling.

Finally, never cook pasta too far in advance. If you have to keep it hot for a little while before serving, set the colander over a saucepan containing 25 mm /1 in of boiling water and cover with a damp cloth until ready to serve.

Sauces for pasta

After the pasta recipes in this chapter, you will find two delicious sauces; remember to keep the size and shape of the pasta in mind when selecting a sauce to serve with it.

A fresh tomato sauce is tasty served over pasta or try this simple idea. Mix one egg yolk with 150 ml /5 fl oz thick cream and season. Mix with 500 g/1 lb hot pasta — the heat of the pasta will make it a creamy sauce.

Fresh egg pasta

In Italy this pasta is called *pasta gialla*, which means yellow pasta.

🕐🍴 1¾ hours including 1 hour drying, then 1 hour or overnight drying

Makes about 500 g /1 lb
500 g /1 lb strong flour
5 ml /1 tsp salt
4 eggs
15 ml /1 tbls olive oil

1   Sift the flour and salt into a heap on a pastry board or into a large bowl. Make a well in the centre.
2   Break the eggs into the well. Add the olive oil and 45 ml /3 tbls cold water. With the fingers of one hand, gradually beat flour from the sides of the well into the liquid ingredients. Now work the dough until it holds together in a very stiff ball. Add a little more water if necessary, but remember the dough will soften quite a lot after kneading and resting.
3   Knead the dough, pushing the ball down and away from you with the heel of your hand. Next, lift up the end of the oblong with your fingers as you draw your hand back and slap the dough into a ball. Now give the dough a quarter turn so that the next time it is stretched in a different direction. Push it out again in the same way, like this every part of it is kneaded. Knead for about 15 minutes, or until the dough feels smooth and elastic; little air blisters under the surface of the dough mean that it is ready.

Pasta with Bolognese sauce

4   Roll the dough into a ball. Wrap it loosely in a polythene bag and leave it to relax at room temperature for at least 1 hour. If you want to leave it overnight, put it in the refrigerator, but do not seal the bag.
5   When you are ready to roll the dough, divide the ball into 4 equal pieces and return 3 of them to the polythene bag. Dust your working surface and rolling pin with flour and roll the dough out as thinly as possible. Use short light strokes, in one direction only, and always work outwards from the centre. Use more flour as necessary to prevent the dough sticking to the working surface. Roll the dough paper thin. If you press the surface with a finger, it should leave only the faintest mark.
6   If cutting noodles by hand, it is best to leave the sheet to dry for 10–15 minutes at this point so that the ribbons do not stick together. Alternatively, flour the surface well. Use a sharp knife to cut the pasta (see picture) so that it does not drag or squash the dough. If you are making noodles or strips, these should then be left for 1 hour or, better still, overnight to dry. Lay them on a clean, floured cloth covered by another cloth, or hang them from a bar — a well-scrubbed broom handle balanced between two chairs will fit the bill. Leave the pasta in a warm room, such as the kitchen.
7   To cook, bring 3.5 L /6 pt salted water to the boil. Add the pasta and bring the water back to the boil. Fresh pasta cooks very quickly so start testing it almost immediately. When cooked, it should be al dente, that is, cooked but still firm between the teeth when a little is tested.

Fresh green pasta

⏱️🍴 40 minutes, 1 hour resting,
15 minutes, then overnight drying

Makes about 500 g /1 lb
250 g /8 oz frozen chopped spinach
350 g /12 oz strong flour
4 ml /¾ tsp salt
2 eggs
15 ml /1 tbls thick cream

1 Cook the spinach according to the directions on the packet.
2 With a slotted spoon, remove the spinach from the saucepan, *not* draining it too thoroughly, and blend it to a smooth purée in an electric blender. (There should be enough liquid left on the spinach to allow it to blend without clogging up the blades.)
3 Sift the flour and salt into a heap on a pastry board, or into a large bowl. Make a well in the centre.
4 Break the eggs into the well and add 75 ml /5 tbls puréed spinach and the thick cream. Continue to make the dough and knead it as for Fresh egg pasta, adding an extra 15–30 ml /1–2 tbls puréed spinach, or cold water, if you cannot get the dough to hold together without it.
5 Wrap the dough loosely in a polythene bag and leave to rest for at least an hour at room temperature — or chill overnight. Roll the dough and cut it into the required shape and dry it as for Fresh egg pasta.
6 Cook in about 3.5 L /6 pt boiling salted water until just al dente; drain thoroughly.

Home-made red pasta

⏱️🍴 30 minutes, 1 hour resting,
15 minutes, then overnight drying

Makes about 500 g /1 lb
500 g /1 lb strong flour
5 ml /1 tsp salt
4 eggs
45 ml /3 tbls tomato purée
15 ml /1 tbls olive oil

1 Sift the flour and salt into a heap on a pastry board. Make a well in the centre.
2 Break the eggs into a blender and add the tomato purée. Blend until the eggs and purée are mixed. Add the olive oil and 45 ml /3 tbls cold water. Blend again.
3 Pour the tomato mixture into the well in the flour. Continue to make the dough and knead as for Fresh egg pasta, adding a little more water, if necessary.
4 Wrap the dough loosely in a polythene bag and leave to rest for at least 1 hour at room temperature — or chill overnight. Roll the dough and cut it into the required shape, then dry it as for Fresh egg pasta.
5 Cook the pasta in 3.5 L /6 pt boiling salted water until al dente, then drain.

Bolognese sauce

🍴 1½ hours

Serves 4
25 g /1 oz butter
60 ml /4 tbls olive oil
125 g /4 oz fat salt pork, or unsmoked bacon, finely chopped
1 onion, finely chopped
2 carrots, finely chopped
1 celery stick, finely chopped
250 g /8 oz sirloin of beef, minced
1 strip of lemon zest
1 bay leaf
60 ml /4 tbls tomato purée
275 ml /10 fl oz beef stock, home-made or from a cube
150 ml /5 fl oz dry white wine
salt and freshly ground black pepper
freshly grated nutmeg
60 ml /4 tbls thick cream
For serving
500 g /1 lb pasta, freshly cooked
freshly grated Parmesan cheese

1 Heat the butter and olive oil in a thick-bottomed saucepan; add the finely chopped fat salt pork (or unsmoked bacon), onion, carrots and celery and fry, stirring from time to time, until the meat browns. Stir in the minced beef and brown.
2 Add the lemon zest, bay leaf, tomato purée, beef stock and dry white wine to the pan. Season with salt, black pepper and freshly grated nutmeg to taste. Cover and simmer very gently for 30 minutes, stirring occasionally. Check the seasonings.
3 Remove the lemon zest and bay leaf from the sauce and simmer, uncovered, for a further 30 minutes, or until the sauce has slightly thickened. Stir in the thick cream and simmer for 2–3 minutes more.
4 Pour the sauce over the pasta and serve with Parmesan cheese.

Siciliano sauce

🍴 15 minutes

Serves 4
50 g /2 oz canned anchovy fillets in oil
olive oil
400 g /14 oz canned peeled tomatoes
120 ml /8 tbls finely chopped fresh parsley
1–2 garlic cloves, finely chopped
50 g /2 oz walnuts, chopped
125 g /4 oz button mushrooms, chopped
salt and freshly ground black pepper
For serving
500 g /1 lb pasta, freshly cooked
freshly grated Parmesan cheese

1 Drain the oil from the anchovies and make it up to 150 ml /5 fl oz with the olive oil. Pour this oil into a saucepan, add the anchovies and heat them gently, stirring and mashing until well blended.
2 Drain the tomatoes and chop them coarsely. Add them and the rest of the ingredients to the pan. Season with salt, if it is necessary (the anchovies will probably have made the sauce quite salty enough), and pepper to taste. Continue to stir until the sauce heats through, but do not let it boil.
3 Pour the sauce over pasta and serve with grated Parmesan cheese.

NOUVELLE CUISINE

In nouvelle cuisine the presentation of the dish is almost as important as its preparation. Serve sautéed chicken breasts garnished with mango and surrounded by a delicate lime sauce — tempting to eye and palate.

The French have created one of the world's most superb cuisines and have elevated cooking to a fine creative art. Their greatest dishes are classics, rising above nationality to become universal in their appeal. In traditional *haute cuisine* restaurants these dishes were prepared according to strict rules, originated by Carême and Escoffier, but now a whole new movement has swept the kitchens of France — *nouvelle cuisine*.

It began when the late Fernand Point (of La Pyramide, in Vienne) began experimenting with a lighter style of cooking bearing the adage 'make it simple'. André Guillot, author of *Ma Cuisine*, chef at the Auberge du Vieux Marly near Paris, and one of the most exciting chefs I have ever known, followed along the same lines as Point to create an even simpler cuisine. It enhanced the natural tastes of the ingredients, producing some supremely delicate sauces without adding a trace of flour, but by reducing meat essences, wines and stocks.

Today's nouvelle cuisine leaves plenty of room for the personality of the chef, and that applies as much to the creative amateur with a sense of adventure as it does to my colleagues within the profession.

Nouvelle cuisine principles
The first tenet of the new cuisine is an insistence on the best-quality ingredients. Gone are the days when the menu was settled in advance and the shopping done to fit the menu. Now the marketing is done first and the menus selected according to what is freshest and best.

Having chosen the materials, the new-style chefs then insist that everything is cooked for the absolute minimum amount of time so that the true flavours of the food come to the surface. There is no overseasoning of the sauces, no overpowering aromas from the food, and every dish must be as pleasing to the eye as its delicate flavours and crisp textures are to the taste buds and tongue. The chef works as an artist, combining and blending all he knows to produce the finished picture.

The nouvelle cuisine movement has its roots in the cuisines of past and present. From the cookery books of 17th- and 18th-century France comes the inspiration for lighter sauces. The ideas for garnishing are borrowed from the modern masters of Japanese cooking and arrangement. The ancient cuisine of China adds the concept of fast cooking and crisp textures. The whole brings to us — elegantly and almost magically — the true taste of food.

New sauces
With this new mode of cooking, gone are the complicated 'mother' sauces of the classic French kitchen. The word *roux* has been eliminated from cooking terminology.

Nouvelle cuisine sauces are thickened by reduction — a simple process of boiling the cooking liquids with wine and stock to concentrate and intensify the flavours. They are finished in various ways — butter or cream whipped in at the last moment is the simplest and commonest. A spoonful of Glace de viande (*page 22*), or Quick meat glaze (*page 21*) for ease, is a favourite way of adding extra flavour.

Gone are the days of thick coating sauces which disguised the food. Nouvelle cuisine sauces, particularly the opaque ones, are often served alongside the meat, fish and poultry or spooned onto the plate before the food to make a bed on which the central ingredient will nestle. Those sauces spooned over the food are so light and translucent that they act as a glaze and the true colour of the food shows through.

Methods of cooking
There are many different methods of cooking used in nouvelle cuisine, but these fall into two general categories. For fish, meat, poultry and whole vegetables the emphasis is on short cooking times, to retain the full flavour of quality produce and, in vegetables, the crispness of texture. When you are making sauces, the cooking time will be longer and the same applies to pâtés, mousses and vegetable purées where a complete smoothness of texture is the desired result.

Blanching and steaming are two methods of cooking which are frequently used with vegetables. To blanch vegetables, quickly submerge them in boiling, salted water so that they are briefly cooked but still crisp, with their colour and flavour preserved. This is a suitable preparation for vegetables which are to be served cold as a salad accompaniment. Steaming vegetables will cook them slightly more but the texture will still be crisp and the individuality of flavour and appearance of each vegetable will be retained in presentation, as in my recipe for Légumes panachés.

En papillote: again, this method of cooking ensures the maximum flavour of the ingredients. Literally 'cooking in a bag', the food, along with any herbs or other flavourings, are sealed into a container, made from foil or parchment paper for example, and cooked in the oven or submerged in boiling water. All the goodness and flavour is kept with the food, which is normally served in individual parcels (see page 96).

Sautéeing is a natural choice for the nouvelle cuisine cook. This is a traditional method of cooking in hot fat in a shallow pan; it is also a quick method, depending for success on the quality of the produce. I like to use unsalted butter as the main fat with a little oil added to reduce the risk of the butter burning. In nouvelle cuisine the pan juices from a sautéed dish are often used as the

basis for an accompanying sauce, adding colour and extra savour. This is why I prefer unsalted butter because it is less likely to leave the juices in the pan too salty to incorporate into a sauce.

Blending flavours
As I have said, using the pan juices will add extra savour to a sauce, but in nouvelle cuisine it is also paramount that the sauce should be free of any trace of burnt fats. If in any doubt, it is often safer to start the sauce from scratch using fresh butter in a clean pan. As a general rule there should only be a small amount of sauce to serve with each individual portion, 30–45 ml /2–3 tbls each is usually plenty.

The old custom of presenting fruit with meat has come back into favour and, if the fruit is slightly exotic, so much the better. It adds the pleasure of the unexpected to the already accepted pleasures of taste and visual aesthetics. A purée of fruit or vegetables often forms part of the accompanying sauce.

Presentation

Presentation is an integral part of a nouvelle cuisine dish. It is so important that in restaurants specializing in nouvelle cuisine most of the dishes are prepared as individual servings by the chef, so that he has complete control over the appearance of the food when it reaches the diner.

In domestic terms, serving individual portions removes all the trauma of carving in front of your guests and of trying to keep the dish hot while you serve everybody at the table. You can now prepare each individual serving in the privacy of the kitchen and bring it to the table piping hot.

Arrangements are delicate and precise, after the style of the Japanese. A professional will not hesitate to use his (washed) fingers to arrange the food on the plate and will carefully wipe away any stray drops of sauce from the side of the plate with absorbent paper. Portions are small and the dish is never crowded.

Vegetables can play an important part in the presentation of nouvelle cuisine food. They may be served as a delicate garnish to the main dish, shaped or moulded and carefully arranged, or they may be served as a separate dish to accompany the main course. But gone are the days when you served a heap of tumbled greens on a plate with the prime purpose of nourishment. Now the colour and shape of the vegetables, as well as their flavour and texture, are used to tempt the eye as well as the palate.

Certain vegetables such as mange tout need no special preparation, their shapes being small and regular anyway. Green beans need only trimming into even lengths, broccoli and cauliflower cutting into natural florets. But other vegetables are more clumsy to look at, their shapes are irregular and they may be large. These are cut and shaped to look as attractive as possible on the plate. They may be served as a delicate garnish to the meat: cut into flower shapes, tiny batons or olives

Chicken breast with mango

or puréed and set into small moulds. Occasionally a julienne of mixed vegetables may be served, poached for minutes only to a light, crisp texture and arranged on the plate alongside the main dish.

Or an attractive method of presentation is to 'turn' the vegetables. Carve firmer vegetables with a sharp knife into regular oval shapes, about 25 mm /1 in long and 15–20 mm /½–¾ in wide at the middle. This way several different vegetables can be cut to the same shape for a dish, or various vegetables can be cut to contrasting shapes to lie alongside each other. Remember that vegetable accompaniments to nouvelle cuisine sautés should be simple plain dishes that do not clash with the carefully blended flavours of the main dish.

The same principles of presentation, and indeed preparation, can be applied to nouvelle cuisine desserts. Again, the key word is 'purity'; do not smother flavours or textures with mounds of cream or sweet sauces — although both are still used in moderation.

Chicken breast with mango

⏱ 35 minutes

Serves 4

4 × 125 g /4 oz boneless chicken breasts, skinned
60 ml /4 tbls sesame seeds
salt and freshly ground black pepper
50 g /2 oz butter
30 ml /2 tbls olive oil
1 mango
juice of 2 limes
30 ml /2 tbls chicken stock, home-made or from a cube
150 ml /5 fl oz thick cream

1 Lay the sesame seeds in a flat container and season them with salt and pepper.
2 Lay the chicken breasts flat on the sesame seeds and turn them to coat them evenly with seeds on both sides.
3 In a large frying-pan, heat 25 g /1 oz butter and the olive oil. Add the chicken breasts and sauté them over a high heat for 4 minutes, or until the chicken is tender but still moist, turning once during cooking.
4 Meanwhile peel the skin from the mango and cut it into 16 thin segments.
5 Remove the chicken breasts from the pan and keep them warm. Add the remaining butter to the pan. Sauté the mango segments until they are soft but not coloured. Remove them with a slotted spoon and keep warm, while you prepare the sauce.
6 Add the lime juice and the stock to the pan and simmer until reduced to half the original quantity. Stir in the thick cream, bring to the boil and season with salt and freshly ground black pepper.
7 Spoon a helping of sauce onto each of 4 individual heated serving plates. Place a chicken breast in the centre of each plate and garnish the top of each with a spray of sautéed mango segments.

French fish terrine

 1¾ hours

Serves 6 or more

*600 ml /1 pt or 1 lb mussels, scrubbed and
cleaned*
500 g /1 lb pike, sole or turbot fillet
3 egg whites
2.5 ml /½ tsp salt
freshly ground white pepper
350 ml /12 fl oz thick cream
butter, for greasing
1 green pepper, diced
*12 spinach leaves, trimmed, blanched and
dried*
100 g /4 oz cooked prawns, shelled
6 sprigs of dill, to garnish

For the French tomato sauce

25 g /1 oz butter
25 g /1 oz ham, finely chopped
½ Spanish onion, finely chopped
1 celery stick, finely chopped
30 ml /2 tbls flour
*300–425 ml /10–15 fl oz hot beef stock,
home-made or from a cube*
400 g /14 oz canned peeled tomatoes
5 ml /1 tsp tomato purée
2.5 ml /½ tsp sugar
1 bouquet garni
salt and freshly ground black pepper

1 Heat the oven to 150C /300F /gas 2.
2 Put the mussels with 5 mm /¼ in water in a heavy-based saucepan with a tight-fitting lid. Cover and cook over a high heat, shaking the pan frequently, for about 5 minutes or until the mussels open. Discard any that remain closed. Leave them to cool a little, then remove them from their shells and blot them on absorbent paper.

3 To make the fish *mousseline*, pat the pike or other fish dry with absorbent paper. Put it through the finest blade of a mincer 3 times.

4 In a medium-sized bowl, mix the minced fish and the unbeaten egg whites until well blended. Place the bowl over a large bowl of crushed ice, add the salt and season with freshly ground white pepper to taste. Work the mixture well with a wooden spoon: the salt will make the fish stiffen and change in its consistency. When stiffened, add the thick cream, a little at a time, working the paste gently.

5 To assemble the terrine, line the base of a 1.2 L /2¼ pt loaf tin with greaseproof paper. Lightly butter the paper and tin sides. Divide the fish mousseline among 3 bowls. Fold half the diced green pepper into the first bowl of mousseline. Spread it evenly over the base of the tin. Arrange 6 spinach leaves over the mousseline and green pepper layer, ensuring that they show at the edges. Arrange half the mussels on the spinach leaves. Fold the prawns into the second bowl of mousseline. Spread the mixture over the mussels. Over this layer, arrange the remaining mussels, then the remaining spinach leaves. Fold the

French fish terrine

remaining diced green pepper into the third bowl of mousseline and spread this evenly over the spinach leaves as a final layer.

6 Cover with buttered greaseproof paper. Place the terrine in a baking tin and pour boiling water into the tin to a depth of 25 mm /1 in. Bake for 1 hour.

7 Meanwhile, make the French tomato sauce. Melt the butter in a thick-bottomed saucepan. Add the finely chopped ham, onion and celery and sauté gently for about 10 minutes, until the onion is soft and transparent but not brown.

8 Sprinkle the flour into the pan and stir over a low heat for a further 1–2 minutes.

9 Remove the pan from the heat and gradually stir in 300 ml /10 fl oz boiling beef stock. Add the canned tomatoes and their juice, the tomato purée, sugar, bouquet garni and salt and freshly ground black pepper to taste.

10 Return the pan to the heat and bring the mixture to the boil, stirring constantly. Simmer, uncovered, for about 30 minutes, stirring occasionally, until the sauce is thick and smooth. If the sauce seems to be getting too thick, add a little more hot beef stock.

11 Strain the sauce through a fine sieve into a clean pan, pressing the vegetables firmly with a wooden spoon to extract all their juices. Taste the sauce and adjust the seasoning, if necessary. Reheat gently and then keep warm.

12 To serve, carefully invert the terrine and cut 6 slices. Spoon the hot French tomato sauce onto individual heated serving plates and place a slice of terrine on top. Garnish with sprigs of dill and serve.

Légumes panachés

The name means, literally, 'stylish vegetables', but they are only stylish if they are put into the steamer in the order given!

 40 minutes

Serves 4
2–3 large carrots
2–3 thin courgettes
75 g /3 oz green beans
salt
125 g /4 oz tiny new potatoes, scraped
50 g /2 oz tiny new turnips, about 25 mm /
   1 in in diameter
50 g /2 oz mange tout
50 g /2 oz broccoli florets
freshly ground black pepper

1 Using a sharp knife, 'turn' the carrots and courgettes by carving them into smooth olive shapes, about 25 mm /1 in long. Leave the green skin on the outside of the turned courgettes. When prepared, there should be 75 g /3 oz carrots and 50 g /2 oz courgettes.
2 Cut the green beans into even, 5 cm /2 in lengths.
3 Half fill the base of a steamer with salted water and bring it to the boil. Place the new potatoes in the top part of the steamer, cover and steam for 8 minutes.
4 Add the turned carrots, cover and steam for 1 minute.
5 Add the turnips to the top part of the steamer, cover and steam for 30 seconds.

Légumes panachés

6 Add the green beans, mange tout and broccoli florets, cover and steam for 1½ minutes.
7 Finally add the courgettes, cover and steam for a further 2 minutes. Check all the vegetables; they should all be cooked through but still *al dente* — slightly crisp to the bite.
8 Arrange a selection of the vegetables on each of 4 heated, individual serving plates. Season with salt and freshly ground black pepper. Serve them immediately as a side dish accompaniment for a meat or fish main course.

Melon rings with fresh fruit salad

40 minutes, plus
2 hours chilling

Serves 4
juice of 1 lemon and 1 lime
1 small honeydew melon
1 small bunch white grapes
2 bananas
2 ripe peaches
15–30 ml /1–2 tbls caster sugar
4 sprigs of fresh mint

1 Combine the lemon and lime juice in a large bowl.
2 Cut the melon in half widthways and carefully scoop out the seeds with a metal spoon. Cut two 25 mm /1 in thick rings from each melon half and cut off the skin. Brush the melon slices all over with lemon and lime juice to preserve the colour, and wrap them in cling film. Chill in the refrigerator until ready to serve. Reserve the remaining melon for another recipe.
3 Peel the grapes, cut them in half and remove the seeds with the point of a sharp knife. Place the grape halves in a bowl and toss with a little of the lemon and lime juice. Chill.
4 Peel the bananas and slice them into the bowl with the remaining lemon and lime juice mixture. Toss them to preserve their colour.
5 To peel the peaches, place them in a sieve and pour boiling water over them, until the skins are loosened. Now hold each peach in a soft cloth to protect your fingers, and peel. Cut each peach in half and remove the stones. Slice into wedges and place in the bowl with the banana slices. Add sugar to taste, and toss the fruit in it, gently. Chill for 2 hours.
6 When ready to serve, remove the cling film from the melon rings and place one ring on each of 4 dessert plates. Spoon the prepared banana and peaches into each ring, mounding the fruit up in the centre. Garnish each serving of fruit salad with grape halves, and place a sprig of fresh mint beside each melon ring.

Melon rings with fresh fruit salad

TEMPURA

Tempura is a Japanese speciality which has become famous worldwide without losing any of its original Oriental flavour. Discover in this chapter how to make and use this light-as-air batter.

The Japanese have a way of turning the simplest food into an exotic adventure. Tempura menus are based primarily on seafood — slices of fish, prawns, crab, cuttlefish and any of the other numerous foods from the Japanese coastal waters. Vegetables are included in abundance, plus a little meat, usually chicken. Every ingredient is dipped in tempura batter and deep-fried to a pale gold. The succulent morsels are then served with a savoury dipping sauce and a dressing that includes grated *daikon*, the giant Japanese white radish.

Good tempura is so important to the Japanese that most ordinary restaurants in Japan do not serve it. This deep-fried delight is left for speciality restaurants where the chef and staff are geared to serving the batter-dipped food straight from the hot oil. By the same token do not expect to serve tempura dishes as part of an ordinary dinner party; you will have to make a feature party of them as you would a fondue or a barbecue.

Ingredients

Tempura food should always be very fresh. In Japan the shellfish, as well as the fish, would be raw. As it is sometimes difficult to buy raw prawns I have compromised by using cooked ones but if you can get raw prawns, so much the better. Vegetables, too, should be really fresh and in the best possible condition, so choose your tempura ingredients by the season and buy what is best in the shops.

For the dipping sauce you will need some special ingredients from a Japanese shop. The most important of these is instant *dashi* powder. Dashi is a strong fish stock made from dried bonito fish and seaweed; it forms the basis of many sauces and soups in Japanese cooking and provides the characteristic flavour for the sauce served with tempura. Making your own dashi is a long, complicated process so take the easy way out and buy instant dashi powder which you reconstitute with hot water. If you cannot buy dashi, you can substitute a strong chicken stock, although the superb fishy flavour will be lost.

You will also need soy sauce. There are many types of soy sauce but the Japanese variety has quite a different flavour from the Chinese or European and should be used for preference; however, it is expensive.

By way of special vegetables you will need daikon and fresh root ginger. Daikon (also known as mooli) has a strong, hot taste and is always included in tempura menus because it contrasts so well with the mild flavour of the fried food; the Japanese also believe it aids the digestion.

Tempura batter

The typical batter used for tempura is very different from the traditional batter most of us are used to. It is much lighter than the batters used for deep-frying in the West; the ingredients are combined just before frying and then they are mixed very lightly. Ideally the batter should be mixed with chopsticks; this will leave you with a batter that does not look properly mixed — which is exactly what you want. There should still be the traces of unmixed flour round the bowl and on top of the batter. Never leave the batter standing, mix it in small batches as you cook the food.

Frying oil

Tempura restaurants use a frying oil specially composed to give the best results; it is a vegetable oil not too highly refined, mixed with up to 50 per cent sesame seed oil. Buying special tempura oil outside Japan is prohibitively expensive so I use ordinary vegetable oil, but make sure that the oil you use is fresh and clean.

Preparation and cooking

Most tempura foods are cut into bite-sized pieces before cooking. Some will be cut decoratively — for example prawns may be 'butterflied' and vegetables may be cut into flower shapes. Prepare all the ingredients before you start to cook and arrange them on a tray beside your cooking area.

In Japan a tempura *nabe* is used for frying. This is a large *wok* with a draining shelf attached to one side. The food is fried quickly, lifted from the oil and placed on the

shelf to drain while the next batch of food is cooked. But there is no need to buy special implements. Use your normal deep-fat frier with a frying basket and place a wire rack next to it; line the rack with absorbent paper and replenish it as necessary.

The food must be fried, served and eaten as quickly as possible. It is not possible to cook everything in the privacy of the kitchen, keep it hot and serve it as you normally would for a dinner party. Therefore arrange your cooking area close to the eating area and then serve your guests in turn as you cook. Arrange a sort of production line so that you can cook the food and serve it efficiently.

Have all of your prepared ingredients arranged in groups on a tray, according to the length of cooking time required for each type of food (see the chart). Have a bowl ready for

Tempura cooking times

Cook only one portion at a time

Ingredient	Time in minutes
Sweet potato, sliced 5 mm /1/4 in thick	4½
Asparagus tips	3
Carrots, sliced 3 mm /1/8 in thick	2½
Green pepper rings	2
Aubergines, sliced 5 mm /1/4 in thick	1½
Courgettes, sliced 5 mm /1/4 in thick	1½
Green beans, 5 cm /2 in long	1½
Onions, sections	1½
Prawns, cooked	1½
Squid, 25 mm /1 in squares	1½
Chervil, bunch	1
Fish strips	1
Mange tout, whole	1
Mushrooms, quartered	1
Onion rings	1
Scallops, sliced	1
Spring onions	1

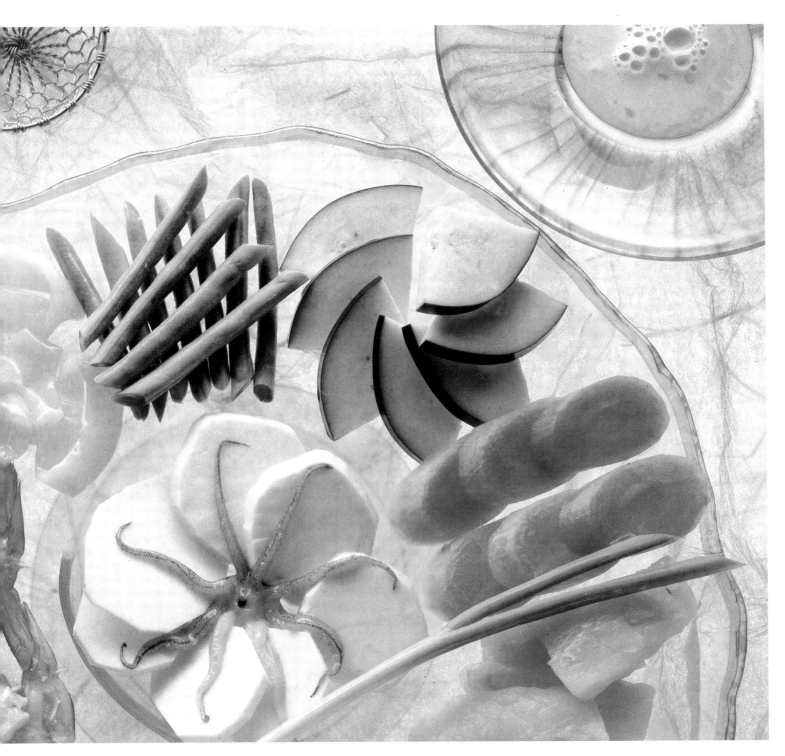

mixing the batter, with the measured ingredients for the batter to hand. Place the paper-lined draining rack on the other side of the deep-fat frier and put the serving plates to warm.

Prepare the bowls of dipping sauce and daikon dressing and place them on the table. Heat the oil to the right temperature. When your guests are ready to eat, mix the first batch of batter and start to cook a portion for one person. Using chopsticks or two forks, take a piece of food and dip it into the batter. Let the excess drain off, then drop the food in the hot oil. Start with the food requiring the longest cooking and time carefully, adding quick-cooking items at the last moment. When the batter is a pale gold colour and the food inside cooked but still crisp, lift out all the pieces with the frying basket and drain on the paper-covered rack.

Presentation
In any Japanese meal each dish is an artistic composition in itself. The plates, the shapes and colours of the food and the way it is arranged are as important as the taste. Tempura is no exception. Choose the plates carefully in a colour to complement the golden colour of the fried food. As soon as you have cooked a single portion, arrange the different pieces carefully on the plate and serve it at once, carrying on cooking for the next person as quickly as possible.

Cooking times
The recipes in this chapter are for tempura menus with accurate cooking times for each portion. But you may wish to vary the ingredients according to what is best in the shops, and to help you judge the cooking times, use the chart on the opposite page.

Carefully prepared ingredients for Seafood tempura

Basic tempura batter

5 minutes

Makes 425 ml /15 fl oz
2 eggs
75 g /3 oz flour

1 Put the eggs in a bowl with 215 ml /7½ fl oz cold water and beat until frothy.
2 Add the flour, unsifted, and beat (preferably with chopsticks) until just blended. Take care not to overbeat.

Tempura dipping sauce

 7 minutes

Serves 4
10 ml /2 tsp instant dashi powder
300 ml /10 fl oz boiling water
60 ml /4 tbls soy sauce
60 ml /4 tbls sake
2.5 ml /½ tsp sugar
a pinch of ground ginger

1 Put the dashi powder in a pan and pour the boiling water onto it. Stir until dissolved. Stir in the remaining ingredients.
2 Place the pan over a medium heat and bring to the boil; simmer for 5 minutes and then remove from the heat.
3 Divide the sauce among 4 heated bowls and put one bowl before each guest.

Soy tempura batter

 5 minutes

Makes 425 ml /15 fl oz
1 egg
15 ml /1 tbls soy sauce
125 g /4 oz flour

1 In a medium-sized bowl, whisk together the egg, soy sauce and 225 ml /8 fl oz water until smooth.
2 Gradually sift in the flour and beat lightly, with chopsticks, until it is just blended. Take care not to overbeat.

Vegetable tempura

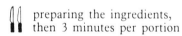 preparing the ingredients, then 3 minutes per portion

Serves 4
½ aubergine, halved lengthways
salt
1 carrot
6 green beans
8 mushrooms
½ Spanish onion
8 mange tout
4 asparagus tips
Tempura dipping sauce (see recipe)
Daikon dressing (see recipe)
oil, for deep frying
850 ml /1½ pt Basic tempura batter (see recipe), unmixed

1 Slice the half aubergine lengthways into 4 slices, discarding the end; cut each slice into quarters. Put the pieces into a colander and sprinkle with salt. Leave to drain for 30 minutes. Rinse the slices under cold water and dry well with absorbent paper.
2 Cut 16 rounds 3 mm /⅛ in thick from the carrot. Cut the green beans in half and trim them to even 5 cm /2 in lengths. Quarter the mushrooms. Slice the onion 6 mm /¼ in thick and open out into rings.

Trim the mange tout. Arrange the prepared vegetables and the asparagus tips on a tray next to the cooking area.
3 Prepare the dipping sauce and daikon dressing and place a bowl before each guest.
4 Heat the oil in a deep-fat frier to 180C / 350F.
5 When your guests are ready to eat, prepare 425 ml/15 fl oz of the basic tempura batter. Prepare one portion as follows: using chopsticks or 2 forks, dip 1 asparagus tip in batter and drop it in the hot oil; fry for 30 seconds. Dip 4 carrot rings in batter and drop into the hot oil; fry for 1 minute. Dip 3 pieces of green bean and 2 pieces of aubergine in batter and drop them in the hot oil;

fry for 30 seconds. Dip 2 quartered mushrooms, 3 onion rings and 2 mange tout in batter and add to the oil. When all the vegetables are in the oil, fry for 1 minute.
6 Remove the cooked vegetables from the oil with a frying basket and drain on a paper-covered wire rack.
7 Arrange the vegetables in groups on a heated plate and serve immediately, then continue cooking the remaining portions. Make up the second batch of batter when the first one is used up or if it starts to look gluey.
8 Each guest eats his or her portion as it is served, dipping the food in the sauce and the dressing with chopsticks.

Daikon dressing

🍴 10 minutes

Serves 4
1 daikon (mooli)
1 piece of fresh root ginger

1 Trim the daikon and grate it finely. Peel the ginger and grate it into the grated daikon to taste.
2 Divide the Daikon dressing among four small serving bowls and place one before each guest.

Curried chicken tempura

🍴 preparing the ingredients, then 3–4 minutes per portion

Serves 4
24 chicken wings
Tempura dipping sauce (see recipe)
Daikon dressing (see recipe)
oil, for deep frying
½ beaten egg
90 ml /6 tbls cornflour
90 ml /6 tbls flour
5 ml /1 tsp salt
10 ml /2 tsp sugar
10 ml /2 tsp curry powder

1 Cut the chicken wings off at the first joint and use just the first large section (the wing tips and centre sections can be used for making stock).
2 With a sharp knife, cut the meat from the bone from the narrow end of each portion, leaving the meat attached to the bone at the wide end. Dry the wings on absorbent paper, then place them on a tray next to the cooking area.
3 Prepare the dipping sauce and the daikon dressing and place a bowl before each guest. Heat the oil in a deep-fat frier to 180C / 350F.
4 In a small bowl, combine the beaten egg, 150 ml /5 fl oz water, the cornflour, flour, salt, sugar and curry powder. Mix with chopsticks or 2 forks until just blended.
5 Hold a chicken piece by the bone and dip it into the batter, drain it briefly then put it into the hot oil. Repeat with 5 more pieces. Cook for 3–4 minutes until a pale golden brown, turning several times to ensure they are thoroughly cooked. Lift out with a slotted spoon and drain briefly on the paper-covered wire rack.
6 Arrange the cooked chicken wings on an individual heated plate and serve at once, then continue to cook the remaining portions in the same way. Each guest starts to eat as soon as the portion is ready, dipping it in the sauce and the dressing to his or her own individual taste.

● If you prefer the plain batter to one with a curry flavour, marinate the chicken wings first. To make the marinade, combine 5 ml / 1 tsp grated horseradish, 5 ml /1 tsp dry mustard, a pinch of ground ginger and 15 ml /1 tbls rice vinegar. Mix them to a smooth paste, then stir in 15 ml /1 tbls vegetable oil and 150 ml /5 fl oz soy sauce. Add the chicken wings, toss to coat well, then leave to marinate for 2 hours. Drain the chicken wings, dip them in batter and fry them as described above.
● The Japanese radish, *daikon*, sold as mooli in Europe, is used in the dressing served with this dish. It is milder than the more common red radish and has a less peppery taste. If you are unable to buy *daikon*, you will find that turnip is the best substitute for it.

Vegetable tempura

Seafood tempura

🍴 preparing the ingredients, then 4½ minutes per portion

Serves 4
1 aubergine
salt
8 large prawns
4 small squid
500 g /1 lb haddock fillet
1 sweet potato, weighing about 225 g /8 oz
1 carrot
4 green beans
4 spring onions
Tempura dipping sauce (see recipe)
Daikon dressing (see recipe)
oil, for deep frying
850 ml /1½ pt Basic tempura batter (see recipe), unmixed

1 Cut the aubergine lengthways into 8 slices, 6 mm /¼ in thick, discarding the end slices which are mostly skin. Cut each slice into quarters. Put the slices into a colander, sprinkle with salt and leave to drain for 30 minutes. Rinse the slices and dry them well on absorbent paper.
2 Shell the prawns if necessary. Interlink them head to tail in pairs to make a circle; secure each pair with a cocktail stick.
3 Clean the squid, removing the blade and the dark external membrane. Cut the flesh into rings or 25 mm /1 in squares.
4 Skin the haddock and cut the flesh across into 16 fingers.
5 Peel the sweet potato and cut 8 slices, 6 mm /¼ in thick. Peel the carrot and slice into 3 mm /⅛ in rings. Halve the green beans and trim to even 5 cm /2 in lengths.
6 Arrange the fish, prepared vegetables and spring onions on a tray next to the cooking area. Prepare the dipping sauce and daikon dressing and place a bowl of each before each guest.
7 Heat the oil in a deep-fat frier to 180C / 350F.
8 When your guests are ready to eat, mix 425 ml /15 fl oz of the basic tempura batter and fry one portion as follows: with chopsticks or two forks, dip 2 slices of the sweet potato in the batter and drop them into the hot oil; fry for 2 minutes. Dip 2 carrot rings in batter and drop them in the hot oil; fry for 1 minute. Dip 2 lengths of green beans, 8 aubergine pieces, a quarter of the squid rings and 2 prawns in the batter, and drop them in the hot oil; fry for 30 seconds. Dip 4 haddock fingers and 1 spring onion in the batter and add to the oil.
9 When all the ingredients are in the oil, fry for 1 minute longer, then remove them all at once with the frying basket and drain them on absorbent paper on a wire rack.
10 Arrange the fried portion on a heated plate and serve immediately. Then cook the remaining portions in the same way, making up the remaining batter when the first batch runs out, or when the batter starts to look gluey in consistency.
11 Each guest should start to eat his or her portion as soon as they are served, dipping the fried food into the sauce and the daikon dressing according to taste.

COOKING EN PAPILLOTE

A papillote is a case — made of paper or, these days, foil or a roaster bag — in which an individual serving of meat, poultry, fish or vegetables is cooked, thereby preserving all its savoury goodness, flavour and aroma.

Cooking *en papillote* is one of the great French cooking techniques of the early 19th century. It is, literally, 'cooking in a bag'. Originally the papillotes were made of paper, cut into heart shapes or ovals and brushed on both sides with melted butter or oil. They were used to enclose the food and were then fried in oil to puff them up before being baked in the oven to cook the enclosed food.

Today, cooks use foil and roaster bags to make this cooking technique work its wonders without fuss and bother.

There is an element of surprise, too, for your dinner guests. Serve papillotes straight from the oven, and let everyone unfold or cut them open at the table with a knife. Or you can open the papillotes a little and pop a garnishing sprig of watercress in the opening.

Cooking meat and fish en papillote

Meat and fish to be cooked en papillote are first sealed in a little hot oil or butter to give them colour and flavour. They are then seasoned and wrapped in foil or oiled grease-proof or parchment paper, or placed in a roaster bag. Sometimes herbs and vegetables, or other flavouring ingredients, are added to the packages before they are cooked.

During cooking, the ingredients simmer in their own juices, which are all inside the tightly sealed papillotes. When you come to unwrap them, you'll be surprised at the abundance of rich juices that will have collected in the bottom of each papillote.

Island paper-wrapped beef garnished with spring onion 'flowers'

Cooking vegetables en papillote

Instead of drawing out all the flavour of your vegetables into the cooking liquid and then discarding it, seal the flavour inside the vegetables by cooking them, in individual portions, in little foil wrappings.

The vegetables are blanched, seasoned with salt and pepper, flavoured with herbs and then beef or chicken stock enriched with butter. Next they are wrapped securely with foil. If you have other papillotes or the Sunday roast in the oven, the vegetables en papillote can be slipped in next to these. If you do not want to use the oven, you can simmer tightly sealed foil parcels in a pan of gently boiling water; not a drop of water need enter the parcels once they are sealed. Whichever way you choose, the flavour and sweetness of the vegetables will be totally unimpaired.

How to make papillotes

Foil: the development of foil for home use has led to one of the most intriguing mini-revolutions in the kitchen, yet a generation later a surprisingly large number of otherwise innovative cooks still seem unaware of its full potential. It is the ideal material to use in conjunction with food because it is moisture-proof, greaseproof, odourless, non-flammable and totally impervious to dust and dirt. It can be moulded quickly and easily into any conceivable shape and is therefore ideal for making papillotes.

Always cut foil into heart shapes, ovals or squares large enough to enclose the food completely but loosely. It is safest to cut the foil generously rather than skimpily — there is nothing more irritating than to find that the ends of the foil will not meet around the food or that you have to wrap it so tightly that you puncture the piece of foil with a protruding drumstick or sharp bone. And even if you do make the ends of a skimpy sheet meet, you will be in trouble again when you come to unwrap the parcel; the foil is likely to break and all the delicious juices you intended trapping inside the parcel will spill out into the baking tin. By using a good-sized piece of foil you will avoid these disasters, and — with the food enclosed in its loose wrapping — the heat is able to circulate freely inside, thus ensuring that the food cooks evenly.

Paper or parchment: greaseproof or baking parchment paper is cut into a heart shape or oval large enough to enclose the food and leave extra paper around the edge to fold up to seal.

The food is lightly sautéed and placed on one half of the lightly oiled or buttered paper shape. The other half of the paper shape is folded over to cover the food and the edges are then folded up together to make a tight seal.

Usually the packages are fried in hot oil for a minute or two to puff up the papillotes. They are then baked in the oven at 190C / 375F /gas 5, and the papillotes keep their puffed-up shape while the food is cooking.

Roaster bags should be floured before the food is put inside them. The filled and sealed roaster bag is then placed in a roasting tin, and 1 or 2 tiny holes are made in the bag, on the top, to prevent it exploding.

Island paper-wrapped beef

 45 minutes

Serves 4–5

500 g /1 lb sirloin steak
30 ml /2 tbls sake (or dry sherry)
45 ml /3 tbls soy sauce
15 ml /1 tbls cornflour
1 Spanish onion, finely chopped
oiled greaseproof paper
oil, for deep frying
spring onion 'flowers', to garnish

1 Slice the beef thinly across the grain discarding any fat or gristle. In a small bowl, combine the sake (or dry sherry), soy sauce, cornflour and finely chopped onion. Add the beef, toss to coat well and leave to marinate for 10–15 minutes, stirring from time to time.
2 Cut 20 or 24 10 cm /4 in squares of oiled greaseproof paper. Divide the marinated beef among them and then fold securely into little packets.
3 Heat the oil in a deep-fat frier to 180C / 350F, when a day-old cube of bread takes 60 seconds to go golden brown and crisp. Deep-fry the packets in 2 batches for 2 minutes and serve very hot, still in their paper packets.

Foil-baked broad beans and lettuce

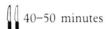 40–50 minutes

Serves 4–6

450 g /1 lb fresh or frozen shelled broad beans
12 tiny button onions
1 small or ½ large head lettuce
50 g /2 oz butter
2.5 ml /½ tsp crumbled savory or thyme
1.5 ml /¼ tsp caster sugar
salt and freshly ground black pepper
60 ml /4 tbls beef stock
a dash of Worcestershire sauce
a dash of soy sauce

1 Heat the oven to 190C /375 F /gas 5. If you are using fresh broad beans, remove the skins from any beans that are large and tough. Peel the button onions, place them in a saucepan with cold water to cover and bring them to the boil. Drain.
2 Wash the lettuce and drain it thoroughly. Cut the lettuce into strips, about 10 mm / ½ in wide.
3 Melt the butter and sauté the blanched button onions until golden brown. Add the broad beans, cover the pan and sauté for 2 minutes if you are using frozen broad beans and 5–6 minutes if you are using fresh beans. Remove the pan from the heat.
4 Add the shredded lettuce to the pan, the savory or thyme, sugar and salt and freshly ground black pepper to taste. Moisten with the stock, Worcestershire sauce and soy sauce.

5 Cut 4–6 pieces of double thickness foil, large enough to hold one-quarter or one-sixth of the mixture. Divide the vegetable mixture among the foil pieces. Seal the foil packets neatly and securely and place them on a baking tray, join upwards. Cook in the oven for 5–10 minutes if you are using frozen broad beans and 20 minutes if you are using fresh beans.
6 Serve the vegetables immediately, in their packets.

Sole en papillote

 1 hour

Serves 4

4 lemon sole, filleted into 16 and skin removed
25 g /1 oz flour
salt
freshly ground black pepper
25 g /1 oz butter
15 ml /1 tbls olive oil, plus extra for greasing
25 g /1 oz mushrooms, thinly sliced
50 g /2 oz boiled peeled prawns, defrosted if necessary and well drained
150 g /5 oz jar cockles, drained
1 garlic clove, finely chopped
15 ml /1 tbls finely chopped fresh parsley
150 ml /5 fl oz dry white wine
150 ml /5 fl oz thick cream
4 sprigs of watercress, or flat-leaved parsley, to garnish

1 Heat the oven to 170C /325F/ gas 3.
2 Sprinkle the flour on a plate and season it well with salt and freshly ground black pepper. Coat the sole fillets with the seasoned flour. Heat the butter and olive oil in a large frying-pan. When the foaming subsides, add 4 sole fillets and fry them for 30 seconds on each side. Remove them from the pan with a fish slice and drain on absorbent paper and keep them warm. Repeat, 4 at a time, with the remaining fillets until they are all cooked.
3 Add to the fat remaining in the pan the mushrooms, drained prawns, drained cockles, finely chopped garlic, parsley and dry white wine. Bring to the boil and boil for about 5 minutes, until the liquid is reduced to about half its original quantity.
4 Add the thick cream, season to taste with salt and freshly ground black pepper, lower the heat and simmer gently for about 10 minutes.
5 Cut 4 pieces of foil, each large enough to envelop 4 fish fillets completely. Brush one side of each piece of foil with oil and place 4 fillets on each. Spoon some of the mushroom-prawn-cockle mixture onto each fillet and divide the sauce among the parcels. Fold the foil over the fish and seal the edges securely and neatly by rolling them in on themselves.
6 Place the papillotes, folded side up, in an ovenproof dish. Bake them in the oven for 10–15 minutes.
7 Arrange the foil packets on a serving dish, open each one a little and poke a sprig of watercress or parsley into the opening. Serve immediately.

CHINESE STEAMING

Steaming food in the Oriental manner not only saves time and fuel, but also produces food with a special flavour and tenderness, so take a tip from the Chinese and try this method of cooking meat, vegetables and rice.

The Chinese method of steaming food produces delicately flavoured meat and vegetables or minced food in parcels which is eaten with a pungent sauce, such as soy.

Types of steamer

The Chinese use bamboo baskets to steam all manner of food, which is either placed straight in the basket or, in the case of food with sauce, in a dish in the basket. Sometimes several baskets containing different foods are stacked up on one pan; the steam filters through the baskets and the various foods so that several dishes can be steamed at once. Put the food needing the most cooking at the bottom nearest the steam and the ingredients needing the least cooking at the top — using this method saves both time and fuel.

Although the bamboo basket is the traditional Chinese steamer, you will often find that in the restaurants stainless steel or aluminium steamers are used which consist of steamer pots, perforated metal steamer baskets and tightly-fitting lids. These are much easier to keep clean. Alternatively you can use either a trivet which will stand in or hook over the side of a large saucepan or flameproof casserole, or a wok if you possess one. Or use an expanding metal basket with a perforated bottom made of interleaving panels; this will stand above the water and is designed to fit saucepans of varying sizes.

Cooking in a steamer

Fill the saucepan with water to come 5 cm / 2 in below the steamer basket, bring to a rolling boil, put the steamer basket on top, cover with the lid and steam over rapidly boiling water for the time stated in the recipe. A very strongly flavoured bouillon or

Bamboo steamer baskets can be stacked over one saucepan; the metal steamer (front left) stands inside the saucepan

tock, flavoured with soy sauce, ginger, spring onions and garlic, is sometimes used in place of the boiling water to create a more fragrant steam.

The food for steaming can either be placed directly on the floor of the basket or in a dish in the steamer basket. Whole pieces of fish, poultry and meat or minced food wrapped up in parcels can be cooked on the floor of the baskets. The little parcels can have wrappings of lettuce or spinach leaves, or *won ton* pastry (a paper-thin pastry, available from Chinese supermarkets, which becomes almost translucent when steamed), while rice can be wrapped in a lotus leaf. (Lotus leaves are also available from Chinese supermarkets.)

Another very popular steamed food, especially in the Cantonese region of China, is *dim sum* — sweet and savoury stuffed dumplings. Finely chopped meat or vegetables or sweet paste can all be wrapped in dough. *Dim sum* are frequently eaten as a snack between meals or served as a savoury or light luncheon.

Placing food directly on the floor of the basket allows condensation from the steam and the excess juices from the food to drain into the pan of boiling liquid below. This prevents the food becoming too wet or soggy.

If you are cooking food in a sauce, place it in a gratin or other heatproof dish and put this dish in the steamer basket. The sauce gains liquid from the condensed steam, which drips into it from the underside of the lid.

Rice is steamed without a dish, but on a wet towel or napkin so that it does not fall through the holes of the steamer basket. Food wrapped in spinach or lettuce leaves, or in thin *won ton* pastry, can be placed on top of the rice while it is steaming. The juices of the wrapped food will flavour the rice as it cooks.

The rules for steaming

1 When improvizing a steamer, the cooking pot should be large enough to hold comfortably the stand and the dish containing the food. Ideally its diameter will be 25 mm–5 cm /1–2 in larger than that of the dish so that steam can circulate and reach all the food.

2 If you are using a dish, heat it. Place the food in the hot dish and put it in the pan or steamer basket only when the water is boiling rapidly and the steam rising. To cook, immediately cover the pan with a tightly fitting lid and turn up the heat so that the steam is at its height.

3 Food cooks quickly by steaming so keep your eye on it to make sure you catch it when it is just cooked. All meat — except pork, which must be well done — should be a little pink inside when removed from the steamer. Vegetables should be slightly crisp.

4 Because of the intense heat the food absorbs during the steaming, the cooking process continues even when it has been removed from the heat. Therefore steamed food should be served at the moment it is considered cooked, otherwise it will be overdone. Steam-cooked food to be served cold should be cooled as quickly as possible to stop the cooking process.

Chinese steamed rice

Rice is a staple food for the Chinese and is served at nearly every meal. Steamed rice has a slightly unusual but very pleasant loose-grained texture.

 45 minutes

Serves 4
1 Chinese bowl of rice
700 ml /1¼ pt boiling water

1 Place the rice in a sieve. Wash the rice under cold running water, rubbing the grains between the fingers. Rinse until the water runs clear, then drain it well.
2 Put the rice in a large saucepan and pour in the boiling water. Bring to the boil and boil for 10 minutes, then drain.
3 Place the rice on a wet tea towel or napkin in a steamer basket and steam over rapidly boiling water for 30 minutes. Transfer the rice to a heated serving dish.

Hot Chinese steamed chicken

Serve the reduced bouillon over which the chicken has been steamed as a tasty sauce or, as the Chinese would probably serve it, as a soup to be eaten at the same time as the chicken dish.

1½ hours

Serves 4–6
1.4 kg /3 lb chicken, trussed
2 spring onions, thinly sliced
15 ml /1 tbls soy sauce
15 ml /1 tbls peanut oil
30 ml /2 tbls sake or dry sherry
For the bouillon
1 chicken stock cube
10 ml /2 tsp soy sauce
30 ml /2 tbls sake or dry sherry

1 Place the chicken in a large saucepan and add enough cold water to just cover it. Bring slowly to the boil then simmer for 30–40 minutes, skimming the surface as necessary. At this stage the chicken will be half cooked.
2 Remove the chicken from the pan. Reserve the cooking liquid.
3 Transfer the chicken to a heatproof dish which will fit into your largest saucepan or flameproof casserole, but is large enough to hold the chicken comfortably.
4 Combine the thinly sliced spring onion, soy sauce, peanut oil and sake or dry sherry. Rub the sauce into the chicken.
5 To prepare the bouillon: crumble the chicken stock cube into 575 ml /1 pt of the reserved cooking liquid. Pour this stock into the saucepan or flameproof casserole you have chosen to steam in, and add the soy sauce and sake or dry sherry. Bring the bouillon to the boil, then stand a trivet in the saucepan or casserole. Put the dish containing the chicken on the trivet, cover the pan

and steam for 30 minutes over the boiling bouillon. Add more of the reserved chicken cooking liquid to the pan, if necessary. Serve immediately, with the steaming bouillon as a sauce or a soup.

Chinese steamed pork with ginger

 20 minutes

Serves 3–4
450 g /1 lb pork fillet
4 thin slices fresh ginger root, cut into narrow strips
4 button mushrooms thinly sliced
4 spring onions, including green parts, finely sliced
10 ml /2 tsp cornflour
30 ml /2 tbls soy sauce
30 ml /2 tbls peanut oil

1 Thinly slice the pork fillet and place in a shallow gratin dish with the ginger strips, mushrooms and spring onions.
2 Blend the cornflour with the soy sauce and peanut oil. Pour this mixture over the pork and vegetables.
3 Place the gratin dish in a steamer basket, cover and steam over rapidly boiling water for 10 minutes, or until the pork is cooked through. Alternatively, place the dish on a trivet in a large flameproof casserole, cover and steam.

Chinese steamed trout

30 minutes

Serves 2
2 fresh trout, each 350 g /12 oz
8 button mushrooms, thinly sliced
8 thin slices fresh root ginger, cut into narrow strips
4–6 spring onions, thinly sliced
For the sauce
15 ml /1 tbls sake or dry sherry
5 ml /1 tsp sugar
15 ml /1 tbls soy sauce
10 ml /2 tsp cornflour

1 Combine the sauce ingredients in a small bowl.
2 Clean then gut the fish. Using a sharp knife, make a slit along the belly of the fish. Place your fingers under the gills and pull out all the entrails, working down the belly. Place the fish in a long oval gratin dish just large enough to hold them, then pour over the sauce, rubbing it into the fish both inside and out.
3 Decorate the fish with the thin slices of mushroom, ginger and spring onion. Place the dish in a steamer basket, cover and steam over rapidly boiling water for 15 minutes, or until cooked. Alternatively, place the dish on a trivet in a large oval flameproof casserole, cover and steam.

Steamed beef with green pepper

🥄 20 minutes

Serves 3–4
450 g /1 lb sirloin steak
1 green pepper, cored and seeded
10 ml /2 tsp cornflour
20 ml /4 tsp soy sauce
30 ml /2 tbls dry sherry
15 ml /1 tbls peanut oil
5 ml /1 tsp vinegar
2 spring onions, thinly sliced
a spring onion tassle, to garnish

1 Cut the sirloin steak, across the grain, into slices about 3 mm /⅛ in thick. Arrange the slices in an oval gratin dish. Cut the green pepper into thin strips and then add them to the beef.
2 Blend the cornflour with the soy sauce, dry sherry, peanut oil and vinegar and pour the mixture over the beef and green pepper. Sprinkle the sliced spring onions over the top, then toss with a fork or two chopsticks to ensure all the ingredients are coated in the sauce.
3 Place the dish in a steamer basket, cover and steam over rapidly boiling water for 8 minutes, until the beef is tender. Alternatively, place the dish on a trivet in a saucepan or flameproof casserole, cover tightly and steam. Serve immediately, garnished with the spring onion tassle.

Steamed pork in lettuce leaves

🥄🥄 soaking the mushrooms, then 35–40 minutes

Steamed beef with green pepper

Serves 4–5
20 lettuce leaves
For the filling
225 g /8 oz raw minced pork
4–6 Chinese mushrooms, soaked in hot water for 30 minutes
4 canned water chestnuts, finely chopped
2 slices of fresh root ginger, finely chopped
2 spring onions, finely chopped
15 ml /1 tbls sake or dry sherry
15 ml /1 tbls soy sauce
15 ml /1 tbls peanut oil
freshly ground black pepper
For the sauce
30 ml /2 tbls soy sauce
30 ml /2 tbls sake or dry sherry
90 ml /6 tbls chicken stock, home-made or from a cube
2 spring onions, thinly sliced

1 First make the filling. Drain the soaked dried mushrooms, discard the woody stems and press the caps dry in absorbent paper. Chop the mushrooms finely and place them in a bowl along with the rest of the filling ingredients; mix well.
2 Steam the lettuce leaves, 4 or 5 leaves at a time, over rapidly boiling water for 1 minute, then remove from the steamer.
3 Lay the steamed lettuce out on a clean, flat surface, stem ends towards you. Place about 15 ml /1 tbls of the mixture in the centre of each leaf. Fold the stalk end of the leaf over the filling, fold in the sides, then roll up to enclose the filling completely.
4 Place the lettuce rolls, join downwards, in a single layer in a steamer basket. Cover and steam over rapidly boiling water for 5 minutes. Cook in batches if necessary.
5 Meanwhile, combine all the sauce ingredients in a saucepan and mix together. Heat through gently.
6 Serve the lettuce rolls hot, with the sauce poured over.

Steamed green peppers with pork filling

🥄 45 minutes

Serves 4
2 green peppers, each 150–175 g /5–6 oz
60 ml /4 tbls peanut oil
For the filling
400 g /14 oz lean pork
50 g /2 oz pork fat
4 spring onions, including green parts, finely chopped
4 thin slices fresh root ginger, finely chopped or grated
2.5 ml /½ tsp sugar
2.5 ml /½ tsp cracked black peppercorns
15 ml /1 tbls cornflour
30 ml /2 tbls soy sauce
15 ml /1 tbls dry sherry
4–6 Chinese dried mushrooms, soaked in hot water for 30 minutes
For the sauce
1 garlic clove, finely chopped
15 ml /1 tbls cornflour
30 ml /2 tbls Chinese fermented black beans (optional)
For the bouillon
275 ml /10 fl oz chicken stock, home-made or from a cube
15 ml /1 tbls soy sauce
15 ml /1 tbls dry sherry

1 First make the filling. Mince the pork and the fat, then mix them with the finely chopped spring onion, ginger, sugar, black peppercorns, cornflour, soy sauce and dry sherry.
2 Drain the soaked dried mushrooms, discard the woody stems, press the caps dry in absorbent paper and chop them finely. Add them to the filling mixture; mix well.
3 Cut the green peppers in half lengthways and remove the stems and seeds. Stuff the pepper halves with the pork filling, levelling the tops with a spatula.
4 Heat the peanut oil in a large frying-pan and sauté the stuffed pepper halves on all sides, until the peppers begin to go soft and the meat is golden brown. Remove from the pan with a slotted spoon and reserve the oil in the frying-pan.
5 Combine the ingredients for the bouillon in a heavy-based saucepan, and bring to the boil. Put the peppers into a steamer basket and place it over the saucepan of bouillon. Cover and steam over the rapidly boiling bouillon for 15 minutes. Transfer the cooked peppers to a serving dish and keep them warm while you make the sauce.
6 Reheat the oil in the frying-pan and sauté the finely chopped garlic until transparent. Blend in the cornflour. Add the bouillon which was used for steaming to the frying-pan and bring to the boil, stirring. Simmer for 2–3 minutes, stirring continuously. Add the black beans, if using.
7 Spoon a little of the sauce over the stuffed peppers and serve the remaining sauce separately.

Preserves

BOTTLING FRUIT

As each season's fruit becomes plentiful, it is satisfying and simple to preserve some by bottling. Preserved in syrup, whole or sliced fruits can be used in flans, pies, mousses and other delicious puddings.

You can preserve all types of fruit by bottling, with the exception of bananas. Bottling is very effective, it gives you a delicious syrup to serve with the fruit and also saves valuable freezer space for other items which can only be preserved by freezing. Correctly bottled, the fruits will be preserved with their shape, their colour and their texture unimpaired.

There are several methods of preserving.

Some of them are especially suited to particular fruits, but mostly the method you use will be a matter of your own personal choice.

Each method of preserving fruit achieves the aim of all preserving processes — the destruction of the micro-organisms present in the fruit which would otherwise allow the fruit to decay. During heating, the bottling process creates a vacuum so that other

organisms cannot enter the bottles and damage the fruit. The vacuum seal is essential to successful preserving.

Preparing the fruit

Always choose fresh, firm fruit that is just ripe but never over-ripe. Prepare and wash the fruit. Cherries, damsons, small plums and greengages can be bottled whole but, if you wish, stone the cherries. Large fruits should be halved or sliced for the best flavour. Crack a few of the stones and include the kernels to give a nutty flavour.

Dip peaches, apricots and nectarines in boiling water for 1 minute, then in cold water; the skins will rub off easily. Halve pears and peel, core and slice apples. Keep

Preparing fruit for bottling

pears and apples, until ready to bottle, in a bowl of water acidulated with lemon juice, to preserve their colour.

Hull soft fruits, top and tail gooseberries and currants. Wash soft fruits in a colander under a light sprinkling of cold water so that they are not bruised. Shake the colander gently to remove excess water. Halve extra-large strawberries.

Peel, core and cut pineapples into rings or cubes. Trim and slice rhubarb into even lengths. Peel and segment or slice citrus fruits, removing all pith and pips.

Liquid for bottling

Use water or unsweetened fruit juices such as orange or apple juice. Generally a light sugar syrup is used for both hard and soft fruits. For extra-special preserves, replace some of the syrup with a fortified wine such as sweet sherry, or brandy or a liqueur.

To make the syrup, put 225 g /8 oz sugar into a pan with 600 ml /1 pt water or fruit juice. Bring to the boil over a low heat, stirring until the sugar has dissolved, then boil for 1 minute. If it is more convenient you can make the syrup in advance, storing it in a covered container in the refrigerator for 1–2 days. It is then used (with alcohol added if wished) hot or cold according to the preserving method.

Flavouring

Flavoured sugar adds something extra, particularly to apples, pears and quinces. To prepare it, simply leave a vanilla pod or a few bay leaves in a covered jar of sugar for a few days before use.

Spices, or even fresh flowers, can be tied into a small piece of muslin and boiled with the syrup. Try a piece of lightly bruised root ginger, whole cloves, allspice or juniper berries, or strips of thinly pared orange or lemon zest. These add an extra flavour to apples, pears, rhubarb and stone fruits. For gooseberries, try to find a head or two of elderflowers. For really memorable strawberries, steep a few black peppercorns in the syrup. Remove and discard the bag of flavourings when the syrup is ready and use fresh ones if you want to include them with the preserve.

Preserving jars

Gradually invest in a stock of special heat-resistant preserving jars; these will last a lifetime. Preserving jars come in two standard sizes, 500 g /1 lb and 1 kg /2 lb.

A screw-band fastening fits over a flat metal lid lined with non-corrosive material, with a rubber gasket attached, or with a separate rubber ring. The gasket or ring must be new each time you use the jar.

A clip-fastening fits over a glass or metal lid. The lid may be separated from the top of the bottle with a rubber ring or it may have a gasket attached. These also must be new each time. The clip has two positions, one of which holds the lid, the other which clamps it when fully tightened.

Ordinary jam jars can be used for bottling by any method except in a pressure cooker. You can buy non-corrosive lids with fitted rubber gaskets or loose rubber rings to suit the standard-sized jars.

Fruit bottling by different methods

Method Fruit	Pressure cooker Minutes*	Water bath		Moderate oven	
		Cold start Temperature and Minutes**	Warm start Minutes*** at 88C /190F	Minutes ½–2 kg / 1–4 lb	over 2 kg / 5 lb
Apples, sliced	1	74C /165F 10	2	30–40	45–60
Apricots	1	83C /180F 15	10	40–50	55–70
Blackberries	1	74C /165F 10	2	30–40	45–60
Cherries	1	83C /180F 15	10	40–50	55–70
Citrus fruit, segmented	1	83C /180F 15	10	40–50	55–70
Currants	1	74C /165F 10	2	30–40	45–60
Damsons	1	83C /180F 15	10	40–50	55–70
Figs	5	88C /190F 30	40	60–70	75–90
Gooseberries	1	74C /165F 10	2	30–40	45–60
Greengages	1	83C /180F 15	10	40–50	55–70
Loganberries	1	74C /165F 10	2	30–40	45–60
Mulberries	1	74C /165F 10	2	30–40	45–60
Peaches, halved	3–4	83C /180F 15	20	50–60	65–80
Pears, halved	5	88C /190F 30	40	60–70	75–90
Pineapple, sliced	3–4	83C /180F 15	20	50–60	65–80
Plums, whole	1	83C /180F 15	10	40–50	55–70
halved	1	83C /180F 15	10	40–50	55–70
Quince, halved	5	88C /190F 30	40	60–70	75–90
Raspberries	1	83C /180F 15	10	40–50	55–70
Rhubarb	1	74C /165F 10	2	30–40	45–60
Strawberries	1	83C /180F 15	10	40–50	55–70

*Minutes after the correct pressure is reached
**May take 1½ hours to reach bottling temperature
***May take 30 minutes to reach bottling temperature

Preparing jars: the jars must be without chips or cracks — and clean. Wash them well in warm soapy water, scrubbing if necessary. Rinse and drain. Soak new, loose rubber rings in cold water immediately before use. Preheat the jars in a low oven for 10 minutes, then dip them in boiling water to sterilize them immediately before use. Preheat the jars in a low oven for 30 minutes if you are using either the moderate-oven method or pressure-cooking method.

Filling jars: jars should be well filled but not to overflowing with fruit. As you pack in the fruit, give the jar a shake so that the fruit settles into the jars. Pour on the liquid at the temperature given for the method and add any extra flavourings you choose.

Put on the lids. Clips and screw-bands must not be tightened before processing. When fruit is bottled by the moderate-oven method, they are not put on the bottles until after they are removed from the oven.

Methods of preserving

Follow the temperatures and times for processing given in the chart above. Oven processing times vary not only according to the type of produce, but also according to the amount being bottled in a batch.

Moderate-oven method: heat the oven to 150C /300F /gas 2 and warm the jars for 30 minutes. Pack them with the prepared fruit. Bring the syrup to the boil and pour it over the fruit to come 25 mm /1 in from the top of the jar. Place the lids in position but do not put on the screw-bands or clips. Stand the jars well apart on a padded tray or board and put in the oven for the time given in the chart. Remove the jars to an insulated surface and immediately screw on the bands tightly, or fix the clips. Leave the jars to cool.

Cold-water-bath method: for this you will need a large pan deep enough to immerse a number of jars. Prepare the pan with a trivet or false base made of a folded cloth. Pack the fruit into jars, as described above, and fill them with the cold syrup. Put on the lids and then the screw-bands. Tighten these fully, then unscrew them a one-quarter turn. Alternatively, put the spring clips in position without tightening them.

Put the jars in the pan, so they do not touch, and pour in cold water to cover the jars, or at least up to the necks. Suspend the thermometer in the water and cover the pan with a lid. Put the pan over a low heat. The water must reach 55C /130F in 1 hour so adjust the heat from time to time. During the next 30 minutes it must reach the appropriate temperature shown on the chart. Maintain this temperature for the time given in the chart, then turn off the heat. Remove the bottles from the pan, and tighten the screw-bands at once. Leave to cool.

Warm-water-bath method: a deep pan, prepared with a trivet or false bottom, is again needed. Temperatures are given as a rough guide, but they are less critical than for the cold-water-bath method. Pack the jars with the prepared fruit. Heat the syrup to about 60C /140F and pour it onto the fruit, to cover, as described above. Put on the lids and fastenings, unscrewing the bands by a quarter turn. Heat water to about 38C /100F and pour it around the jars to cover them completely. Cover the pan and adjust the heat so that the water reaches simmering point within 30 minutes. Maintain a temperature of 88C /190F for the time given. Remove the jars from the water immediately, tighten the screw-bands and leave to cool.

Pressure-cooker method: you will need a deep pressure cooker and specially heat-resistant jars (not jam jars). Fit the trivet or false base into the cooker and pour in at least 5 cm /2 in cold water. Check the manufacturers' instructions for your particular pressure cooker. Warm the jars in a low oven for 30 minutes. Pack them with prepared fruit and fill with boiling syrup to 25 mm / 1 in below the rim. Fit on the lids and screw-bands and then unscrew the bands by a quarter turn. Do not tighten the clips. Stand the bottles in a large bowl of boiling water for 5 minutes.

Arrange the bottles with spaces in between in the pressure cooker and pack newspaper between each jar so that they do not clink during the processing. Put on the pressure cooker lid and turn on the heat.

When the steam starts to rise, make the necessary adjustment to cook at Low /5 lb pressure. Bring the cooker to pressure in 5–10 minutes, then lower the heat to maintain the pressure for the given time. Turn off the heat and leave the pressure cooker to cool for 10 minutes. Remove the bottles, immediately tighten the screw-bands and leave the bottles to cool.

Final stages

Testing for seal: wait for 24 hours, then test for seal. Remove the clips or screw-bands and, placing your thumb and second finger on either side of the rim, try to lift the bottle by the lid. If the vacuum seal is complete, the lid will stay on the jar. If it comes away in your hand, eat the fruit within a day or two or start the process again. This will mean sterilizing the jars again, using fresh rubber rings and, where necessary, reheating the syrup.

Label the jars with the type of fruit used, the date and make a note of the flavourings.
Store the bottled fruit in a cool, dry place. They have a long shelf life and will keep for much longer than a year.

Ideas for bottled fruit

● Chop bottled cherries, pears or plums and stir them into yoghurt. Halved strawberries, whole currants or raspberries are delicious served this way.
● Make a purée or use bottled fruit purée and mix it with an equal quantity of thick custard or whipped cream. Freeze it and you will have a special ice cream, or chill it and serve as a fruit cream.
● Simmer cherries with a stick of cinnamon in equal quantities of red wine and fruit syrup. Chill and serve as a refreshing cold cherry soup. Try raspberries and plums in this way, too.
● Use bottled soft fruits for trifles.
● Drain pineapple rings or apple slices, dip them in batter and deep dry for golden fritters.
● Use for making upside-down sponge puddings, steamed suet-crust puddings and crumble-topped hot fruit puddings, or for traditional pies, flans and tarts.

Bottled greengages

Orchard fruit can be bottled successfully in syrup by the moderate-oven method. Use greengages in a deep pie.

1 hour 15 minutes, then 24 hours

Makes 1.4 kg /3 lb
1.1 kg /2½ lb medium-sized greengages
225 g /8 oz sugar
a piece of root ginger, peeled and bruised
a long strip of thinly pared orange zest

1   Heat the oven to 150C /300F /gas 2 and warm the jars for 30 minutes.
2   Wash the greengages, remove the stalks and halve them if you wish, if they are large. Crack a few stones and pack some kernels with the fruit in the jars.
3   To make the syrup, put the sugar into a pan with 600 ml /1 pt water. Tie the ginger and orange zest in a piece of muslin and add them to the pan. Stir to dissolve the sugar, then boil for 1 minute. Now remove and discard the muslin bag.
4   Pour the hot syrup over the fruit to come 25 mm /1 in from the top of the jars. Place the lids in position but do not seal them.
5   Stand the jars well apart on a padded tray or board and put them in the oven for 40–50 minutes.
6   Remove the jars from the oven and place them on an insulated surface. Immediately screw on the bands or fix the clips. Leave for 24 hours to cool. Test for seal, label and store.

Surprise strawberries

Delicate strawberries are preserved by the cold-water-bath method. Use them as a filling for crêpes — make a sauce with a little of the syrup.

1 hour, then 24 hours

Makes 1.4 kg /3 lb
225 g /8 oz sugar
6–8 black peppercorns
30 ml /2 tbls kirsch (optional)
1.1 kg /2½ lb strawberries

1   Prepare the pan with a trivet or insulated base.
2   To make the syrup, put the sugar into a pan with 600 ml /1 pt water. Tie the peppercorns in a piece of muslin. Immerse them in the water. Stir to dissolve the sugar, then boil for 1 minute. Remove the muslin bag and discard. Add the kirsch, if using. Leave the syrup to cool.
3   Hull the strawberries and wash them in a colander under gently running cold water. If they are large, halve the strawberries. Pack them into jars.
4   Fill the jars with cold syrup to within 25 mm /1 in of the top. Put on the lids, then the spring clips without tightening them, or the screw-bands, unscrewing them by a one-quarter turn.
5   Arrange the bottles in the pan so that

they do not touch and cover them with cold water. Suspend a cooking thermometer in the water and cover the pan with a lid. Put the pan over a low heat. Adjust the heat from time to time so that the water reaches 55C / 130F within 1 hour.
6   In the next 30 minutes the water must reach 83C /180F. Maintain this temperature for 15 minutes, then turn off the heat.
7   Remove the bottles from the pan and immediately stand them on an insulated surface. Tighten the screw-bands at once and leave the strawberries for 24 hours to cool. Test for seal, label and store.

Bottled cherries

These cherries are bottled in a deep warm-water-bath. Use them in a tart or heat them and serve with ice cream.

1 hour, then 24 hours

1 Heat the oven to 150C /300F /gas 2 and warm the special heat-resistant jars for 30 minutes. Fit the trivet or a false base into the pressure cooker and pour in 5 cm /2 in cold water.
2 Dip the peaches in boiling water for 1 minute, then in cold water, then remove their skins.
3 To make the syrup, put the sugar in a pan with 600 ml /1 pt water. Tie the allspice berries, if using, in a piece of muslin and add them to the pan.
4 Stir to dissolve the sugar, then boil for 1 minute. Discard the allspice berries. Stir in the brandy and simmer but do not boil.
5 Pack the peaches into jars and fill the jars with the hot syrup to 25 mm /1 in below the rim. Put on the lids and spring clips, without tightening them, or put on the screw-bands and unscrew by a quarter turn.
6 Stand the bottles in a large bowl of boiling water, then arrange them in the pressure cooker so that they do not touch each other. Pack newspapers between each jar so that they do not clink during the process.
7 Put on the cooker lid and turn on the heat. When the steam starts to rise, make the adjustment to cook at Low /5 lb pressure. Bring the cooker to pressure in 5–10 minutes.
8 Lower the heat and maintain the pressure for 3–4 minutes. Turn off the heat and leave the cooker to cool for 10 minutes.
9 Remove the bottles, immediately tighten the screw-bands and leave for 24 hours to cool. Test for seal, label and store.

Vanilla apples

This sliced, hard fruit is bottled in a warm oven. Use it for pies, crumbles or to serve hot with custard.

1 hour 30 minutes, then 24 hours

Makes 1.4 kg /3 lb
1.1 kg /2½ lb cooking apples
juice of 1 lemon
225 g /8 oz sugar
a vanilla pod

1 Heat the oven to 150C /300F /gas 2 and warm the jars for 30 minutes.
2 Peel, core and slice the apples into a bowl of water acidulated with the lemon juice.
3 To make the syrup, put the sugar and the vanilla pod into a pan with 600 ml /1 pt water. Stir to dissolve the sugar, then boil for 1 minute.
4 Drain the fruit and pack it into the jars.
5 Remove the vanilla pod from the syrup. Pour the hot syrup over the fruit to come 25 mm /1 in from the top of the jars. Cut the vanilla pod into 3 pieces and then put a piece in each jar. Put on the lids but do not seal.
6 Stand the jars well apart on a padded tray or board and put them in the oven for 30–40 minutes.
7 Remove the jars from the oven and place on an insulated surface. Immediately screw on the bands or fix the clips. Leave to cool for 24 hours. Test for seal, label and store.

Makes 1.4 kg /3 lb
225 g /8 oz sugar
4 whole cloves
6 allspice berries, lightly crushed
1.1 kg /2½ lb cherries, stoned

1 Prepare the pan with a trivet or insulated base.
2 To make the syrup, put the sugar into a pan with 600 ml /1 pt water. Tie the cloves and allspice berries in a small piece of muslin. Immerse them in the pan. Stir to dissolve the sugar, then boil for 1 minute. Remove and discard the spices.
3 Pack the jars with the fruit and pour hot syrup over the fruit to cover — the syrup should be at 60C /140F. Put on the lids and spring clips, without tightening them, or the screw-bands, unscrewing them by a one-quarter turn. Arrange the jars in the pan so that they do not touch.
4 Cover the jars with water at about 38C /100F. Cover the pan and adjust the heat so that the water simmers (88C /190F) within

Use bottled fruit for cherry soup or an upside-down sponge pudding

30 minutes. Maintain this temperature for a further 10 minutes.
5 Remove the jars from the water immediately the processing time has finished. Tighten the screw-bands and leave for 24 hours to cool. Test for seal, label and store.

Party peaches

These peaches are bottled whole in brandy syrup for a dinner party dessert.

1 hour, then 24 hours

Makes 1.8 kg /4 lb
1.1 kg /2½ lb small peaches
225 g /8 oz sugar
6 allspice berries (optional)
150 ml /5 fl oz brandy

MAKING JAM & MARMALADE

Apart from being an enjoyable pastime, making jam and marmalade provides you with a shelf full of bright, colourful confections to use as sweet sauces, fillings for cakes, glazes — and a topping for bread and toast.

The traditional method of making jam is so straightforward that it is hard to simplify it. The image of gleaming pans bubbling away on the cooker, with scents that are the very essence of summer rising from them, is the same today as it was centuries ago. This is one area of cooking that has remained virtually unchanged.

Marmalade is usually made in January and February because this is the time when Seville oranges are in season. With their rough, orangy-red skins, these bitter Spanish oranges make a delicious tart-sweet preserve. However, you can make marmalade at any time of the year, from sweet summer oranges, grapefruit, lemons or limes, or delicious variations with two or more types of fruit. The yield is high, except for jelly marmalade, so the cost is low. Always use fruit that is just ripe, never over-ripe.

Equipment
All you need in the way of equipment for making jam and marmalade is a large preserving pan or an enamelled or non-stick pan (a saucepan is fine for small quantities), a long-handled wooden spoon, measuring jugs and pouring jugs, and a slotted spoon to skim off the foam as it rises. You can use old jam jars or coffee jars, washed and rinsed until they are scrupulously clean. Seal them with waxed paper discs and screw-top lids.

Choose a large pan as it should be no more than half full after you have added the sugar. A sugar thermometer is the most accurate means of testing the setting point of jam or marmalade.

Pectin content
Fruit that is high in pectin — the natural setting agent which is present to a greater or lesser extent in all fruit — includes cooking apples, crab-apples, damsons, plums and gooseberries. These are cooked with the addition of a little water. Currants and raspberries cook in just their own juices.

The delightful partnerships in jams — blackberry and apple, marrow and damson, cherry and redcurrant, strawberry and gooseberry — originate from the need of low-pectin fruit with poor setting potential to 'borrow' pectin from the others. Apart from blackberries, marrow, cherries and strawberries, other low pectin fruit include pears, peaches and rhubarb. To make jam from low-pectin fruit alone, you can add, to each 1.75 kg /4 lb of fruit, 30 ml /2 tbls lemon juice; 5 ml /1 tsp citric or tartaric acid; commercially prepared pectin in liquid or crystal form, according to the maker's instructions; or 150 ml /5 fl oz strained apple, gooseberry or currant juice.

All citrus fruits are high in pectin, which is present in the skin, white pith and pips, so there is rarely any problem in getting your marmalade to set.

As a general rule, you can estimate that 1.3–1.6 kg /2½–3 lb citrus fruit will have enough natural pectin to set 3 kg /6 lb sugar. This will give you approximately 5 kg /10 lb marmalade — so you will know how many jars to prepare.

To extract the maximum amount of pectin, tie the pips into a piece of muslin and add them to the pan of boiling fruit. If the pith is not included in the marmalade, tie this in with the pips as well. Then, when the fruit has finished boiling, squeeze the bag of pips and pith over the pan before you discard the bag.

The addition of extra acid in the form of lemon juice or citric acid or tartaric acid in recipes where there are no lemons helps to work on the natural pectin and to prevent the marmalade from crystallizing while it is being stored.

The methods
When you are making jam, select top-quality fruit that is just ripe. Over-ripe or badly damaged fruit should not be used, although if a fruit has one or two small blemishes, these can be cut out with a sharp knife. Remove the stalks, leaves, hulls or stones. Put the fruit into a pan with any water and acid that is called for and cook until the fruit is completely tender. At this stage add warmed sugar. To warm the sugar, spread it out on a baking tray and heat for 20–30 minutes in a cool oven (110C /225F /gas ¼). The warming helps to dissolve the sugar more quickly without lowering the temperature of the jam too much. When the sugar is added, the fruit must be completely tender, otherwise the result may be bullet-hard fruit and a quite unspreadable jam — fruit stops tenderizing the moment you stir in the sugar. Stir the jam over a low heat until the sugar has dissolved, then increase the heat and boil the jam for 10–20 minutes, or until it will set.

If you have a sugar thermometer, you will know that setting point is reached when the temperature reaches 104C /220F. If not, test by spooning a little jam onto a saucer. Cool it quickly, then push the blob of jam with a finger. If it wrinkles, it is ready. If not, bring the preserve back to the boil, then test it again in a few minutes.

Pour the jam into warmed jars — the jars may be warmed by washing and drying off in a cool oven just before the potting stage. The jars should be warm, otherwise the hot jam may crack the glass. Cover immediately with a waxed paper circle, wax side down on the surface, then cover the jar with a screw-on lid. Allow to cool. Label each jar, clearly marking the date, and store in a cool, dark, dry and airy place. Heat and dampness adversely affect the keeping quality of jam or marmalade.

There are two distinct types of marmalade, which are made in quite different ways. One includes the whole peel of the fruit, either chopped thickly to give 'chunky' marmalade or thinly for the 'shred' kind. The other type is jelly marmalade, which is made like any other fruit jelly preserve. The juice is strained off and measured and 400 g /1 lb sugar is added to each 500 ml /1 pt juice. Very finely shredded and blanched zest (but no pith) is usually added.

The method for making marmalade is very similar to that for jam. Following the recipes in this chapter you can make up your own fruit combinations according to which fruits are readily available, but keep the total weight of the fruit the same or in the same proportion to the water, acid and sugar. For example, instead of using all Seville oranges, substitute one grapefruit or two lemons to make the same weight.

When lemons, which are high in acid, are included there is usually no need to add extra acid. Otherwise, add up to 2.5 ml /½ tsp citric or tartaric acid or 15 ml /1 tbls lemon juice to each 2 kg /4 lb fruit for marmalade, twice the quantity for jelly.

Testing, bottling and storing are exactly the same for marmalade as for jam-making.

Jam and marmalade notes
● As a general rule, the sugar represents about 60 per cent of the total weight of the finished jam. Knowing this helps you calculate the number of jars to have ready.
● You can use granulated or cube sugar, or preserving crystals, which dissolve more quickly. Natural soft brown sugar deepens the colour and gives a slightly cloudy appearance but it is especially good in apple, apricot, quince and rhubarb jam.
● Never leave fruit to stand in a metal pan overnight. By all means soften the fruit a day in advance, but transfer it to a non-metal mixing bowl — china or glass is preferable — before you leave it overnight.
● The pan should not be more than half full after the sugar is added — jam spits!
● You can use a pressure cooker to speed up the process of cooking the fruit. You need less water for this method — usually only 1 L /3 pt to each 1 kg /3 lb of fruit, but check the capacity of your pressure cooker first. When steam begins to rise from the pan, put on the high pressure valve, bring to high pressure and cook for 20 minutes; allow the pressure cooker to cool for 10 minutes before opening the vent and removing the lid.

Next add the sugar to the softened fruit, leave off the lid and use the open pan to boil the jam or marmalade to setting point.
● Rubbing the base of the pan with glycerine before adding the fruit helps to prevent sticking and minimize the scum.
● The stones and pips are often included in the recipes to add pectin and flavour.
● You can freeze citrus fruits and make your marmalade at a future date. Open freeze the fruit in roasting tins, then store it in sealed bags. Thaw the fruit before cooking.

Ingredients for jam and marmalade

- You can leave the chopped peel and pith for marmalade soaking in part of the water overnight — this cuts down on the cooking time.
- To quicken the preliminary preparation of the fruit, cook the fruit whole to soften it and then cut it up with a knife and fork. Put it in a saucepan with all or part of the water and simmer on top of the cooker for about 2 hours. Alternatively, cook in a covered ovenproof dish at 150C /300F /gas 2 for about 4 hours (economical if you are slow-cooking a casserole at the same time).

Strawberry and gooseberry jam

about 1 hour

Makes about 3 kg /6½ lb
500 g /1 lb gooseberries
1.5 kg /3½ lb strawberries
1.8 kg /4 lb sugar

1   Wash the gooseberries, top and tail and put them into a pan. Wash the strawberries, hull them and add them to the pan.
2   Stir the fruit over a very low heat until the juices start to run, then bring it to the boil and cook it for about 20 minutes, stirring occasionally. Meanwhile, heat the oven to 110C /225F /gas ¼. Spread the sugar on a baking tray and warm it in the oven for 20 minutes.
3   Add the warmed sugar and stir over a low heat until the sugar has dissolved. Increase the heat and bring the jam to the boil. Boil rapidly for about 15 minutes, until the jam has reached setting point.
4   Pour the jam into warmed jars, cover, label and store.

- An alternative method is to cook the gooseberries first, strain them and then cook the strawberries in this juice. Cool the preserve in the pan for 10–15 minutes, stir well and then pour into the jars. This gives you the setting property of the gooseberries but the appearance of strawberry jam.

Cherry and redcurrant jam

about 1½ hours

Makes about 3.4 kg /7½ lb
500 g /1 lb redcurrants
2.5 kg /5½ lb black cherries
2 kg /4½ lb sugar

1   Wash the redcurrants and strip them from the stalks into a pan, using the prongs of a fork.
2   Wash the cherries, remove the stalks and any leaves and stone them. Tie the cherry stones in a piece of muslin.
3   Using a long-handled wooden spoon, stir the redcurrants over a very low heat until the juice starts to run.

4   Add the cherries and the bag of stones, stir well and bring to the boil. Cook for about 40 minutes, stirring occasionally, until the fruit is tender. Taste the fruit to be sure. Squeeze all the liquid from the bag of cherry stones into the preserving pan. Discard the bag of stones. Meanwhile, heat the oven to 110C /225F /gas ¼. Spread the sugar on a baking tray and place it in the oven for 30 minutes to warm.
5   Add the warmed sugar to the fruit and stir until it has dissolved. Next increase the heat and boil rapidly for about 15 minutes, or until the jam has reached setting point.
6   Pour the jam into warmed jars, cover, label and store.

Raspberry and orange jam

Here is a version of raspberry jam that makes that precious fruit go further.

about 2¼ hours

Makes about 3.7 kg /8 lb
2 large sweet oranges
2.25 kg /4¾ lb sugar
2 kg /4½ lb raspberries

1   Wash the oranges. Squeeze out the juice and pour it into a medium-sized saucepan. Tie the orange pips in a piece of muslin and then add them to the saucepan, together with 300 ml /10 fl oz water.

2   Cut the orange peel and pith into very thin strips. Add it to the pan, cover and bring to the boil. Cook for about 1–1½ hours until the peel is tender. Meanwhile, heat the oven to 110C /225F /gas ¼. Spread the sugar on a baking tray and place it in the oven for 30 minutes to warm.
3   Pour the contents of the saucepan into a larger pan, add the raspberries, stir and bring to the boil. Cook until the raspberries are tender.
4   Squeeze all the liquid from the bag of pips into the saucepan, then discard the bag of pips. Add the warm sugar to the tender fruit. Stir over low heat and boil rapidly for about 10 minutes to setting point.
5   Pour the jam into warmed jars, cover, label and store.

Apricot jam with brandy

This is a lovely filling for sponge cakes or a delicious topping for desserts.

about 1½ hours

Makes about 4.5 kg /10 lb
2.7 kg /6 lb fresh apricots
2.7 kg /6 lb sugar
75 ml /5 tbls brandy

1   Remove any stalks from the apricots, then wash, halve and stone them. Put the prepared apricots in a large pan. Crack open

Once you have a good stock of preserves, you can use them for all kinds of desserts—open lattice tarts, cheesecakes with toppings, ice cream with jam sauces; or serve them as a treat with scones and cream

a few of the stones, soak the kernels in boiling water, remove the skins and put them in the pan with the apricots. They will give the jam a lovely almondy flavour.

2 Add 600 ml /1 pt water, bring to the boil and cook for about 40 minutes, stirring occasionally, until the apricots are tender. Meanwhile heat the oven to 110C /225F /gas ¼. Spread the sugar on a baking tray and place it in the oven for 30 minutes to warm.

3 Add the warmed sugar to the pan and stir over a low heat until it dissolves. Increase the heat and boil rapidly for about 15 minutes, or until the jam has reached setting point. Stir in the brandy.

4 Pour the jam into warmed jars, cover, label and store.

Greengage jam

about 1 hour

Makes about 4.5 kg /10 lb
2.7 kg /6 lb greengages
2.7 kg /6 lb sugar

1 Wash the greengages, then halve and stone them. Put them into a large pan. Crack a few of the stones, dip the kernels in boiling water and peel off the skins. Add them to the pan.

2 Pour on 700 ml /1¼ pt water, bring to the boil and cook for about 25–30 minutes,

stirring occasionally, until the fruit is tender. Meanwhile, heat the oven to 110C /225F / gas ¼. Spread the sugar on a baking tray and place it in the oven for 30 minutes to warm.

3 Add the warmed sugar to the cooked fruit and stir over a low heat until it has completely dissolved. Increase the heat and boil rapidly for about 15 minutes, until setting point is reached.

4 Pour the jam into warmed jars, cover, label and store.

Lemon marmalade

about 2–2½ hours

Makes about 4.5 kg /10 lb
1.5 kg /3 lb lemons
2.7 kg /6 lb sugar

1 Wash and dry the lemons. Cut them in half and squeeze out the juice.

2 Thinly pare the zest from half of the lemon shells and cut it into fine matchstick shreds. Roughly cut up the pith and tie it with the pips in a piece of scalded muslin.

3 Cut the remaining lemon shells into very thin matchstick shreds, cutting the peel and pith together.

4 Put the lemon juice, shredded peel and zest and the muslin bag into a pan, with 3.1 L /5½ pt water. Bring to the boil and simmer for 1½–2 hours, or until the peel is tender and the contents of the pan are reduced by about a half.

5 Meanwhile, warm the sugar — spread it on a baking tray and place it in an oven heated to 110C /225F /gas ¼ for 30 minutes.

6 When the contents of the pan have been reduced, turn the heat down to low. Squeeze the muslin bag over the pan, then discard it. Add the warmed sugar to the pan and stir until it is dissolved.

7 Increase the heat, bring the marmalade to the boil and fast-boil it for about 10–15 minutes, or until setting point is reached, skimming off the foam as it rises. Remove the pan from the heat and leave the marmalade to stand for 20 minutes.

8 Stir the marmalade to distribute the peel evenly, then ladle it into warmed jars, cover, label and store.

Marmalades from left: Coarse Seville, Jelly and Five-fruit

Coarse Seville orange marmalade

 2–2½ hours

Makes about 4.5 kg /10 lb
1.2 kg /2½ lb Seville oranges
2.5 ml /½ tsp citric or tartaric acid, or
15 ml /1 tbls lemon juice
2.7 kg /6 lb sugar

1 Wash the oranges, cut them in half and squeeze out the juice. Tie the pips in a piece of scalded muslin.
2 Slice through the remaining peel and pith with a sharp knife. Put it in a pan with the orange juice, acid or lemon juice, 3.4 L /6 pt water and the bag of pips.
3 Bring it to the boil and boil gently for about 1½–2 hours, or until the peel is tender and the contents of the pan are reduced by about a half.
4 Meanwhile, warm the sugar — spread it on a baking tray and place it in an oven heated to 110C /225F /gas ¼ for 30 minutes.
5 When the peel is tender, and the contents of the pan have reduced, turn the heat down to low. Squeeze the bag of pips over the pan, then discard it. Add the warmed sugar to the pan and stir until dissolved.
6 Increase the heat, bring to the boil and boil rapidly for 10–15 minutes, or until setting point is reached, skimming off the foam as it rises. Remove from the heat and leave to stand for 20 minutes.
7 Stir the marmalade to distribute the peel evenly, then ladle it into warmed jars, cover, label and store.

Jelly marmalade

 about 3½ hours, plus draining time

Makes about 2.3 kg /5 lb
1 kg /2 lb Seville or sweet oranges
5 ml /1 tsp citric or tartaric acid, or
30 ml /2 tbls lemon juice
1.4 kg /3 lb sugar

1 Wash and dry the oranges. Thinly pare the zest and cut it into very thin matchstick strips. Put it in a saucepan, cover with 600 ml /1 pt water, bring to the boil and cover the pan. Simmer for 1½ hours, or until the zest is tender. Drain the shreds and reserve the liquid.
2 Roughly cut up the orange pith and flesh into segments. Put it in a pan with the acid or lemon juice and 2 L /3½ pt water. Bring to the boil and simmer for 2 hours.
3 Add the strained juice from the shreds, boil and simmer for a further 20 minutes.
4 Scald a jelly bag and hang it over a large bowl. Tip in the fruit and juice and strain, without squeezing the bag, for about 2 hours, or overnight if more convenient.
5 Measure the strained orange juice and pour it into a pan. Weigh 400 g /1 lb sugar to each 500 ml /1 pt juice, spread it on baking trays and warm it in an oven heated to 110C /225F /gas ¼ for 30 minutes.
6 Bring the orange juice to the boil, add the warmed sugar and stir over a low heat until it dissolves. Add the reserved strips of orange zest, bring to the boil quickly and fast-boil it until the jelly sets. Skim off the foam as it rises. Remove the pan from the heat and leave the jelly to settle for 20 minutes.
7 Stir the jelly to distribute the peel evenly and ladle it into warmed jars. Cover, label and store.

Five-fruit marmalade

 about 2–2½ hours

Makes about 4.5 kg /10 lb
1.4 kg /3 lb citrus fruit — 2 Seville oranges,
1 sweet orange, 1 grapefruit, 2 lemons,
2 limes
2.7 kg /6 lb sugar

1 Wash and dry the fruit. Cut each in half and squeeze out the juice.
2 Thinly pare the zest from the oranges and grapefruit and cut it into thin matchstick strips. Cut up the pith roughly and tie it with the pips from all the fruits in a piece of scalded muslin.
3 Cut the lemon and lime peel (with the pith) into very thin strips.
4 Put the fruit juice, cut up peel and zest, muslin bag and 3.4 L /6 pt water into a pan. Bring it to the boil and simmer for 1½–2 hours, or until the peel is tender and the contents of the pan reduced by about a half.
5 Meanwhile, warm the sugar — spread it on a baking tray and place it in an oven heated to 110C /225F /gas ¼ for 30 minutes.
6 When the contents of the pan have been reduced, lower the heat. Squeeze the muslin bag over the pan, then discard it. Add the sugar to the marmalade and stir until it is dissolved.
7 Increase the heat, bring to the boil and fast-boil for 10–15 minutes, skimming off any foam as it rises, until the setting point is reached. Remove the marmalade from the heat and leave to stand for 20 minutes.
8 Stir the marmalade to distribute the peel evenly, then ladle it into warmed jars, cover, label and store.

Index